A GRANDFATHER'S GIFT

Papaw's life and times in rural Mississippi.

James E. Smith, Sr.

iUniverse, Inc.
New York   Bloomington

A GRANDFATHER'S GIFT
Papaw's life and times in rural Mississippi.

iUniverse books may be ordered through booksellers or by contacting:

iUniverse
1663 Liberty Drive
Bloomington, IN 47403
www.iuniverse.com
1-800-Authors (1-800-288-4677)

Because of the dynamic nature of the Internet, any Web addresses or links contained in this book may have changed since publication and may no longer be valid. The views expressed in this work are solely those of the author and do not necessarily reflect the views of the publisher, and the publisher hereby disclaims any responsibility for them.

ISBN: 978-1-4401-4144-7 (pbk)
ISBN: 978-1-4401-4146-1 (cloth)
ISBN: 978-1-4401-4145-4 (ebook)

Printed in the United States of America

iUniverse rev. date: 6/25/09

Contents

Introduction

I was born in Knoxville, Tennessee, on March 18, 1944. My parents had moved there from Mississippi. Dad was helping build the Oakridge nuclear bomb plant. On August 6, 1945, one of those bombs was dropped on the city of Hiroshima, Japan, bringing an end to World War II. After that, Dad's work was done, and he, along with hundreds of others, was laid off. We moved back to Jefferson County in rural Mississippi. My parents had been born and raised in Jefferson County. My wife and I married on May 23, 1965. We have two children and four grandchildren. That brings me to the reason for writing this book.

Maybe my descendants and other people as well might like to know how we and other farmers lived in the rural areas of Mississippi when I was a boy. For several years, I pondered the idea of writing a book. I simply wanted to record our family history for our descendants. As I was trying to research our family history, I would wonder why one of our grandparents hadn't written some information for us and our grandchildren. That got me to thinking, *Why don't I do just that and leave some information for my grandchildren about where and how we lived and how life was back then?* We knew where our grandparents lived, but nothing much about our great-grandparents.

My parents loved each other and their children and passed very important common information on to us concerning how to live and get along with each other as well as other people. We have passed that on to our children in the hopes they will pass it to our grandchildren.

I am proud to say, my parents married and stayed together, being there for their children.

Worrying, that I was not a writer, I was reminded of the words of a famous writer, P. L. Travers, who once said, "A writer is, after all, only half his book. The other half is the reader and from the reader the writer learns." From this quote, I realized everyone has the potential to be a writer if he writes what someone else enjoys reading. My mother's youngest brother, Uncle Bennie Beesley, let me read some stories he had written about his childhood, and I thought, *I enjoyed reading those simple stories very much.* I thought there would be many young descendants who would treasure these writings someday.

This book is about my experiences and contains the stories I have heard my folks tell while sitting on the front porch after supper at night. For many years, my grandfather Pearl Beesley lived with us. He and my dad would swap old tales about towing wagons and logging with oxen and mules. They talked about the "dummy line" railroads that ran through the forest and told my parents' childhood tales and many other stories I would long for later in life. How I wish I would have taken notes, but it didn't seem important at the time. Television had come along when I was still a young boy, and we moved inside and sat in silence watching the tube. Not many more stories would be told in such a quiet setting, as the front porch deep in the country, with only the interruptions of whippoorwills, hoot owls, screech owls, and such making pleasant noises in the distant woods. I was about twelve years old when we bought the television.

My life experiences and those of my parents and grandparents have shaped my personality. The best things in life are free, but there is a certain amount of morality required for a peaceful, happy and fulfilling life. I give all the credit to my parents and grandparents for inspiring me on what I like to think is the correct path of life. I thought this might be worth passing on to my descendants. Some of the names in here have been changed, except for family names, of course, because friends of my family might not think a certain thing is funny. I notice we think a lot of things are funny, unless they are about us. We have been blessed with two wonderful children: James Edward Jr. (Jim), born February 22, 1970, and Kimberly Lea (Kim), born December 31, 1974.

As you read these pages, keep a few things in mind. The writer is a novice with not a day's education in journalism; there is no plot, no beginning, and no ending. There is no high point of interest except where the reader happens to find one. The book is broken down into chapters. Each chapter stands alone. I thought it might be better to do it this way, rather than write it in story form. If one gets bored with a particular chapter, he or she can simply move to another chapter without interrupting the storyline. Writing in story form, I found myself jumping around and getting off subject. One may wonder how I remember some things in such vivid detail. It has been surprising how I can remember a certain event, but the details are not clear until I start to write and focus on the subject and words on my computer screen. Some of these stories may not be exactly as the events occurred, but they certainly are as I remember them. There is no attempt to add details for emphasis to these writings, and in no case do I intend to write fiction here.

Ruthie and I have lived in several places around Mississippi over the years. We raised our children; they moved on, and we became empty nesters. In 2003, Ruthie and I moved to Olive Branch in North Mississippi in order to be close to our children and grandchildren who lived in Memphis, Tennessee. We wanted to attend our grandkids' activities, birthday parties, sporting events, and other such things. Most of all, we just wanted to watch them grow up. It is such a pleasure to watch our grandchildren grow up and a real pleasure to spend time with them. Jim and Ashley have three: Jackson Parker (Jack), born May 3, 2002; Samuel Thomas (Sam), born December 13, 2004; and James Benjamin (Ben), born March 13, 2007. Kim and Seth have one, Shane Alan, born May 13, 2008. We now know why they call grandchildren "grand".

I hope all of you will appreciate this book and the effort that has been put into it. If that occurs now or in the future, no matter how far, then my efforts will have been rewarded. To my grandkids, "Happy reading!" from Papaw.

Thomas and Annie Mae Smith
My parents
Circa: 1968

1

The Beginning

Thomas James Smith, my father, was born December 16, 1905, to John and Annie Smith in Jefferson County, Mississippi. One day, when he was twenty-eight and still single, he was over at Clark, Mississippi, at the post office talking to Hollis Segrest, the postmaster. Hollis asked, "Tom, when are you going to get married?"

Daddy said, "Well, I'm not against the idea, but I just ain't found the right girl yet."

Mr. Segrest said, "Well, Pearl Beesley has a beautiful young gal up yonder," referring to a house up the hill to the rear of the store/post office. He continued, "Her name is Annie Mae, and I think she is about marrying age."

Daddy said, "Well, I'll have to talk to her one day when I get a chance."

Later on, Daddy heard that one of those parties that the folks called a "dance" was taking place at a friend's house. There would be live music, if the local musicians were available to play. The music makers played for food and whiskey or whatever alcoholic beverage was offered. Moonshine whiskey (homemade whiskey) was the mainstay of alcoholic drinks. If the musicians were not available, the dance would have to be held at someone's house who owned a wind-up record player. No invitations would be sent out. Everybody around the neighborhood had an open invitation to every dance. The dance would begin, and the house would fill with guests. There would be no cars parked in the yard, because few people had horses to ride, let alone cars to drive. Some rode work mules, but maybe they didn't have a saddle. Some just walked over. The Blue Hill and Clark communities were densely populated in those days, so the walk wouldn't be more than a mile or two. The couples would meet at some location and walk two by two down the trail to the dance. They would be spaced out several steps, so sweet talk could be exchanged as they walked along and not be overheard by the others.

Some brought 78 RPM records to the party if they had them, though there weren't many who did. Owning a record player was a luxury around the neighborhood in 1934, and the Depression had everybody hunting rabbit tracks to keep from starving to death, as Mamma's brother, Uncle Lewis Beesley, used to say. Uncle Lewis said they couldn't afford shells to shoot rabbits, so they would take a piece of charcoal and rub a black spot on the side of an old dry log, and the rabbit would think it was a hole. When they chased the rabbit, he would try to jump into the fake hole and would knock himself out, and that was how they harvested their rabbits. He told us kids that sometimes they didn't have shoes to wear. When they went to church, they would be walking as quietly as a cat on the hardwood floor, and people would know they didn't have shoes. They would put hickory nuts between their toes so they would tap on the floor as they walked in and people would think they were wearing shoes and wouldn't look down at their feet. We never believed all that, but we laughed until our sides hurt at Uncle Lewis. Uncle Lewis said they called rabbits "Hoover Hogs" because the Depression was blamed on President Herbert Hoover. Back then, the blame or credit was always on whomever was president, the same as today. Times were hard, and music recordings were hard to come by. Daddy said some people would do without flour to buy a Jimmie Rogers record. Jimmie has been given the credit for being the father of country music.

At those dances, the same records would be played over and over, and when they got tired of hearing those, they would sing themselves. Mama said some of those ole country boys and gals were good singers. Daddy fit that description, and he knew a lot of Jimmie Rogers's songs. Daddy and Mama were both attending one of those dances. Daddy noticed this pretty young girl and went over to ask her for a dance. It was Mama, and she accepted. They spent a lot of time talking together as the party continued. That was referred to as courting. If you were seen talking to a member of the opposite sex and no one else was around, well, you were courting. Maybe you didn't want to admit it, but you were and there was no use in trying to deny it.

My father lived almost on top of a famous spot in that part of the country called Blue Hill, and my mother lived about three miles east of Blue Hill just beyond the Clark Post Office and General Store. Clark is no longer a town, but it was a town with a post office back then. Mom and Dad walked to dances together and to Bethesda Baptist Church together on Sundays. After a reasonable courtship, Daddy proposed the big question, and Mama said yes. At seven o'clock on a Wednesday night, December 26, 1934, in my mother's grandpa Klar's house, they were married.

The old custom of dressing for your wedding was, "Something old, something new, something borrowed, something blue, and a sixpence in his shoe." This custom was observed in their wedding. They didn't have an old British sixpence, so Daddy put a silver dime in his shoe. Mama wore a brown dress and brown shoes that she borrowed from her sister-in-law. Daddy wore his blue navy serge suit. Each of those items was supposed to be good luck. The "something old" was for continuity with the bride's family. "Something new" was for the bride's new life ahead. "Something borrowed" was from a happily married friend or family member with hopes the good fortune in marriage would carry over to the new bride. "Something blue" was worn because blue symbolized love. The "sixpence in his shoe" was for wealth and security. I'm not sure if both could wear these things or if it was meant just for the bride, but between the two of them, all these things were used in their wedding. I guess the "sixpence in his shoe" referred to the groom. Daddy's shoes were new.

Mr. Porter Sanders from Union Church, Mississippi, the local justice of the peace, performed the ceremony. There were so many people there, they decided to have the wedding out in the front yard, but there were no lights other than the light from the fire. Somebody held a lighted pine splinter over Mr. Porter's head so he could read the scripture. He finally finished the ceremony and pronounced the couple married. Mr. Porter never got around to signing the licenses, and they never did get around to getting the licenses signed afterward. So, technically speaking, my parents were never married. Union Church, Mississippi, was about six miles south at the intersection of Highway 550 and Highway 28.

Their honeymoon was at my father's parents' house on Blue Hill. Daddy still lived with his parents. At one point, they moved into the smokehouse and/or barn located at the rear of the house, so they could enjoy making their own home together. They lived there until the next crops of cotton, corn, etc., were finished. That was the rest of that year. After living there for a few months, they moved to the Truly farm near Church Hill and around Truly Lake in Jefferson County. They were working under the FSA (Farm Security Administration) that was enacted by President Franklin D. Roosevelt in 1935. One of the activities performed by the FSA was having farmers live together under the guidance of government experts and work a common area. The government owned the land. There were many government programs in those days, such as the CCC (Civilian Conservation Corps), WPA (Works Project Administration), TVA (Tennessee Valley Authority), and many others. In this FSA program, the government furnished houses. Some had two rooms and some three rooms. They also furnished a mule for farming. This was life for many people during the Great Depression.

My parents had a dream of owning their own farm someday. Their dream seemed so distant during those times. Farms were coming up for sale. Lending agents were foreclosing on farms all round the country. Still, even though many acres of farms were up for sale, they needed money for the purchase. Banks and other lending agents would loan money, but my parents would need collateral to secure the loan. Mom and Dad had neither money nor collateral. They were barely making living expenses, let alone saving any money.

Their first child, John Pearl, was born September 30, 1936 while they lived at Truly Lake. They named him after his Paternal Grandpa John Smith and Maternal Grandpa Pearl Beesley, he was called J.P. or Pete. They moved from there to Terry, Mississippi, just south of Jackson sometime after that. Some friends helped them move, and they told a story about one of Mama's remarks. It seems the house had cracks in the floors wide enough for snakes to crawl into the house. She had pulled out a dresser drawer one day and found a rat snake or chicken snake coiled up on the clothes in that drawer. Somebody who didn't know about this incident just simply asked, "Annie Mae, why are ya'll moving?"

Mama replied, "Let me tell you something, when snakes start getting in your drawers, it's time to move!"

One can imagine the wonder the other person had when she asked, "What in the world are you talking about, Annie Mae?!"

In Terry, they lived on the same type of government farm project, FSA, and raised a cabbage truck crop. The government was trying to help people in order to get money flowing again. In Terry, they furnished a house, barn, mule, farming tools, canning utensils, etc. All my parents had to do was supply the labor. The government supplied an overseer to provide instructions on how to farm and provided the market for the cabbage. Their second son, William Arthur, was born on August 29, 1939, while they lived in Terry. In 1941, the United States entered WWII, and jobs suddenly became plentiful. There were military bases to build, and weapons, ammunition, ships, vehicles, and everything a country needed to fight a war to produce. With the money flowing, people were buying things, and that created more jobs. Our nation was pulling out of the Depression. Daddy left his family with relatives and moved to Hattiesburg, Mississippi, for a better job.

There were so many construction people coming into Hattiesburg to build Camp Shelby, an army base, he couldn't find a room. He got on the list to move into a new boardinghouse that was under construction. He had a cot under a shade tree and put his suitcase underneath his cot. He was there several days. He said he got in from work one day and they were ready for him to move in. He got everything inside just as it started to sprinkle rain. He had gone to work as a plumber's helper for a construction company that was building Camp Shelby. His pay was seventy-five cents per hour, and the folks back home just couldn't believe he was making that much money. It was unheard of in that part of the country in those days. With that kind of money, maybe his farm dream just might come true. They might have extra money to save.

After a while, Mama and her two kids moved to Hattiesburg with Daddy. When he had moved to Hattiesburg, Mama couldn't live in the house in Terry anymore. She had moved back home with her two children, waiting for Daddy to send for them. After he got settled and found room for them, Mama and her two kids moved to Hattiesburg with Daddy. Mama said she could buy a pound of hamburger meat, a dozen eggs, and a loaf of bread for one dollar. All those groceries required a little over an hour's work, so you can see why the folk back home were so excited about Daddy's pay scale. Even though one of their major dreams was owning a farm, they wanted a family even more. Raising children was far more important to them than owning a farm. They felt that if they put their heart and soul into it, they could do both, raise a family and save up to buy a farm.

The base was finished, and Dad was laid off, so they moved from Hattiesburg to Jackson, Mississippi, to another job. Daddy was laid off from that job, so they moved to Oak Ridge, Tennessee. The United States had the formula to build the atomic bomb, so a plant was needed—and in a hurry. Daddy and Mama moved their family to Knoxville, Tennessee, sometime around 1943, and he hired on at the Oak Ridge atomic bomb plant. I'm not sure just when the plant was started, but they moved there that year. The plant wasn't named at the time. It was top secret. They only knew it was a military facility. Their plan was to work there until they could save enough money to buy their farm and build a house on the new farm back home. They lived in Knoxville, Tennessee, in a so-called apartment house. That was a very large old home with the owner and his wife living in one bedroom, living room, and kitchen. The rest of the rooms were rented out to tenants. Each tenant lived in just one room. They had to cook and sleep in the same room.

During that raging war and traumatic economic depression, in the Knoxville General Hospital, Knoxville, Tennessee, on March 18, 1944, I saw my first light of day. The doctor held me up by my feet and announced to my mother, "He is ready for the army." The hospital stay for my mother was five days. The doctors didn't get the mothers up the next day as they do now; they kept them in the hospital bed for at least five days. That ran the hospital bill and doctor bill to fifty dollars. Mama had to make room for one more in that one-room apartment. The rooms were much larger in the older homes, than they are in homes today. This room was big enough for a double bed, a baby bed for me, and a pallet for J. P. and William. There was room for a two-burner kerosene stove for cooking. They shared a refrigerator with one of the neighbors or the landlord, I'm not sure which. There was one bathroom downstairs and the landlords used it for themselves only.

There was one bathroom upstairs, and all six of the families had to share that one bathroom.

Finally, Knoxville and the nearby town of Oakridge had enough housing for the influx of people who were constructing the plant. Other businesses had grown into the area, due to more working families coming there. A mobile home became available for rent in Oak Ridge near the plant. We moved from Knoxville to the rented mobile home. Because of the war, a lot of products were rationed. Many things that were in good supply were rationed to save a necessary quantity for the military. Each family received a book of ration stamps each month for each member of the family. These stamps were very important. Without them, one could not buy whatever they needed, regardless of the emergency. If the stamp book was used up, they had to wait until next month to buy whatever they needed. On one of the trips home to visit the home folks, we stopped in Birmingham, Alabama. Mama went into the restroom and put her purse on the floor in the stall. She walked out and left it sitting there on the bathroom floor. We were several miles down the road when she remembered her purse. The ration stamps were in the purse. Without them, we couldn't buy a replacement tire, gasoline, or oil. They were very upset, but we drove back. The purse was at the cash register and still intact with every ration stamp still inside. Another lady had turned it in to the service station attendant, knowing someone would return for it.

Since the job was secret, one wonders how they managed to build the plant. The workers would report to a certain place each morning. A truck would come by and pick up a certain number of workers. These men would be shuttled out to a building under construction. There might be pipes sticking through walls. Daddy and the other plumbers would be told to tie a pipe onto that, run it over, and stick it through another wall. There might be a machine in the room, in which case, they would be told to connect the pipes to it. They didn't know from where the pipes came or where they were going or what the machine's purpose was. The next day, they might be taken to a different building to complete some work there. They were told not to ask questions, so they didn't. There was a line of people outside the gate wanting a job. If a person was caught asking questions, he might be fired on the spot and replaced by someone waiting for a job. They were told that military spies were wandering around the plant. Maybe the spies were working along with the men, they didn't know. Even if a worker knew the person he might be talking to, he didn't carry on any conversation about the job.

One day, Daddy had an attack of the mumps. Another person on the job had an attack of the measles the same day. They were sent home and were riding in the same car. When they reached the gate, they had to stop for the guard to release them to leave the site. The guard told them that they would have to wait while he searched the car. Daddy told the guard to please hurry, because he had the mumps and the other fellow had the measles. The guard fell back away from the car and told them to go ahead. Daddy and the other guy, laughing, talked about how easy it would be to sneak anything out of the plant. Just tell the guard that you had some disease and he would get out of your way and let you go on through.

Mama told us it wasn't proper to be caught away from home at night. They had warning sirens that would be sounded. The sirens were a warning that they were blacked out. That meant turn off every light in your house and your car. If you were headed home in a car, the lights had to be turned off. One either walked on home, drove home in the dark, or spent the night in the car. Those sirens were a bone-chilling sound. It meant that enemy planes had been discovered and more than likely they were bombers coming to bomb whatever it was they were building. Later in the night, the sirens would be sounded again, and that meant all clear. Lights could be switched on again. Of course there were never any bombings in America, so these were probably just tests. We think they were just having the people practice, just in case.

Finally, one night, they were riding down the road and the car radio was playing. A news flash came on the radio. An atomic bomb had been dropped on Hiroshima, Japan. It went on to say the bomb had been manufactured in a secretly built plant in Oak Ridge, Tennessee. That was how Daddy and the other folk learned what they had been doing. They had mixed feelings. The plant had been successful, but they would lose their jobs. They were no longer needed there either. It was August 6, 1945, and the bomb had been dropped that very morning. I was in the car sitting in my mother's lap when the news came over the radio. I would be eighteen months old in twelve days.

Fortunately, my parents had managed to save enough money to

make a down payment on a farm back home and start building a house. The dream was coming true. The farm was located in Jefferson County, one mile south of Highway 552 on the left side of Lucky Hollow Road heading south. On February 15, 1943, Daddy bought mama a farm for her 26th birthday February 7th, their dream was coming true. Daddy had made a deal with Krause and Company to buy a farm with one hundred acres, more or less (it was actually 128 acres), in Jefferson County. That later became our home place and still is until this day. They bought the place for $10.00 per acre or $1,000.00 for the farm and two old houses and a barn.

He was out of work, but he had his own house for his family. He could make some amount of money farming and raise most of the food they would need on the farm. He would need to find public work, if possible, for extra income. He had learned a skill while building all those military bases. His skill might land him a nice job in construction someplace. There was a lot going on in Natchez, Mississippi, after the war. The country had pulled out of the Depression and factories were being built in Mississippi.

The area was populated mostly by small farmers. The farms were anywhere from a few acres to several hundred acres in size. Mr. John Shelton had owned a very large farm in that area. He had sold a one-hundred-acre tract of land to someone. That farmer had borrowed the money from a bank run by a Jewish man named Krause to buy the land. He had gone bankrupt, and Krause had foreclosed on the property. My parents bought that tract of land. John Shelton had willed the rest of his property to his children, one of whom was Mr. Clint Shelton and his wife Mrs. Catherine. They were in their late fifties. Mr. Clint drove the school bus, farmed cotton, and raised beef cattle. Farther on that way was a farm owned by his sister, Mrs. Mattie and her husband, Mr. Cash Garrett. Being the baby of the family, she had inherited her father's house. Mr. John had willed the next tract south to his son Mr. Charles Barret (Buck) and his wife Mrs. Velma. Since I can remember, a good number of these families were old enough to draw Social Security and farmed for extra income. All that is except Mr. Clint, he wasn't quite sixty yet.

Lee Dee, my black friend, lived with his grandparents between Mrs. Mattie's and Mr. Buck's farms on Mrs. Mattie's farm. They were farm tenants. Another black family, Mr. Jerome Trevillion's, were tenants who lived on Mr. Clint's farm. North of our farm was Mrs. Mary Bailey's farm. She was the mother of Mrs. Velma and Mrs. Catherine Shelton. Mrs. Bessie Lea was another one of Mrs. Mary Bailey's daughters. Mrs. Bessie Lea and her husband, Mr. W. L. Dickerson, lived with Mrs. Mary. The Bailey house was a very large house, and the Dickersons had retired from a road-building business. Eastward on Highway 552 was the farm of Mr. Bud and Mrs. Janie Short. Past their farm were the farms of Uncle Bill and Aunt Lennie, then Mr. Charles Shelton, then Mr. Grover Goza, and my wife's parents, Mr. and Mrs. Bennie and Earline Goza. Westward on 552 were Mrs. Mosel and Mr. Holly Segrest, then Uncle Jack and Aunt Maggie, and just down the hill from them were Grandpa John and Grandma Annie. Farther on that way were Mr. and Mrs. Lester and Mollie Tanksley, Mr. and Mrs. Jim and Mildred Nesler, Mr. and Mrs. Hiram and Mary Alice Norton and Mr. and Mrs. Guy and Stella Kelly. North of the Bailey house were Mr. James and Mrs. Janie Cole, then Mr. Wilton and Mrs. Mable Brown. Mr. Wilton was the game warden for the county. Mr. James Cole was a carpenter, and they all farmed on the side. Most of them had inherited their farms. They just wanted to live in the country and enjoy farming. All farms were cotton, cattle, and timber, but mostly cattle. There were no row crops or truck crops around there, except for the farmer's own use. There were no so-called truck farmers.

Daddy would be working in different towns around the state of Mississippi and would send money home to Mama for the purpose of paying for the farm. They could pay the interest and any amount on the principal they wanted. Mama would take the money to Krause's office in Fayette, and he would tell her, "You don't have to pay all that much at once, Mrs. Smith, just use that money for something else." He sounded like a real nice guy, but he wanted two things: One, he wanted the loan to run as long as it could so he could collect more interest; second, he had foreclosed on a loan that had been borrowed to buy that very tract of land that Mama was paying for. His second reason stemmed from the fact she might not be able to pay for the land and he would foreclose. Krause accumulated a lot of land by loaning people money on their land and foreclosing when they failed to pay the loan. This is not to say he was a bad person; it was just business. However, that is just the way a lot of mortgage companies operated. It might be good and proper business, but trying to talk someone out of paying for their property while they have the money is just plain wrong, in my book.

He wasn't about to pull that on Mama. She had a dream to own a farm, and she wouldn't own it until it was paid for. She had a debt, and the first thing she wanted to do was pay the debt off as quickly as possible. That came before anything else, except bare living expenses. The debt was structured for farmers, so they could pay the interest once per year after the crops were harvested. They could then pay any amount on the principal they wanted. Then the interest would be accumulated on the balance of the debt the next year. Mama would follow that procedure each time, but she didn't wait the full year; she paid weekly or monthly as the money accumulated. When Krause would tell Mama to keep the money and buy her or the kids some clothes, toys, or something, she would ask, "Do you want this money or not?"

He would then turn to his secretary and say, "Opal, write her a receipt." They paid that ten-year debt off the first year.

Their dream was coming true, and it was a tremendous good feeling. My mother had never been raised on her own land or lived in her own house while growing up. She now had the farm, bought and paid for. The next step was the house. Mom and Dad needed their own house on their own farm. There wasn't enough money to build the house someplace on the farm. There wasn't even enough money to build the house. They would need some help to get that done. Daddy had a great idea. He would move his family into one side of the old farmhouse he was living in. They had lived in cramped quarters before, so they could do it again. Then, the vacated half of the house could be torn down. Next, they could rebuild the part they had razed. That would be easy; since a house had stood on that spot, there would be no necessary groundwork. After rebuilding that half of a new house, they could move over there and tear down the rest of the old house. After that was out of the way, they could build the rest of the house and connect it together, making a completely new house.

After giving that plan much thought, he decided to give it a try. If it didn't work, there was enough room in his parents' house, and they could move in there. Grandpa and Grandma Smith lived about three miles up the road. Once one half of a house is built, the other half has to be exact in many ways. One, it has to be the same level. This would take some extreme engineering since the house was sitting on pillars. The new house has to connect in the correct alignment. This young man, just now forty years of age, was taking on a major carpenter task. He had done odd carpenter jobs during his day, but he was now a skilled plumber and experienced farmer. It might be too much for him, but he had promised his darling wife that she would have her own farm and house someday. He had to fulfill that commitment; besides that, he wanted those things himself. If he waited to save up enough money to build the house, it would take years. He might be pushing fifty before he reached his dream. Many country folk had built their own houses, and they weren't carpenters. He could do it. How would he know he couldn't if he didn't give himself the chance?

The old house had real good lumber. It had been built during the days when trees were big and a lot of lumber came from the choice part or center of the tree. By pulling and straightening nails, they could reuse them also. The doors in the old house were still good. The hinges and doorknobs could be reused. Uncle Jack and Grandpa Smith would help with the labor for free. With the money that had been saved up and the reusable parts of the old house, they just might be able to get it done.

My parents moved into one half of the existing farmhouse, tore down half the house, and built a new half. Then, they moved into the new half, tore down the other old half, and replaced that space with a new half, completing the new house. When asked where we lived while we built the new house, Daddy liked to laugh and say, "We lived in it." He was so proud of himself for pulling that off. He had never heard of that being done before. We did live in the house, but Mama said it was a real mess. They had no electric tools, so they sawed every board with a handsaw or crosscut wood saw. Much of the rough-cut outside lumber was stacked and sawed with a crosscut two-man saw all at once. All outside boards were nailed up on a forty-five-degree angle for bracing strength then covered with a heavy tarpaper that had brick-sized brown blocks of grit on it. This gave the outside a bricked look. Inside, walls and flooring were all one-by-six-inch tongue-and-groove dressed pine lumber. The roof was corrugated, galvanized tin, and the house had front and back porches. They screened the back porch. The house was built with a living room, dining room, kitchen, one bath, and three bedrooms. They heated the house with wood until sometime in the late fifties, and the cook stove was a wood burner until the late sixties. Daddy did not want to give in to modern appliances. I overheard him talking to a neighbor once saying he still liked to cut wood. It also gave us kids something to do, and he seemed to like keeping us busy. The house turned out well and required very little maintenance. It was about 1,200 square feet in size not including the porches. It cost something like $800.00. Their dream was finally fulfilled. They had the house and farm they had been dreaming about, and it was all paid for. Oh, what a feeling!

Mama had a fourth boy not long after the house was finished on Wednesday, August 18, 1948. He was stillborn. There were strange coincidences concerning the birth of that child. My oldest brother, John, had been born on a Wednesday; my brother William had been born in August, and I had been born on the 18th of March. That child was connected to all three of us by days and dates. I thought that was a strange amount of coincidences. My sister, Bessie Mae, was born May 23, 1952, in Port Gibson, Claiborne County, Mississippi.

The house was wired with electricity when it was built, I think, but indoor plumbing was not added until around 1949. We had a cistern for a water supply. The rainwater drained off the roof of the house through gutters and into the cistern. During dry spells, we had to conserve water until we built a six-thousand-gallon tank on the other side of the house. When the cistern was low on water, we hooked a garden hose onto the tank and drained it into the cistern. After we added the tank, I don't remember having to conserve water quite as much. The cistern was a hole dug into the ground about twenty feet deep and ten feet across. It was bricked and concreted inside to hold water. It worked very well, but I never did the math to find out how many gallons it held. I do remember a bucket that hung in the cistern and drawing water as needed, a bucket at a time. On wash day, it was a real job. Plumbing was added, and that consisted of a pipe entering the wall of the cistern and turning down almost to the bottom. There was an electric pump under the corner of the house near the cistern, and pipes ran out of the pump output into the bathroom and kitchen sink.

Our house was built off the ground so the pipes were suspended and exposed to the outside temperature. During the winter, we would listen to the weather report at ten o'clock in the evening, and if the temperature was going below thirty degrees, we would hear one of our parents shout, "One of you young'uns better drain the water pipes." We would always argue about who would go out into that cold night, crawl under the house, turn off the main valve, and open the drain valve. Everybody had done it the last time, so it was someone else's turn. Finally, Mama or Daddy would select a kid. The selected kid would gripe all the way out and under the house and mumble coming back inside. This, of course, would bring a snicker from one of the other kids and a fight would start. Funny, I never saw the Waltons, Griffiths, or the Cleavers behave that way (popular TV shows).

As time passed, the old galvanized pipes were replaced with copper pipes; this time, the copper pipes were buried so only the riser pipes were exposed to the weather. We wrapped those with insulation. It had to get below twenty degrees before they would tell us to drain the pipes, and that does not happen very often in Mississippi. Yes, indeed, we were moving on up, as they say. To heat the water during the woodstove era, we had a woodstove-type water heater. The water heater was located near the stove. A pipe ran from the upper part of the water tank (which held about thirty gallons) through the firebox of the old Home Comfort stove, then back to the lower part of the water tank. This pipe was full of water, of course, and when the cook stove heated, the hot water rose up through the tank, causing a circular motion. That's how the water tank worked without a pump.

We realized the power of the water heater system one day while Mama was canning vegetables. She had had a hot fire in the Home Comfort that day pretty near all day, and we were not using any hot water from the tank. The water was getting hotter and hotter. Finally the safety valve, which was called the "pop-off valve," melted out to keep the tank from exploding, and hot water and steam sprayed out into the kitchen. No one was home except Grandpa Pearl Beesley, Mama, and me. We did not know what to do, but I suddenly remembered Daddy telling the others how to turn off the water at the pump, and I saved the day by closing that valve. Everybody was impressed that I knew how to do that, being probably six or seven years old. I was proud that I had saved the cistern from being pumped dry. I'm sure they just let me think that, because both Mama and Grandpa at least knew how to turn the power off to the pump. Of course, my idea was better.

You are probably wondering what we did for hot water if the stove had not been used for a while. Well, water had to be heated on the stove or we just used cold water. Before the water heater was installed, we used water from the reservoir on the stove. The reservoir was a tank installed inside the stove on one end of the Home Comfort that held about ten gallons of water, maybe less, and heated when the stove had a fire inside. One thing I remember was how glad everyone was that no longer did we hear, "Somebody fill up the reservoir." Yeah boy, we had moved up in the world. That stove stood out a couple of feet from the wall, and the overhead part, to which the stovepipe was attached, came back to the wall, making a cubbyhole on one end. One of my fondest childhood memories was hiding in that cozy, warm compartment on a cold winter's day while Mama was busy in the kitchen. My older brothers would be in school, and I would entertain myself playing in that compartment behind the stove. I also remember one time when I tried to squeeze into that space, it was strangely cramped. It had been quite a while since I had been behind there. At first, I wondered if the stove had been moved some way, but then it dawned on me that I had outgrown my favorite space. Just one of life's turns I would have to get over. I would soon learn that other simple enjoyments would have to be placed into the past.

Under one end of the house, we partitioned off about sixteen square feet and filled it with pine straw making a sweet potato house, or yam house. (Just doesn't sound right ... yam house.) When our little friends would come over and we played hide-and-seek, the tater house, as we called it, made a great hiding place until we were found the first time, then it became the first place to look. Anyway, to store potatoes in there, we placed a layer of straw and a layer of potatoes then straw over that and potatoes over that until the house was full. Every now and then, Mama would say, "One of you young'uns go out to the sweet tater house and bring me some taters." I don't remember arguing about that chore, because Mama would lay those potatoes on the rack in the oven of that old Home Comfort and turn them every now and then until they were baked tender. There were always some baked taters lying on the shelf on the back of that old stove. That was snack food. We would peel one, open it up, fill it with butter (real cow butter), and reheat it in the oven and yum, yum. Besides being baked in potato pies, those potatoes would be sliced, rolled in sugar, and fried in the skillet with a little grease (real hog lard). Sometimes, they were sliced and simmered in sugar water and candied.

A crib was located on the right side and out to the rear of the house about a hundred feet or so. The crib was about fourteen feet square and was covered with corrugated tin like the barn and house. In early summer, the supply of corn and/or hay that was stored there for cow/hog/chicken/horse/mule feed would be depleted so the crib would be cleaned and swept out. The Irish potatoes would be dug and placed on the floor of the crib. No potato could touch another potato, because if one rotted, it would rot all the potatoes it was touching. You've probably heard that "one rotten potato would spoil the whole barrel"? Mama would send one of us kids out to the crib to gather some potatoes and bring them in for a meal. She would make the best potato salad you ever ate and mashed potatoes, fries, and boiled potatoes in with the snap beans, etc. After the potatoes were gone or at least half gone, we kids would set up an old iron bed frame, a card table and chairs, and a radio, and the crib would be our camp house until the corn or hay was ready to harvest. We had a lot of good times in that old crib with friends and kinfolk.

The barn stood to the far rear of the house for corn and hay storage. It had a side room on the right end for storing tack, harnesses, and other farming tools. The left side of the barn was boarded up on three sides with chicken wire and a wire gate on the front. That was the chicken house, and it had a hen nest on one side. One of the chores was gathering the hens' eggs. Most of the time, we could gather about half a dozen eggs or so each day. When the hens were laying well, hardly anybody wanted eggs, but when they slacked off, everybody wanted eggs for breakfast and sometimes supper too. It was something psychological about not caring for something when there is plenty of it. When an old hen quit laying, we would sneak into the henhouse at night and catch her on the roost. Then we would have chicken and dressing or chicken and dumplings. I never knew just how Mama knew a hen was past laying age, but she was pretty good at it.

About twenty-eight acres of the farm was fenced in and set aside for a cornfield. When the corn grew roasting ears, we would gather, shuck, silk, and cut the kernels off and store it in the freezer. Mama would fry the corn in a big cast-iron skillet with a little grease. She would stir until the corn had brown flakes, then it was done. That fried corn was the best I have ever had. After the corn matured, it was gathered and stored in the barn and crib. Some corn would be shelled for the gristmill. Mr. Clint Shelton lived about three quarters of mile down the road south from our house. He ran a gristmill on his farm. We would take the shelled corn over there, and he would hook his H Model Farmall tractor to his mill with a belt. The belt ran around the belt pulley on the tractor and around the pulley of the gristmill. There were two stones inside the mill, and at least one stone was spun by the pulley. There was a big tapered wooden hopper on top of the mill where the corn was poured in. Mr. Clint would pour our shelled corn into a foot tub, about a four or five-gallon galvanized bucket. This galvanized container was called a foot tub because it was about the proper size in which to wash one's feet. If you were ready for bed and had been going barefoot, you would wash just your feet before bedding down for the night. The foot tub was filled with shelled corn then emptied into the hopper. He would scoop a syrup bucket (a small tin bucket that held a little less than a gallon) out of the hopper and empty that into a wooden box located in one corner of the mill house. That was his toll for grinding the meal. We usually had two foot tubs full of shelled corn. That made a pretty good sack of meal, maybe forty or fifty pounds. I don't think we ever weighed one.

Mr. Clint would use his toll corn to make chops for the chickens, meal for his use, and so on. After he poured the corn into the hopper and the meal started coming out the chute, he would catch some in his hand and inspect it to be sure it was the right texture. Some wanted a fine meal, and others wanted a course meal. He never asked us kids how we wanted it, but he must have known Mama's preference, and if that was the case, nobody else mattered. There was an adjustment under the hopper to control the flow of corn into the mill. There was another adjustment on the side of the red wooden box to set the distance between the stones. This was how he ground the meal to perfection. Wider apart would grind chops and a little closer together would grind grits. Tighter would grind course meal, and real tight would grind fine meal. If those grooves in the grindstones were not right, you never knew what you were going to get.

Sometime around 1948, Daddy bought an M-Model John Deere

tractor. That was a small, one-row 14.65 horsepower tractor. A couple of fellows went joyriding on it one night, ran the M into a bank on the side of the road, and broke that tractor half in two. The tractor had been parked at one of the men's houses for the night. They were hired help, and Daddy didn't want to be too hard on them about the damage. He let them work out the expense by cutting stove and house wood. Of course, they would have been a long time cutting wood to pay for damages, but Daddy was easy on them, they didn't mean to do anything wrong. After the tractor was repaired, Daddy traded it for the 1951 big B Model John Deere, packing 24.62 horsepower. I tell you that would make any country boy proud. It was among the largest tractors of its day. Maybe other manufacturers made larger tractors back then, but I'm not sure if they did. John Deere made a Model A that had a bit more horsepower.

Mr. Roy Lutz came down our driveway with that brand new shiny tractor sitting on the bed of a truck in 1950. It was bright green with yellow wheel hubs. I had toy tractors and seeing that real one so beautiful was amazing. I have always thought that occurrence is the reason until this day, my favorite color is green.

That old B was a joy for us kids as well as a workhorse. One kid could ride on one hub, another on the other hub, one in the seat, and one on the drawbar. We would go down the road running ten miles per hour. When we went over the top of Clanton Hill, we knocked it out of gear. Clanton Hill was about a three-to-one grade or something like that and a little steeper halfway down. Then, at the bottom, there was a three-hundred-yard stretch. A few yards down that stretch was a driveway into the field and a wire gap. After we knocked the tractor out of gear, it would start coasting and running real fast. I would love to know just how fast that tractor traveled when it flattened out in that stretch. I do know it was extremely fast for a tractor. When the tractor reached the field driveway, the driver would catch the right brake, locking that one wheel, and steer the tractor into the driveway, then catch the other brake, locking both rear wheels, and slide up to the gap. Rocks would be flying and dust boiling. It was a beautiful thing.

We never realized the danger until one day, I had cranked the tractor and started to move when the right rear axle broke almost in two. It hung enough to keep the tractor from hitting the ground, and I let out on the clutch to stop it. I don't even let myself think about what would have happened if that axle had broken going down Clayton Hill with three or four kids hanging on it.

We had a Bush and Bogg disk that actually belonged to my uncle Bill Smith, but he never used it, because he didn't have a tractor. Why would Uncle Bill buy a disk if he didn't own a tractor? you might ask. Well, we sometimes wondered, but I don't remember asking him that question. He more than likely just wanted to buy it for his brother and his brother's kids to use for farming. Then again, he might want a little farm work done on his place, and he might get a family discount. Uncle Bill thought like that most of the time. He had a hundred acres located a few miles from us that his wife, Aunt Lennie, had inherited from her father. The disk cut about six feet of ground on the first trip around the field. On the second trip, and all trips thereafter, we had to place the left edge of the disk in the middle part of the first round, re-disking half of the plowed ground. We continued around and around the field, disking about three feet of ground with each round. The tractor had to be placed in second gear to pull that big disk. The tractor moved at 2.5 miles per hour, clucking at 1,250 RPM, about walking speed or less. We'd sit on that thing hour after hour, day after day, in that hot Mississippi sunshine until we had disked twenty-eight acres of field.

Then we hooked the pulverizing disk to the tractor and made little circles over the field in third gear traveling at 3.6 miles per hour. This circling motion was a good break from the trips around the field and took much less time. The corn was then planted. After it grew a few inches high, it was cultivated; then at about two feet high, it was cultivated again with larger plows on the cultivator. That cultivation was called "laying by." Then there was no more work in the field until the roast ears were ready to be harvested for boiled and fried corn. When the corn matured in the fall, around October, it was gathered and stored in the barn and the crib. Daddy grew shoe-peg corn, because the cob was small and the grain long. That made for more actual corn on the cob compared to the larger ears that had a larger cob and shorter grain. Another reason he liked the shoe peg was that it was easier to shell. He also liked it because the ears were smaller and made mostly nubbins (short small ears of corn) that were used to feed the cows. A cow could put the entire ear into her mouth, shuck and all, and chew it. The large-eared corn would have to be chopped with a cane knife or hatchet into pieces to enable a cow to get it in her mouth.

A corn crop meant feed for the chickens, and chickens meant fried chicken, eggs, chicken and dumplings, and chicken and dressing. This was at no cost, except the cost of growing the corn. The expense was only gasoline and fertilizer, once the tractor was paid off. The corn also fed the hogs, and from the hogs we got ham, sausage, bacon, pork chops, spare ribs, and lard for cooking, still at no cost except the cost of growing the corn. The corn was fed to the cows, and from the cows, we got beef, milk, cream, and butter at no cost except the expense of growing the corn. We also had a large vegetable garden, and there was no cost, except for the fertilizer. Most of the fertilizer was free cow manure that we shoveled off the barnyard and from around the pasture.

One of our main entertainments on Saturday night was the *Grand Ole Opry*. We'd sit in the living room in the summertime with all the windows raised and front door open, except the screen. That let in the cool summer breeze, and we would listen to the *Grand Ole Opry* on the radio. In the winter, we'd sit by the wood heater listening to the *Grand Ole Opry*. Their sponsors were Martha White Self-Rising Flour and Jefferson Island Salt. Those jingles for the commercials were fun. Mama and Daddy would go to bed around ten o'clock, but we boys would stay up after the Opry and listen to Earnest Tubb's Record Shop. Finally, after buying the television, we got to see the stars on TV that we had been listening to on the radio. The TV show was called the *Grand Ole Opry*. We still listened to the *Opry* on the radio on Saturday nights, though.

Some guy came to stay with us a few days. I think he was some relative, but I'm not sure. He slept in the crib where we boys had our camp house. He left for a visit to one of the other relatives and never came back. He had all his belongings, except for those in his suitcase, in a trunk. He left with the suitcase but left the trunk. I don't know if he forgot his trunk or just didn't think there was anything in there worth keeping. He didn't have a car; he had been dropped off there by some other relative. I took a peek in his old trunk one day and found an old radio in there. The thing looked like a piece of junk, all busted up and worn-out looking. I was about sixteen and really into rock and roll. Our radio was not working at the time, and an AM radio was just what I needed, so I could listen to WNOE in New Orleans. They played all the hot rock-and-roll tunes of the day.

I almost left the radio and closed the trunk but decided that thing just might work. I wouldn't know unless I gave it a try. I plugged it in, and nothing happened. I fooled around with it and found some wires that weren't connected and some tubes that were almost out of the sockets. After a little time, that baby was playing ever so fine. I had to carry it around in pieces, but when I set it down, it played the best rock and roll that any radio could. I listened to Hugh Baby, a disk jockey on a station in Del Rio, Texas. I don't remember the radio station, but he played black soul music, blues, and rock and roll late at night. They didn't call it soul back then, but that was what it was. I liked what is now called Highway 61 blues and Delta blues. He was as much fun to listen to as the music. He came on at 10:00 PM, and I would lie in bed with my trusty old AM on the floor (we never had nightstands). We might have had nightstands if we knew how handy they were, but we never missed what we didn't have. Hugh Baby would come on saying, "This is your main rock-and-roll man, Hugh Baby. I got some records under my arm, and I'm gonna put 'em down, spin 'em around, and lay down some hot rock-and-roll sounds. You gonna be rocking all night with the Hugh Baby!" His main sponsors were White Rose Petroleum Jelly and Lucky Strike Cigarettes. A lot of different soft drinks were sponsoring a lot of radio shows in those days as well. Del Rio was about three airline miles north of the Mexican border. The radio station was nearer to the border than that. They had the station itself sitting within the USA, but the antenna was across the border in Mexico. The reason for this setup was a loophole in the FCC law (Federal Communications Commission).

It was not legal for an AM radio station to transmit more than 50,000 watts within the United States. That was to keep the stations from overriding each other, so each station could advertise for their particular market area. AM (audio modulation) signals travel much farther at night than during the day. The stations were separated according to daytime signal travel. There were too many stations at night; if the transmitters were over 50,000 watts, they would all override each other. Del Rio transmitted 100,000 watts. They got away with it, because they weren't transmitting inside the USA, because the transmission came from the antenna in Mexico. As I said, when the law was written, they didn't think of this being a problem. I think they amended the law, but the radio station was grandfathered in and let stand, because they were within the law when they spent all the money establishing the station. That antenna was directional as all antennas were. They had to beam the signal at night, because radio signals got stronger at night when the weather cooled down. The signals would bounce off the atmosphere, and stations would override each other. They could not be received clearly very far away. Beaming 100,000 watts north out of Del Rio covered Mississippi very well. I don't know how much farther it went. They had different country shows on at night and maybe other shows, but I would be watching television and didn't turn the radio on until after I went to bed at 10:00 on Friday and/or Saturday nights.

I was almost a teenager before we owned an ice cream freezer. When we wanted to make ice cream we borrowed one from our black friend Mahaley Dee. We bought ice from an ice truck that came from town selling ice. He came around with 400 lb. blocks of ice and picked off a 100 lb. and that is how we got our ice before we got the deep freezer. After that we froze our own ice and finally bought our own ice cream freezer.

Thomas J. Smith, my father looking so proud
standing in front of his brand new 1954 Pontiac

2

My Father

James Thomas Smith was named after his two grandfathers, John Thomas Trevillion and James Monroe Smith. Dad didn't like the arrangement of his name, however. His parents wanted to call him Thomas. That meant his name would be written J. Thomas Smith, and he didn't like that. What could he do about it? Well, he would just have to change it, so when he started school, or somewhere about that time, he started writing his name Thomas James Smith, and it stayed that way the rest of his life.

He was born in the house they were living in at the time. It was located on the south side of Harriston Road just about two miles or so west of where that road intersected Highway 552. He was the second son born to John Hiram and Annie Trevillion Smith. His older brother was William George (Uncle Bill), and his younger brothers were John Bennon (Uncle Jack), Uncle Jessie, Uncle Whit, and Uncle Author. He had two sisters, Aunt Lillie and Aunt Bessie. Aunt Bessie died at age two, and Uncle Whit and Uncle Author died at the ages of twenty and eighteen, eight days apart. Daddy's family lived in the Blue Hill community, but their address was Clark, Mississippi. The Clark post office has been closed for many years now. It stood in the fork of Block Foster Road and Highway 552 in Jefferson County, Mississippi.

Aunt Bessie was born with a disease, but I'm not sure what kind. Uncle Whit's and Uncle Author's deaths were extremely strange, but since no autopsy was performed, they never knew the cause of death.

Daddy talked to an old doctor called Buey once about that, and Dr. Buey said, "Tom, you know, during that depression, some folks ran out of food, especially between crops." He went on, "Those boys might have starved to death, because even though they might have had enough to fill their stomachs, they were not getting a proper diet." So, from that, I gather the cause could have been malnutrition, but we will never know. What was so strange about their deaths was that it was the two children who were only two years apart that died one week apart for no known reason.

Daddy grew to about five feet ten or eleven inches and was always slim until he passed the age of sixty. He had black hair and dark green eyes and was very mild-mannered. He was very handsome and had a very good singing voice. He also had a natural talent for building things and had the patience to do the job right. He always had a very gentle personality and a very kind heart. Daddy tried his best to be charming, and most everyone who knew him seemed to enjoy his company. My father paid close attention to anyone he was in conversation with and made the other person feel he was interested in every word he or she had to say. His simple mannerisms and quiet speech seemed to relax people who were in his presence. I learned many common things from my father that have been invaluable throughout my life. The things he taught me have been passed on to my children. Our family was a strong and close family. If a person is lucky enough to be born into a good family, I believe there is a very good chance that person will develop a strong family. My father taught me carpentry, plumbing, gardening, and things like that. Most of all, he taught me to have confidence in my abilities, and that allowed me to do things simply because I had the confidence in myself to try. I have saved a lot of money by building my own house. That was quite an undertaking. I had no carpentry training. I only had what I had learned from him and Vo-Tech in High School. On several occasions, I can remember him teaching me how to observe the way other people had done things. That would give me a general idea to work from. He said, "Don't ever be too proud to ask questions." I soon found that most people like to answer questions that allow them the opportunity to express their intelligence. He told me many times, "If you aren't going to do it right, it is no use doing it." I can't say I actually do everything right due to this advice, but I can say that I still hear his words when I take impatient shortcuts.

I think everybody who knew him liked my daddy. He was very popular around the county, and he would always take time to stop and visit with people. I ran into Mr. Willard Cupit of Union Church, Mississippi, one day, and he said, "I knew your daddy very well." He went on to say, "I was standing on the street in Fayette one day, and your Daddy walked past me a step or two then turned around. Tom asked me, 'Aren't you Willard Cupit?'" Mr. Cupit said yes, but he didn't recognize him at first.

Daddy said, "Well, I'm Tom Smith."

"It shore was good talking to him, because I hadn't seen him in a long time," Mr. Cupit went on. "Your daddy was a fine man." Many of my father's old friends have told me what a good man he was, and I never tire of hearing them say it.

Daddy told stories about his childhood years. He told about how they would plant crops such as cotton and could not afford fertilizer so they didn't do very well. Grandpa John Smith was a blacksmith by trade, and people would come by to have plow points sharpened, ox yokes made, and so on, but wouldn't have the money to pay for the services. Grandpa John would let them have credit, knowing they would probably never be able to pay. Daddy told a story about Grandpa selling Kirby Rushing (his brother-in-law), Grandma Smith's sister Belle's husband, a five-gallon wooden keg of syrup for fifty cents. Daddy said that just the keg was worth fifty cents, but Grandpa told Daddy, "Tom, fifty cents was all the money Kirby had."

Grandpa and Daddy were gathering vegetables in the garden one day when Daddy was a boy, and he saw a snake crawling on the ground. He didn't have a hoe or anything to kill it with. He just had a bucket. So, he started stomping the snake. Grandpa was a couple of rows over and asked, "What you doing over there, boy?"

Daddy said, "I'm trying to stomp a snake."

Grandpa yelled, "You better leave that thing alone, boy! He might bite you!"

Daddy said, "Well, you better look out! He's coming your way!"

Grandpa yelled, "Stomp 'im, Tom! Stomp 'im!"

Daddy would laugh and tell that on Grandpa in front of us kids.

Grandpa would just grin about it. Grandpa John's blacksmith shop was equipped to make cane syrup and grind cornmeal. That's how Grandpa got a lot of their food. He charged a toll for making syrup and grinding meal for other farmers. He would barter blacksmith work for meat, vegetables, fruit, and other necessities.

It was about a half mile through the woods from Grandpa's front porch to the road that ran over Blue Hill. That road later became Highway 552. Oxen would be pulling wagons over the hill after a rain, and their feet would bog into the blue pipe clay from which the hill got its name. When their feet would come out of the clay, the suction would cause a loud pop. They could hear that sound from the front porch. That was a bad hill in those days. Oxen would bog down to their knees when it was wet, and you could hardly drive a nail in it when it was dry. It was very hard to cross with oxen pulling a load and not much better with T Model log trucks. The trucks would make deep ruts when the hill was wet, and when it would dry out, the wheels would run the hard ruts with the high walls so well the driver didn't have to steer. Daddy said they would load the trucks as heavily as possible in dry weather knowing they wouldn't bog down. When they got to Blue Hill, the trucks would sometimes be too loaded to make it over the half-mile grade from either direction. Those old trucks had a lever mounted on the steering column that was called a throttle. The throttle lever was pulled down, and that would lock the accelerator wide open, running the engine at full speed. The driver would have the transmission in the lowest gear on the truck. The vehicle would then be traveling at about walking speed, and the front wheels would be running the ruts keeping the truck in the road. The driver and passengers would all get out and push to help the truck over the hill.

They had an old grey mule named Rock, and he was a very gentle animal. He could be ridden to and from the fields or wherever you wanted to ride. One time, in their youth, Daddy and Uncle Bill were walking back through the pasture toward the house and saw ole Rock and the other mules slowly walking up the path toward the lot because it was feeding time. Uncle Bill said, "Tom, I'm gonna ride old Rock to the house." There was an oak stump near the path which was left after they had cut a tree for house wood. Small limbs had sprouted out and up from the oak stump, making a perfect hiding place. Uncle

Bill jumped up on that stump and squatted down so he couldn't be seen and waited for ole Rock to come slowly walking by on the path. The mule was walking like he was half asleep with his ears flopping downward and his eyes half closed. When ole Rock got even with the stump, Uncle Bill sailed out of those sprouts onto ole Rock's back. Rock didn't know what that thing was that had jumped out of those woods onto him, but whatever it was, he wanted it off and right now. He was bucking and bringing all four feet off the ground, and Uncle Bill, without anything to hold on to, came off the mule and sailed through the air. He hit the ground hard. Uncle Bill jumped up and brushing the dust off his clothes said, "Tom, if I hadn't jumped off that crazy mule, I believe he would have thrown me." Daddy told that story to a lot of people for many years to come.

During the dances, the people would write down words to songs. I have an old song book where a lot of those songs were handwritten, mostly by Daddy, in the most beautiful penmanship I've ever seen. The book is actually an old bookkeeping ledger that belonged to the Wood-Russ Lumber Company in 1921. The Wood-Russ Lumber Company owned a sawmill in Red Lick, Mississippi, along beside the main railroad. They ran a spur out of there that was called the "dummy line." The dummy line ran into the forest around Blue Hill. This railroad was called a dummy line because it was not actually a railroad for any purpose except hauling logs from the forest to the sawmill in Red Lick. There were many dummy lines in South Mississippi in those days. Short leaf yellow pine trees were cut into logs by the Wood-Russ Lumber Company and loaded onto railroad cars. The logs were then hauled down the dummy line to Red Lick where they were sawed into lumber that was loaded onto train cars on the main line and shipped up north for building purposes. In Lincoln County, Mississippi, other timber companies cut long leaf pine timber. There were mills in Pike County, Franklin County, Copiah County, and other areas in South Mississippi where this timber grew. Some say the Yankees saw these virgin pines when they were down here during the Civil War and later came back to harvest this fine timber. I don't know about that, but that's what they say.

Wood-Russ Lumber Company had an office and logging camp located near my father's house, and when the office was closed, they left behind, among other things, this old ledger. The book is about eighteen inches long, fifteen inches wide, and two inches thick. There are about five hundred pages, and only the left pages were used for recording business. That left the pages on the right side available for copying songs. Many of the songs have the author's name and date posted. A label inside the front cover reads "Dameron-Pierson Company, Limited, Manufacturing Stationers and Office Outfitters, New Orleans." A picture of their building is shown on the label and the caption reads, "We occupy this entire building." It was a very large building, six stories high. Their name is written vertically down one corner of the building. There are about thirty songs recorded in the book. The following songs were copied into the book by Daddy: "Song of a Dying Cowboy," March 2, 1931; "Song of a Texas Ranger"; and "When the Work's All Done This Fall." Neither the actual artist nor the original writers of those three songs are recorded in the book. Daddy copied "Hobo Bill's Last Ride" by Jimmie Rogers in the book on March 3, 1931. On March 15, 1931, Daddy copied "The Fatal Wedding," writing with a feather, three hundred and ten words with only one mistake in only one word. With no whiteout or any other way to correct a mistake, he couldn't afford many. As he moved the feather in a circular motion to form the letters, the feather made wide and narrow lines. He had a very unique penmanship. Daddy was left-handed; it is unusual that his pen strokes do not appear to be written left-handed. I observed his handwriting over the years, and he never curved his hand or offset the paper as most left-handed people do. Other songs are "Lonely and Blue" by Jimmie Rogers; "Farewell to the Lighthouse"; "A Little Rosewood Casket"; "The Wreck of the Ole No. 9," a railroad song; "The Wreck of the 1262"; "The Wreck of the 1256"; two other railroad songs; "Twenty-one Years"; "My Sweet Sunny South"; "My Little Darling Pal of Mine"; "Moonlight on the River Colorado"; "Nobody's Darling But Mine"; "Don't Forget Me, Little Darling"; and "Jack O' Diamonds" to name a few. Some of the copiers besides my father are Kattie Bell Davenport, Sarah Clanton, Hattie Clanton, R. C. Jordan, Ruby Lea Martin, and Willard Pritchard.

The folk would sit out on the front porch at night and listen to the steam engine on the old dummy line blow its steam whistle. Daddy said you could tell which engineer was at the throttle by the lonesome sound of the whistle. There were many railroad songs in those days, and the freight train whistles were very popular. The engineers knew people lived all over those woods and liked to hear a train whistle. In the still of night, that whistle could be heard miles away. When the train approached a crossing, they would pull that cord on the steam whistle for a few seconds, let off, and pull it a couple more times more slowly to make sounds that would chill your blood. Then the train would snake on around the hills and approach another crossing and blow that whistle again. As the train traveled farther toward Red Lick, you could barely hear the whistle in the distance. If only that could have been recorded! There are a few Jimmy Rogers records that have that sound on them, and that kind of gives me an idea of how it must have sounded. You can also hear that sound in the movies, but the movie sounds aren't as romantic as the whistles on the records.

In the early forties, Daddy was building a chicken coop, and when he hit one of the nails with the hammer, the nail flew back and hit his right eye. After several years, he lost sight in his eye because of that accident. He was very energetic and never was much of a leisure man. He held a full forty-hour job pipe fitting in construction work, and he still worked on Saturdays on the farm—cutting wood, working in his vegetable garden, repairing fences, and whatever else needed to be done. He would have us kids busy helping with those chores.

Daddy told me once that I could learn a lot of things if I didn't think I already knew whatever it was that I was trying to learn. He said, "If you think you know something, that will keep you from learning what you should know." He said, "If you want to have a lot of friends, one way is to lose a lot of arguments." He told me once that I would become whatever I thought I was. Dad said that the sorriest words he had ever heard were, "If only." He had a dry wit about him and liked to make people smile.

Mr. Clint Shelton came by the house one day when we were on our way to the field to hoe peanuts. Seeing the hoe over Daddy's shoulder, he said, "Looks like you got some hoeing to do, Tom."

Daddy stopped, smiled at Mr. Clint, and said, "Yeah, I got to get that grass out of them peanuts."

Mr. Clint said, "With all this rain we been having, that grass is with 'em, ain't it?"

Daddy said, "Naw, it was with 'em, but it's done past 'em now."

Mr. Clint got a kick out of that.

During his youth, Daddy was hunting one day and came upon Mr. Clint hauling a wagonload of something out of the forest. The steel band around the wagon wheel had come off. That is called the tire. Mr. Clint had wired it back on and patched it as best he could to get it home, so he could repair it properly. It just wasn't working, and he was thinking about taking the wheel off and dragging it home, repairing it, and bringing it back. Daddy happened along during that time and told Mr. Clint that they could fix it right there. He used a method that he had seen his father use in his blacksmith shop. They built a fire in a circle and laid the steel tire on some rocks to hold it off the ground over the fire and got it very hot. They then lifted it with sticks over the wheel that they had held off the ground with rocks. They fitted the tire over the wheel and poured water that they had brought from the nearby creek around the tire. The water caused the hot iron tire to shrink and draw tightly around the wooden wheel. They borrowed a couple of screws from each of the three other wheels and fastened the tire onto the wheel. It was as good as new. The screws would not hold if the tire was loose. As the wheel pressed against the ground, the upper side of the rigid steel tire would push upward and work the screws out of the wood. Daddy explained that the wood had dried and shrunk, making the tire larger than the wheel and that was what made all the screws come out in the first place. With the wheel shrunk tightly around the wheel, this budging action wouldn't occur. Mr. Clint said, "Tom, I can't believe that could be fixed that simply."

Daddy said, "Everything is simple once you understand it, Clint." Smart boy, my Dad.

One day a friend and cousin Pete Maher and I were helping Daddy do some plumbing work under a house in Fayette, and Daddy was crawling under there to help. It was a tight space, and Daddy was grunting as he crawled under the beams.

Pete asked, "Can you make it, Uncle Tom?"

Daddy replied, "Well, Pete, I ain't got no money."

Pete replied, laughing, "When you ain't got no money, you got to make it, right, Uncle Tom?"

Most people I know would not have been in a joking mood in

that situation, but my dear father was like that, he would make light of almost any situation. That made him fun to be around. Almost everybody who knew him very well called him Uncle Tom even if they were no kin at all. I guess he was just too friendly of a guy to be called mister.

His only hobbies were hunting and fishing. He loved to fish for bream in farm ponds around the area. He used a long cane pole with a line as long as the pole and a cork and hook baited with a cricket. He loved to get a bream about hand size on the line. The pole would bend, and he would yell from the other side of the pond, "Awh, looka here!" This would get his fishing companions' attention, and he would let the bream swim and slowly pull him in. You could tell he was really enjoying himself. I would go fishing with him when I was a small boy on Blue Goose Creek. This creek ran across our entire farm. It bent around behind the barn and went out through the woods and across the pasture. Daddy would take my mother and me down there with short fishing poles and lines, and we would bait up with earthworms and sawyers. Sawyers are the larvae of some kind of wood bug that we would chop out of rotten timber lying on the ground. Sometimes, the other kids would go with us, and I remember several different people going fishing with us on the Blue Goose. We would catch catfish and different species of perch. The best fishing holes were in front of log drifts where the water swirled as it flowed past the drifts. We fished with tight lines. The fish would bite, and I would yell, "I'm getting a bite!"

Daddy would say, "Let him go. He will swim under that drift in a minute, and then you pull 'em out." It would be a catfish about ten inches long or a yellow perch about hand size, but to a small boy like me, it was as exciting as if it were a blue marlin. Daddy was having very good luck catching fish in a hole of water one day and called me to come over there. He said, "Throw your hook in here by mine; they are biting pretty good right here."

I said, "Daddy, I don't want to catch your fish."

He said, "I would rather see you catch a fish than catch one myself."

I don't remember making a response to him, but I remember how good it felt to be loved that way by my father. That love has been passed on to my children and other children that I know, because I know kids do appreciate things, but being children, they sometimes don't offer an expression of thanks.

My father always took time for us kids, and if he did not have the leisure time, he would involve us in helping him work. Daddy had an excellent way of correcting us. He would warn us one or two times to behave ourselves, and if that didn't work, he would say, "If I have to tell you again, I'm going to whip you." We knew he meant that, and so we behaved. For that reason, I only got about two or three whippings by him. I was telling him once about someone who always annoyed me. I told him I just couldn't stand that person. He said, "If someone annoys you, that cloud has a silver lining too." He said, "That teaches us things about ourselves that annoy other people."

Daddy told a story about his friend named Bert, who lived near Red Lick. It seems Bert didn't have a horse or vehicle in those days, and that must have been around the twenties or thirties. Bert didn't mind walking, and since he was a small man and in very good physical condition, probably from all the walking, he walked with a fast pace. Bert walked over to Lorman, which was about six miles from where he lived, on a regular basis. Finally, one day, Bert bought himself a horse, and the first day he owned the horse, he rode over to Lorman. Later that afternoon, another of Mr. Bert's friends was sitting on the porch of Mr. Henry Spencer's store in Red Lick and saw Bert walking home from Lorman. Bert was stepping very lively as he passed the front of Henry's store, and he threw up a hand to his friend sitting on the front porch. Bert was about five miles from Lorman at this point, and his friend, knowing that Bert had bought the horse, asked, "Bert, where is your horse?"

Hearing that question, Bert stopped abruptly and snapped his finger saying, "By George, I'll just have to step back over to Lorman and get 'im!"

Daddy told a story about a gentleman in the community who liked to tell lies and became famous for being the biggest liar in Jefferson County. His first name was Louie. One day, he was in town and two or three fellows who knew Louie saw him walking down the street past them. One person yelled, "Hey, Louie, why don't you stop and tell us one?"

They all laughed at the idea, and Louie replied, "I don't have time to stop and tell ya'll one right now, fellows." Looking down at the ground, he continued, "Daddy died this morning, and I'm on the way to the funeral home to get them to go get him."

They all said how sorry they were to hear about Louie's daddy, and Louie walked on down the street. The gentlemen went on home and got dressed. They told some other people about the death and went on out to Louie's house. As they drove up, they saw Louie's daddy sitting on the front porch. He greeted the gentlemen and invited them in. They were amazed at seeing the old man alive and confronted Louie, "Why did you tell us a lie like that, boy?"

To which, Louie replied, "Well, ya'll told me to stop and tell ya'll one, and as I said, I didn't have time to stop and tell ya'll one, so I just told ya'll one while I was walkin'."

Louie told another good one once. He said he was fishing one day, and a stump was out in the edge of the water. He saw a squirrel swim out there and jump up on that stump and start eating a pecan that had been lying on top of the stump. He said a big ole bass hopped out of the water, jumped over that stump, and swallowed that squirrel. He said, "Now, ya'll ain't gonna believe this, but in a few minutes, that bass was back out there putting another pecan on top of that stump."

He said he was fishing one day, and he hooked a real large fish. The fish pulled his line down deep, until the end of his fishing pole was in the water. He couldn't pull him out; it was hung in there. He pulled off his clothes and dove in there to see if he could unhang his line, hoping the fish was still on it. He got down there, and there was an old car on the bottom. That catfish had swam through the open window of that car and rolled the window up. "That's what had my line hung," he said. When somebody said they couldn't believe that, Louie would say, "If you had been there, you would have believed it."

Sometime in the late 1800s, James Monroe Smith, my grandpa's father, and his brothers were in the cotton gin business. They needed a new boiler to make the steam and drive the engines to turn the belts. They ordered the boiler from someplace up north and had it shipped by rail to a town that is now called Pattison, Mississippi. The town in those days was called Martin. Whoever filled out the order and ship-to address made the letter "a" in Martin look like an "o," so the boiler went to Morton, Mississippi. The railroad would not ship the boiler from Morton to Martin free of charge, claiming it wasn't their error. After the cost of the boiler and the cost of freight, their business didn't have enough capital to pay the extra freight. They decided to connect two eight-wheel log wagons together that were pulled by oxen. They had to take a covered wagon pulled by mules with the animal food, human rations, clothes, and other necessary things for the trip to go get the boiler and haul it home. There were approximately eighty-one airline miles between Martin and Morton. There were roads of some type between the two towns, and of course they didn't travel in a straight line, so we will never know just how many miles were traveled, and we don't know the actual number of days that were spent on the trip. They got the boiler loaded onto the two wagons and started home. The wagons bearing the heavy boiler bogged down in the rough terrain and had to be dug out or pulled out any way possible. When they stopped to set up camp at night, they could sometimes see the smoldering smoke from the campfire the night before. That was how much progress they made on some days. They finally reached the mill with the boiler after spending more than two weeks on the trail traveling only about eighty or so miles.

On November 15, 1979, Daddy and Mama were watching a television show; they were laughing as they watched the show. After the show was over, around 7:00 PM, Mama told Daddy to come on into the kitchen and they would have supper. Daddy got up out of his recliner, took a couple of steps, put his hand around to the small of his back, and said to Mama, "Oh, this is it, hon." He staggered backward and sat back in the recliner. He had passed away in a few seconds. I thought that was a proper way for him to go, without a lot of suffering. There had been many times that we would go down for a visit, and Daddy would be in the garden working. Mama would tell us we had better talk to Daddy about taking it easy, because his health wasn't very good anymore. I would tell her that if we picked him up in that garden, we would know he went happy, doing something he loved. He would never be happy sitting around taking it easy.

Daddy had heard two black ladies talking on the street in Fayette one day. One asked the other about some gathering she had been to and the other one said, "Yes, I was there, and we had a large time." Daddy repeated that many times over the years using "We had a large time," rather than the usual cliché, "We had a real big time." At his funeral, a lady said to me, "Ya'll should put that on Uncle Tom's tombstone, 'He had a large time.'" That would have fit his lifestyle perfectly, because he did have a "large time" all his life. We never did that, but we placed a nice stone where he and Mother are buried.

3

My Mother

Where, oh where, do I begin a story about my precious mother. Annie Mae Beesley Smith was born February 2, 1917, in a house on the south side of Highway 552, about three and one-half miles west of Highway 28 in Jefferson County. Mama was a stocky lady but not real overweight and about five feet four inches tall.

She grew up in the Clark, Mississippi, community. Her home most of the time was on Block Foster Road about a mile or so south of Highway 552 across a small creek. It's the first creek crossing the road as one travels south. The road travels up a hill, and on the crest of that hill is an old road barely visible now on the west side. I'm not sure how far down that road it was to the house site. Just past that road still going south on Block Foster Road, probably another mile, is the Singletary place. The Singletarys were my mother's maternal grandparents, Grandma Love's parents. The Singletary Cemetery is located on the left side of the road going south.

Mama and Daddy loved to garden, and one year, Mama canned seven hundred quarts of vegetables and fruit. She hired a black lady, Mrs. Mahaley, to help her with the work. I have mentioned Lee in another chapter. Mrs. Mahaley was Lee's grandmother. Mama would be working most all the time around the house. She had a Maytag wringer-type washing machine for doing laundry. Wire was stretched between posts for hanging out clothes to dry. We boys helped Mama do the laundry, but not nearly as much as we should have. She was too easy on us, and we were too lazy to care.

The laundry was allowed to collect for one week, and then it would be wash day. The Maytag sat on the back porch up against the wall. We would pull it out. It had a caster on each leg. When it was out in the middle of the floor, we would lock one caster that had a locking device on it so it would stay put while the dasher oscillated back and forth. There was a homemade bench on the back porch that Daddy had built. The bench was pulled around near the washing machine and two No. 3 washtubs were set on the bench. The Maytag and both tubs were filled with water. White things were put in the machine first, and after they were washed, the clothes were pulled out of the machine, run through the wringer, and put into one rinsing tub. Then the wringer was pivoted around so it was positioned between the two tubs on the bench. The clothes were pulled out of the first tub, run through the wringer, and then put into the second tub. The clothes were then pulled out of the second tub, run through the wringer, and put into the laundry hamper. The hamper of clothes was carried out to the clothesline and hung out to dry. They had to hang on the clothesline a couple of hours depending on the sun and wind. After drying, they were brought back inside, folded, and put away. On real good sunshiny days, the clothes were left on the line to bleach in the sun. That made them fresher, or supposedly, it did.

Clothes that needed ironing had to be starched and were set aside as they came out of the second rinsing tub. Mama would boil some water on the stove and pour in some starch pellets. The pellets would melt in the hot water and make a starch solution. The clothes were dipped in the starch, wrung out by hand, and carried out to the clothesline where they were hung out to dry. Later, they were brought back inside and ironed. Wash day meant just exactly that—it took all day long. Needless to say, when we came in from school, the first thing we did was pull off our school clothes and hang them up. We were expected to get two days out of a set of clothes. Mama was very adamant about telling us kids not to get our clothes dirty at school. We would be very careful on the first day of wearing fresh clothes, but we didn't have to worry the second day because she didn't expect us to wear the clothes more than two days between washings.

Mama didn't allow any profane language around her, and there was no smoking, except for Daddy's smoking, of course. She insisted we all go to church on Sunday and Sunday night. We never missed a day or night of the church revival services. Mama never took things very seriously; she just believed certain things were going to happen and one should just make the most of it. I think she was right in that respect. If a person reasons things out, they will usually agree. Most problems are no worse than we make them, and we shouldn't get upset about the least little thing that happens. She never made us go to regular checkups at the doctor, and if we did get sick, she tried the old home remedies on us first. Soaking peppermint candy in whiskey made good cough syrup. ST37 stopped bleeding, and a round of black draught two days running (pardon the pun) would clean you out and make you feel better. Now, I do believe there is something to that. Mr. Clint Shelton used to say, "That black draught will sweep your liver off and blow your bottom out!" Liniment was rubbed on sore muscles. If you stuck a splinter under your skin, she placed fat, salted meat on it overnight with a bandage to hold it in place. That would either draw the splinter/ briar/thorn out, or it would fester enough to be picked out with a needle the next day. It worked pretty well most of the time. If you had a cold and your sinuses were stuffed, just boil some pine needles and breathe the vapors. You could also rub Vicks salve on your chest at night. I'm not sure that ever helped, because I only did that one time. I couldn't stand the smell and never allowed that to happen again. Gargling with antiseptic mixed in water was good for a sore throat. An antiphlogistine cream rubbed on a piece of cloth and taped to a sore spot, such as an aching muscle or joint, would soothe the pain.

Mama believed in "live and let live." She might not like the way a person was living, but she didn't consider it up to her to be judgmental. My wife, Ruthie, always said Ms. Annie Mae was an inspiration for her. Many times, a mother-in-law gets a bad rap, but Ruthie wanted to be the same kind of mother-in-law to her in-laws when our children married. Both our son and daughter married several years ago. In all those years, Ruthie has not once told them how to spend their money or how to rear their children. She never told them things they should or shouldn't do or give them any direction or advice that they didn't request, even when she didn't agree with something they were doing.

In other words, like Mama, she minds her own business. For one thing, when one is not telling grown children how to live their lives, it results in happy family gatherings. We directed our children for many years, but there comes a time when they have outgrown the need for our directions. We have to remind ourselves of this until we accept the concept that whatever the child has become, we have to find that acceptable. That is kind of like how my mother thought about things. She said you can talk to a child all you want, but that child is going to live however the parent lives. In other words, setting examples is more important than giving advice to children.

Mama learned to drive a car right after she and Daddy bought one. She was driving their 1939 Ford Coupe one day with her cousin Thelma and my brother William in the car with her. They got to a steep hill on a little gravel road. She said she was talking to Thelma and didn't speed the car up when approaching a certain hill. The car stalled, and she was trying to let it roll back to the flat so she could run at the hill again. She accidentally backed the car off into a deep ditch and rolled it over almost flat on its side. She and Thelma managed to push the car back on its wheels themselves. Neither she nor Thelma thought they could do that, but they gave it a try while they waited for someone to drive by. She said the battery had turned over and the water drained out, so she got a hose pipe that was kept in the trunk, siphoned water out of the radiator, and filled the battery. They got the car started, and it pulled itself out of the ditch. They were lucky it had been dry weather. They were so proud of themselves for taking matters into their own hands and not needing any help.

My mother was a strong woman in many ways. She didn't complain about material things she didn't have. She believed in saving money and making do with what she already had. She felt very blessed, because she had a good, solid roomy house with indoor plumbing, an abundance of food, and so many things she didn't have growing up. She had a good, hardworking husband and four wonderful children (her words). I guess three of them were wonderful. I tried. Mama was a long way from the poverty she had experienced growing up. During her childhood between birth and seventeen, barely getting by was the norm. She was saddened of course when Daddy passed on, but she didn't grumble. She was strong, saying things like he was with the Lord and that she and Daddy had a lot of good years together. Many years after Daddy had passed away, she was diagnosed with bone cancer. The way she handled it still amazes me to this day. Mama didn't think of it as a death sentence; she felt it was the Lord's will and he had given her a very good and happy life. She was determined not to dwell on her sickness. She said to worry about it was nonsense, because she couldn't do one thing about it. Mama made the regular doctor visits and took the prescribed medications, but she never worried. I've never known another person with faith as strong as hers, except my sister Bessie who reminds me of a lot of Mama.

Mama loved to fish for those bream in farm ponds around the country. That was one of the many things she and Daddy had in common, so we all really enjoyed doing that together. My mother loved company, and she was the perfect hostess when mostly uninvited company arrived. My parents never offered an invitation, except to mention to friends, "Ya'll come to see us sometimes." Most of the kinfolk and friends would come near mealtime. We would be eating and just finishing a meal when a carload of people might drive up. She would always ask, "Ya'll want to come have some dinner with us."

The reply would be, "No, we didn't come to eat, but we haven't had dinner yet."

She would insist, "Ah, come on and sit down. I'll put on another pone of cornbread or pan of biscuits. It won't take but a minute." While she was at it, she would open another jar of canned vegetables and make another skillet of gravy or whatever.

I saw her do that many times, and she made the best biscuits I have ever eaten. To hear a lot of people tell it, she made the best biscuits and tomato gravy they ever ate. When our Memphis, Tennessee, cousins Fred and Georgia would come down, Uncle Fred (we called our older cousins uncle or aunt; we thought it was better than Mr. or Mrs.) would ask Mama to make him a couple of pans of those biscuits to take back home with him. She would freeze them so they would keep until he got back to Memphis. He put them in his freezer until Aunt Georgia got around to baking them for him. I think you have got to love somebody's biscuits to go to all that trouble for them. When Uncle Fred said he loved Annie Mae's biscuits, I think he really meant it.

One of Mama's specialties was tomato gravy. She chopped cooked tomatoes and stirred them in regular flour gravy. The tomatoes made it very tasty. She made banana cakes when I was a boy. It was my favorite cake for many years until I finally outgrew it. She placed banana slices between the layers of the cake and more slices on top. We kids also liked Mama's pecan pies, and the three of us boys could eat almost a whole pie at one sitting. Two pies wouldn't last more than a day. We were arguing about sharing the pies one day, and Mama said, "I'll just make ya'll a pie each." And so, she did. We ate pecan pie until we were about burned out on it. Mama also made a yellow cake with coconut icing that was real special.

One time, our Aunt Ruth made a cake of some kind for Mama's birthday and mailed it from Rayville, Louisiana. It arrived well intact. The only instructions on the box was an arrow, with "This side up" written under it. I just wonder how a cake would arrive today in the mail. Even though we hatched our own chickens, Mama ordered some baby chicks from Sears and Roebuck's department store in Memphis, and they arrived in the mail. The only thing different about that from the way other mail was handled was that the mail carrier would bring the chicks down the driveway to the house instead of leaving them beside the road near the mailbox. They were placed in a box about two by three feet in size and about three inches high. It had water and feed in there. I don't know if the feed and/or water was replenished as the freight came along the route all the way from Memphis or not, but I don't remember seeing a dead chicken in the box. I'm sure that if one of the chickens had been dead, Sears would have sent either a credit or another chicken. They trusted people in those days and would never have thought the person was lying.

Mama was big on Christmas. She would bundle us up, and we would go out into the pasture, cut a cedar tree, bring it home, and decorate it. I loved decorating the tree. We had most of the decorations, but we made some of our own. I never remember believing in Santa Claus. Mama wanted us to believe in Santa Claus, but my older brothers somehow let me know he wasn't real when I was very young. They regretted letting me know, but somehow it just came out. I never let Mama know that I didn't believe in Santa, because I thought it might affect my presents. She would get out the Sears and Roebuck catalog in early December. We would go through there and pick out toys. She would order maybe one or two toys, but the rest of that money went for school clothes. We had more than one present, but mostly, the gifts were clothes. Clothes were as exciting as toys. New jeans, socks, T-shirts, and button-down shirts would make a kid very happy. Sometimes, we would get a new jacket and maybe a pair of shoes. We might know when the packages came from Sears if it was a Saturday, but we wouldn't be home during the week, and Mama could hide the presents while we were at school. Even though we didn't believe in Santa, we got a big surprise when we opened our Christmas gifts even though we had selected those things in the catalog weeks earlier.

Daddy would bring home one fruit for each of us from work, usually on payday. We would not be allowed to eat the fruit until after supper. William and I would eat ours pretty quickly right after supper, but J. P. would wait until later on in the evening and peel his and eat it ever so slowly, making William and me gripe about not having ours. How we wished we had more pieces of fruit. Sometimes, it might be only one banana or one apple or one orange. When Christmastime came one year, Daddy brought home a full box of mixed fruit. We had all the fruit we could eat, and we could eat it anytime of the day, regardless of mealtime. Mama had to beg us to eat that fruit before it ruined. We forced some of it down listening to her remind us of all the griping we had done about not having enough fruit to eat. For some reason, I have loved fruit all my days. Maybe that was it. I have always kept some around the house ever since I was grown. I sometimes think about how I enjoyed that one piece of fruit that Daddy would bring home once per week. That one morsel meant much more to me than I could ever realize, until the Christmas that I had an entire box full of fruit. At that point in time, I realized the difference between having only one thing and having all I wanted. Somehow, quantity takes away some of the pleasure.

For several years, Mama attended Home Demonstration meetings in the neighborhood. They were sponsored by a state organization that had something to do with the United States Department of Agriculture. I'm not 100 percent sure, but I think it was a result of the Smith-Lever Act of May 8, 1914, passed by Congress. The idea was to teach farm women how to be homemakers. It was interesting and fun for the ladies to get together and learn things. They would take turns hosting the party in different individuals' homes. The government would furnish the refreshments, and it would always be in the afternoons for two or three hours once per month. There were very good lessons for newlyweds, but it was mostly just a party for the older women. The government lady would schedule these meetings in different parts of the county once per month. She would have a meeting in some neighborhood almost every day.

One day, when I was in high school, another boy and I were selected by the county agent to go out to one of the parties and give a lecture on electrical safety. We talked about extension cord safety and the danger of plugging too many appliances into one receptacle and things like that. Cords weren't as safe as they are today. The cord that attached to an iron would fray where it came out of the iron, because of all the action a lady put the iron through while ironing clothes. Vacuum cleaner cords were also subject to fraying. We advised them to watch for that and have a new cord installed when they noticed a frayed cord. I can't remember all the safety tips we taught, but there were several things around the house that a homemaker might not think about. The agent was selective enough to pick a kid that lived in each neighborhood, so all the ladies attending would know the kids and that helped keep us from being too nervous. It was fun, and we enjoyed it. We were 4-H Club members, and we had learned those things in our club meetings. Sometimes, they would ask for a professional volunteer, like a plumber, electrician, roofer, carpenter, or other household businesspeople to give talks on different things that would be helpful around the house. The professionals readily volunteered, because it gave them a chance to let the people know they were in business. They would give advice about termite control and all that.

Mama had health problems in the 90s. She had moved into a mobile home in her daughter Bessie's backyard sometime in the 80s. She moved there, so Bessie and her family could take care of her. She also liked living there, so she could take care of Bessie's children, especially Casey, who was born after she moved there. Mama was diagnosed with bone cancer. The doctors told us that as time passed, she would start breaking bones easily. She was sitting on the commode one day, and when she started to stand, one of the bones broke in her leg. There was no one else around. She managed to pull the telephone off the nightstand with something that she could reach from the commode. They repaired the bone with steel plates, and she lived for quite a few years longer using a walker.

The home hospice nurses called us all in one day during one of their visits. They explained that the doctors had told them her pain was getting extreme, and she would probably pass away while still on the morphine. She would either have to be fed with tubes or be allowed to come around to eat. If she came out of the sedation, she would be in terrible pain. We decided to just sit with her until she passed. Mama came around enough for us to all tell her good-bye. Of course, we did that without telling her she was dying. All her children were there and several of her grandchildren. About eight o'clock on February 9, 2001, she went to heaven to be with Daddy.

Thomas and Annie Mae Smith family
Rear: Annie Mae and Tom
Front: William, James, Bessie, J. P.

4

Religion

Our mother was very adamant about us kids avoiding sinful living. She and Daddy were members of the Unity Baptist Church a few miles from home. We weren't allowed to say curse words, of course, and she wanted us home on Sundays for church and Sunday school. We were allowed to miss occasionally, but she liked for us to go to church with whomever we were visiting. She especially wanted us home on the Sundays that the reverend came for lunch and dinner. The church had a system for serving the reverend and his family lunch. Since we were out in the rural area of the country, the reverend came from town, sometimes from as far away as Natchez or Jackson even. There were no restaurants around there, of course, so a family would serve him lunch to keep him from having to drive all the way to town.

I experienced several misunderstandings about my religion that I wrestled with all my childhood days. Some of the things I didn't understand arose when watching "men of the cloth." I experienced one that I will mention a little later in this chapter.

We always referred to the reverend as "preacher," so as I continue, preacher will be used in place of reverend. That is what he was called by all the people. We had services from 10:00 A. M. until noon and in the evening, so the preacher would be around all day. The church had a lunch-serving log for inviting the preacher for lunch and supper and to visit with whomever's turn it was to serve him after church. After lunch, he would visit with the family awhile, then go over to visit the other church families. If someone had missed church that day, that was the first house he would visit. If someone was sick or had lost a family member, he would visit them. He would come back to the house for supper before evening services. He would then go back to church for the evening service. It was a good system, and everybody seemed to enjoy it.

I know we kids enjoyed it, because Mama would put the white tablecloth on the table for that meal. She cooked a fine meal and had a pie or cake for dessert, usually both. We had to mind our manners and eat properly, as she would say. It would always be an occasion fit for royalty. It came around about once every three months. Sometimes, Mama would fill in for a family who couldn't take their turn for some reason like being ill or having a child that was ill or something they had to attend to. If they had a good excuse, Mama didn't mind taking their turn. Then they would pay her back by taking her turn the next time. We kids certainly didn't mind having an excellent meal and dining at a well-dressed table. We also had special china for the occasion and special silverware. At other times, we used the chipped, mismatched dinnerware. If we had certain guests, we used the white tablecloth, fine china, and good silverware as well. We would have a couple of different desserts and all that.

When I was eight and William was thirteen, we had not yet joined the church. J. P. had joined several years before, but William and I hadn't gotten around to it yet. There was a church revival that we had once per year. The regular preacher would be there, and he would bring a revival preacher to preach the revival. We would have dinner on the grounds at the church on that Sunday, stay all day, have lunch, sing, and listen to the preacher preach two sermons. The church would have church morning and evening every day of that week. After the morning service, the two preachers would visit the members around the neighborhood.

A preacher named Brother Ball was the revival preacher that year. He came by the house for lunch, and Daddy was at work. I don't remember where everybody else was, but only Mama, William, and I were at home that day. Brother Ball asked Mama if her family was saved. She told him they all were except William and me. He asked us to accompany him out to the woodpile that was out front, so we could have a private conversation. He sat down on a block of wood, and William and I sat on the ground in front of him. He went into why we should be saved and asked why we weren't. I told him I hadn't joined the church, because I was only eight years old and I had planned to get around to it. He asked me why I was waiting, and I told him I didn't know. Later, I was telling Grandma Love about the event, and she told me I should have told him that God takes care of little children. She said that Jesus had said, "Suffer not little children, come unto me." I slapped my knee and told her I wished I had thought of that.

We told him we would accept Christ as our savior that night, and he seemed to be satisfied. William and I were sitting together in the rear of the church that night, and after the sermon, we all sang, "Just as I Am." That was the song they sang when they were trying to get people to join the church. I wasn't going down until William went. William didn't want to go down until somebody else went forward. Nobody went, so we didn't go either. Several kids and a couple of grown-ups had joined earlier in the week and maybe some on Sunday, so there wasn't anybody else left to join except William and me. I told William if we didn't get on down there, that preacher was going to come back and ask us why we had told him an untruth. Mama understood why we hadn't joined, but she wasn't letting us off the hook. She only had two kids to go and her whole family would then be heaven-bound. I knew she needed that. If she lost a child, she would have been heartbroken enough, but knowing they had never witnessed Christ, she would be sick and heartbroken that she might not ever see them again.

The last night, a Friday night, William started on down there just as soon as the song started. I was glad. I wanted to get it over with. I was a young boy and didn't like that manner of attention. We went on down, and after the song was over, the preacher told the congregation who we were and a little about us. Then they started another song, and the congregation filed by and shook our hands and blessed us. A couple of Sunday afternoons later, it was time to be baptized. One of the church members had a farm near the church with a nice large cattle pond. We all went over there and were baptized. I don't remember just how many of us there were, but it was all the ones who had joined the church during the revival. We waded out into the pond with the pastor, and the entire crowd sang a song about a beautiful river. I remember thinking they needed a song about a beautiful pond. He took us one by one and held a handkerchief over our noses as he leaned us backward until we were completely submerged. He then brought us back up, and we waded to the bank and waited until the service was over. We then went up to the farmer's house and changed into dry clothes we had brought for the occasion and went home feeling saved. I remember it being a good feeling.

One Sunday, when I was about ten or twelve years of age, my cousin Johnny and I were riding horses through the woods and we saw a squirrel run up a tree. He had his .22-caliber pump-action rifle. It seemed he always had that rifle with him when he was out riding his horse. He said, "Let's get that squirrel!" With that, he dismounted his horse, hitched him, and ran over to the other side of the tree where the squirrel had climbed up. He ran around the tree with his .22 at port arms. He yelled back at me and said, "I don't see him! Is he on your side?" Meaning could I see the squirrel? I could see the squirrel just as plain as if he were a fresh huckleberry pie sitting in the middle of the dining room table. He was lying flat out on my side of that tree. "Nope, I can't see him over here," I lied.

You see, it was Sunday, and my mama didn't allow any hunting or fishing on Sunday. She had drilled that into us kids all our lives. "Remember the Sabbath and keep it holy," she would say. Being Sunday, it meant guns were not allowed. Now I didn't want to chastise Johnny, but I just couldn't take part in this hunt myself. I had just been born again and was a devout Christian. I had to avoid this temptation the Lord was sending my way. I thought he was testing me to see if I was or was not a real Christian.

John asked again, "You sure you can't see him? That tree is pretty bare, and I can see all over it on this side."

I proclaimed again, "I just don't see him." I was hoping that squirrel would make a move and get me out of my uncomfortable situation. The squirrel wouldn't move, and I just could not lie to my good friend and cousin anymore. "Oh, yeah, there he is about ten feet from the top." I tried to sound surprised. With that, the squirrel made a fast dart down a limb, jumped to the next tree, and was gone. John was a dead shot with that .22, but he missed that one. I doubt if that squirrel could have been hit with a shotgun. He was running very fast on that limb and sailed like a bird to the next tree. We got back on our horses, and I was thinking to myself, *God was testing me today to see if I would hunt on Sunday.* We reined our horses down the path and across the little creek. Coming up the other creek bank, I was wrestling with my conscience. *What else could I have done? I wasn't squirrel hunting in the first place, and after all, I did try to stay out of it.* I continued thinking, *The squirrel wasn't killed, and if the Lord was testing me, well, I just hope I passed the test, and that's just all there is to it.* I just knew anytime now Johnny was going to ask me why I didn't see that squirrel. He never mentioned it again. Letting that squirrel get away wasn't a very big deal. He and I had let many get away before, and that one would not be the last. I never quite made peace with myself about that until I was grown. Had I done the right thing or not? I pondered that question many times during my childhood and over other matters such as that one. I had lied about not seeing the squirrel, and it was a sin to lie. I think the right thing to have done was tell my cousin that we shouldn't be hunting on Sunday, because it was a sin. Then I would be out of the box altogether. I just didn't think of that at the time.

Where the Blue Goose left our farm, it ran onto the Bailey farm and forked into Clark's Creek. The Clark was bigger and had bigger fishing holes. Just before the Blue Goose forked with the Clark, there was a ten-foot-high waterfall over rocks. We would catch fish in the water hole at the bottom of that waterfall. After school was out one year, we all went down to the waterfall to camp out. We had a tent, groceries, fishing poles, and other such things. We stayed Friday night, Saturday, and Saturday night, but Mama had told us to be home for church on Sunday morning. After church, the preacher came home with us for Sunday dinner. We kids were anxious to get back to camp after dinner, and the preacher said he would like to come with us and see the waterfall. Daddy came with us to be with the preacher. So, we all went back to camp. In the big hole of water up the creek from the fall was a big bass on her bed. Well, there we were with a .22-caliber rifle in the camp, a big fish swimming out there just waiting to be shot, and the preacher standing there just waiting to chastise us if we even thought of shooting that fish on Sunday.

Somebody finally said, "We could shoot down beside that fish to knock him unconscious, and we could jump in there and grab it by the gills and pull it out."

Then, to our surprise, the preacher said, "Do ya'll have a gun?"

"Weeelll, yeah," somebody said as we all looked at each other.

"Why don't you shoot him then?" asked the preacher.

John Bailey, one of my neighborhood friends, started for the rifle. The rest of us were stunned, because we knew how Daddy felt about doing such a thing on Sunday, but the preacher was there and it was his idea so, why not? I never remember asking Daddy why he didn't object, but he was in a tight spot. If he told us not to shoot the fish, he would be going against the preacher, and after all, is it really sinful to shoot a fish on Sunday?

Even though it was springtime, that water was still chilly and we had to decide who would jump in and get the fish. John said he would, so somebody shot beside the fish, and the big bass turned up. John jumped in and pulled the fish out. We weren't out of the woods yet on this deal, though. We wanted that fish for our camp supper, but it was the preacher who had said to shoot the fish, and even though we would not have needed his permission if he had not been there, we felt obligated to offer him the fish. He took the fish, and he and Daddy went on back to the house. The preacher hung around the house until suppertime and asked Mama to fry it for their supper. Oh, well, things do turn out that way sometimes. We weren't all that disappointed, because Mama let us miss church that night so we could stay at our camp. I guess she figured if the preacher was going to teach us kids to shoot and fish on Sunday which was against her upbringing, why not let the kids miss church?

Paternal Great-Grandparents John Thomas Trevillion
Fransonia Abigail Humphreys Trevillion.
My father's maternal grandparents
circa: 1930

5

Trevillion Cemetery

Phillip Barnes Trevillion, Grandma Annie Trevillion Smith's grandfather, lived south of Highway 552, about one-half mile west of Blue Hill. He was born December 27, 1819, but I'm not sure where. He had come down the Mississippi River on a homemade river raft with his parents. He and his family settled in Rodney, Mississippi, and later moved to Red Lick and settled on a farm with a Spanish Land Grant. From there, they moved to Jefferson County sometime in the mid-1800s, I think. He lived on a farm he had purchased. It was around six or eight hundred acres. His daughter passed away while they were living there. That was about 1850, and in those days, they usually buried the family member near the home. In this case, they buried their daughter on a ridge just to the rear of the house. A lot of people were buried this way in those days, because it was a real problem taking them to the funeral parlor in town. Besides that, money was a problem in many cases.

Her burial on that ridge was the beginning of the Trevillion Cemetery. Other family members are buried there, and most anyone who wanted grave space was given space. After a few graves, they built a fence around the area and named it Trevillion Cemetery. Phillip Trevillion died during the Civil War of pneumonia and was shipped home for burial in the Trevillion Cemetery. I'm not sure if maybe he was still alive when he got home and later died or just exactly where he was serving in the war when he became ill. Sometime after his death, his son John Thomas inherited some of the land. John Thomas willed one hundred and sixty acres to his daughter who was my grandmother, Annie Smith, and one hundred and sixty acres to her sister, Aunt Inez. He sold the part of the land with the cemetery to O. P. Tanksley. Mr. Tanksley issued a deed for the one-acre cemetery to Great-Grandpa John Trevillion.

The house and cemetery were located on a county gravel road that has since been closed, but the caretakers of the cemetery have kept it open to maintain access to the cemetery. The house was gone before my time, but there are still remnants of the house place. The family members were caretakers of the cemetery on a voluntary basis. They would all meet there on the first Saturday in May to clean the cemetery, clean the stones, and place fresh flowers on the graves. It was an all-day job, so they all brought lunches. If the cemetery needed any upkeep that would cost money, they pooled their own money for the expenses.

Many of the graves were marked with a wooden board. One lady didn't want her grave to be rained on, so a shed was built over it and maintained for many years. An outlaw was killed in Jefferson County around that area, but I don't know just where he lived. He must not have had family around that community, because there was no one to attend to his burial. They buried the man in the cemetery, and a wild plum bush grew from his grave. The old folks said that was because he was wild. The tree finally died, and another one didn't grow there, so I'm not sure just what the wild plum meant, if anything. It was most likely just a coincidence.

Some people would move into the community for a short period, and if a family member passed away, the Trevillion family would allow the person to be buried in the cemetery. There are newborn babies buried there, in some places four or five in a row. Many names are of people that are not relatives and people whose families moved out of the area years ago or maybe shortly after their family member was buried.

As time went on, many people stopped attending the May work sessions, but they would send money to pay whomever was doing the work. Finally, the cemetery was so large with almost one hundred graves that there were more than enough people to do the work. They then decided that everyone who had family buried there would send donations and that would pay for a caretaker. That worked real well, so they started a regular annual meeting for the association. They named the event "May Day" and invited a pastor to preach for the occasion. They built tables for dinner on the grounds and a pavilion for the services. The meeting was all day with one service in the morning. They came all dressed up. They had the service, then had lunch, placed flowers on the graves, and showed their children where their family members were buried. They then had services in the afternoon, and the Trevillion Cemetery Association was born. It was a gathering with over a hundred people who came to visit old friends and family members and at the same time had a memorial service for those who had passed on. My father was caretaker for many years until his death. Now my cousin is the caretaker, and everybody still donates money for the expenses.

A few years ago, the Tanksley family clear-cut the timber off their land and poisoned the remaining hardwood timber with an airplane that sprayed hardwood poison. The plane came too close to the cemetery, and some of the poison drifted over into the cemetery and killed a couple of the large beautiful trees. I contacted the company in charge of the operation and filed a complaint with their insurance company. They sent an adjuster, and we talked about the problem. He asked for an amount of damage and agreed to my estimate. They sent us a few thousand dollars, and we now have that money drawing interest. We use those earnings to help with the expenses of the cemetery.

The ladies bring their favorite recipes and invite the other guests to try them. It's not unlike any other covered-dish meeting. My mother received a lot of compliments for her chicken and dumplings. They got to be so popular that some folks would complain that by the time they got around to Ms. Annie Mae's chicken and dumplings, they were all gone. Mama, being Mama as she was, just couldn't stand not being able to serve all those folks, so she made a dishpan full of chicken and dumplings so everyone could be served. They ate it all every year and bragged about how good they were. Mama was so proud of herself. She liked the idea of knowing her cooking was so well liked.

Different ones offer special singing, and besides that, the entire crowd sings. We used to do that without music, using old church hymnals. Finally, we found a pastor who plays a guitar. He picks the guitar and leads the singing, and we all sing. The special music singers have to furnish battery-operated CD players for their music.

My father made a survey of the cemetery with his mother to determine who was buried in the unmarked graves. He then made a plat measuring the distance from the west fence to each grave then from the south fence to each grave. The name of the person is written where the two measurements meet. That plat is recorded in the Mississippi Archives and History in Jackson. It is filed there under "Trevillion Cemetery." Anyone who wants a copy may get one there.

We have a very good and special time at this memorial gathering every year on the first Saturday in May. Everyone is invited to come and join us.

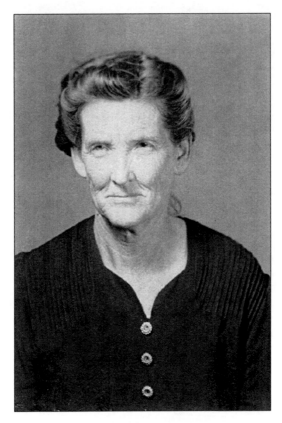

Ada Love Klar Beesley
My maternal Grandmother
Circa: 1960

6

Grandma Love

Most of her grandkids called her Granny Love, but I never did. To me, she was Grandma Love. I don't know why; maybe it was because it wasn't my idea to call her Granny Love. Whatever the reason, Ada Love Klar Beesley, who was born July 12, 1888, and died February 13, 1976, my mother's mother and Grandpa Pearl's wife, was my Grandma Love. Grandma is buried in the Singletary Cemetery located on Block Foster Road in Jefferson County, Mississippi.

Grandma was born in Jefferson County somewhere around Clark, Mississippi. Her mother was Mary Victoria Singletary (1867–1935), and her father was Jacob Klar (1854–1904). Grandpa Klar was a native German. I think it was his parents that immigrated from Germany, but I'm not sure, it might have been his grandparents. His father, whose name was also Jacob, lived in Rodney, Mississippi, and owned some land there. Grandma and Grandpa Klar are buried in the Singletary Cemetery in Jefferson County. Grandma Singletary came from either North or South Carolina. After the crops were gathered in the fall of the year and the weather cooled off, she and her sister would ride horses back home from Jefferson County. They rode sidesaddle, but I don't know how many times they made the trip or how much time the trip required.

Clark, Mississippi, no longer exists, but it was located near the Blue Hill community. Clark had a post office at one time, and just a quarter mile east of Clark on Highway 552 on the north side of the road was where Blue Hill School was located. Before Blue Hill School was built, my mother went to school at Cool Springs about two miles east on the north side of Highway 552. The schools were consolidated, and Cool Springs School was closed.

Grandma Love was of average height, kind of slim, and tough as a nail. She had a very charming personality, and I never knew anyone who didn't think the world of Ms. Love, as she was addressed. She and Grandpa Pearl were married sometime in the early twentieth century and had the following children: Aunt Pearlie Victoria, Aunt Ruth, Uncle Paul, Uncle Lewis Washington, Mama (Annie Mae), Uncle Walter, Uncle John Henry, Uncle Wiley, and Uncle Bennie Volney. Two of their children were stillborn; one was Uncle Walter's twin. The other stillborn child was born after that. He had mongolism. Then Uncle Johnny and Uncle Bennie were born. Aunt Ruth, Uncle Paul, and Uncle Walter had no middle names. Grandma had eleven children in all.

Grandma had an ambition when she was a young girl to own her own farm. Her husband, Grandpa Pearl, didn't share that dream. He was comfortable just living one day at a time. That made her dreams tough to accomplish. She loved Grandpa and was willing to live with him, even though she knew she would probably never own her farm or her own house. Finally, all her kids were grown and had married and moved out, except Uncle Benny. She wouldn't have any further use for Grandpa now and could pursue her dream. Somehow, they were separated. He went to live with his brother Henry in Union Church. She had saved some money and borrowed the rest from her children for a down payment on a farm with an old house on it six miles west of Fayette, Mississippi. The owner of the farm, Mr. Charlie Montgomery, had financed the sale himself. After making the down payment, she had to pay Mr. Montgomery the balance of the money as soon as she could. Uncle Johnny went into the army and would send part of his paycheck home to help make the payments. One time, she and Mr. Montgomery had a misunderstanding about the balance of money owed on the place. Grandma's friend Mrs. Hazel White (maiden name Pritchard) ran a store in Stampley, Mississippi. (We called her Miss Hazel.) Grandma knew Miss Hazel kept a pistol in the store so she asked Miss Hazel if she could borrow it. Miss Hazel said, "You know,

Love, you can borrow anything I have, but what are you going to do with it?"

Grandma said, "I'm going to kill Charlie Montgomery!"

Miss Hazel let Grandma have the gun, but thinking there might be trouble, she notified the county sheriff. The sheriff asked Miss Hazel why she had let Grandma have the gun. Miss Hazel explained, "Why, Sheriff, Love is my friend. She wanted the gun, so I let her have it." When Miss Hazel was telling me this story, she couldn't remember the details, but after the sheriff told Charlie that Grandma was gunning for him, he got their business straight and right away.

She raised a garden and sold vegetables. She also raised cattle and sold butter along with her hen eggs. Somehow, she came up with enough money for the payments to keep Mr. Montgomery satisfied. He didn't need the money, so he could let Grandma give him a little money along on the farm. It was income without a definite payback. That's how many of the people lived in that part of the country in those days. Grandma ran a store in Cannonsburg, Mississippi, for awhile. I used to go down and stay with her in a little side room in that store. The little side room was large enough for a bed and kitchen. She had her house on the farm and would let someone run the store while she went home to see about the farm.

I would visit Grandma from as far back as I can remember. She lived six miles west of Fayette on Highway 61 and had lived there since the late 1930s. I went down one year before I was old enough for school to visit with her in her house on the farm. She wasn't running the store yet, so we stayed there my entire visit. It was the dead of winter, and the old house she was living in at that time, had a fireplace for heat on one side and the kitchen with a wood-burning stove on the other side. She didn't want to build a fire in the stove in the kitchen sometimes, so it was cold on that side of the house. She would go over there, get food, and bring it back over by the fireplace, and we would cook on the fireplace in iron skillets and pots. I had never seen anything like that before, and it was a lot of fun. She showed me how to place a bed of coals and cover them with ashes then place a raw sweet potato on top of that and more ashes on the sweet potato then more coals on top of that. After the potato baked, I would get it out, open it, and fill it with real cow butter. There was always plenty of milk, butter, and buttermilk at Grandma's house because she always kept a milk cow.

She would tell stories about when she was growing up. During the depression of the thirties, they often did not have money to buy sugar to sweeten coffee or canned fruit or anything. So they would sweeten it with sugar cane syrup. I wanted to try that. It tasted bad so I spit it into the fire. She just roared laughing at me. It was a good idea though and was probably better than no sweetening at all. I would hold the fire poker in the fire until the end got red hot, and I would brand my initials or some lettering in a piece of wood. I tell you we had a big time. We would run a wire hanger through bacon and hold it over the fire until it fried. I liked visiting with Grandma Love because she loved children and loved to talk as well. She always kept the coffeepot going by the fire, and I would pour myself half a cup, fill it with milk, and add a lot of sugar. She would say, "Boy, I don't think your mama would want you drinking all that coffee."

Then I would say, "Well, we just won't tell her."

"Well, I don't think you should drink so much coffee either." Then she would break into some story about how I must have taken after one of my ancestors who drank a lot of coffee. It wouldn't matter if the ancestor was directly in line; they could have been an uncle or something. We parched peanuts and shelled pecans and roasted them in butter in the old iron skillet. Butter, lard, fat meat, and other such things weren't a concern in those days like they are now.

The fireplace room had two beds and some chairs, so we would sleep with the fireplace burning slowly, get up in the morning, and cook some eggs, grits, and bacon on the fire. At night, we would sit by the fire and Grandma would once again tell me stories about her life. Her stories were mostly funny and always interesting. She would always date her stories by remembering which one of her children was a baby when the story happened. I would wonder how she raised all those kids with her odd jobs. She earned money by washing and ironing for other people and would sell butter and eggs from the cows and chickens she had on the farm where she lived. She had picked peas for half of what she picked for different farmers in the Blue Hill community. Since I lived in the Blue Hill community, I was familiar with the places she talked about. She had picked cotton for a half a cent per pound.

She and my mother picked some cotton that had not had proper boll weevil treatment. They picked all day, and Grandma got forty cents and Mama got twenty cents. There was no food in the house, so they had brought home some Irish potatoes and boiled them in salt water, and that was supper.

We would sit by that fire and sometimes Baybay, my black friend from across the highway, would stop by and visit with me, and the three of us would talk on up into the night. It didn't matter how late it got, because Grandma and I didn't have anything to do after Baybay went home but go to bed and sleep as late as we wanted the next morning. I remember at least one day we stayed in bed all day. We just got up to put a stick of wood on the fire and maybe fix something to eat, then we would jump back into bed. She and Grandpa Pearl had lived on almost every hill in the Blue Hill area on different farms and in different tenant houses. They had lived on Mrs. Mattie Garrett's farm and Mrs. Jennie Segrest's farm. Grandma and Grandpa Klar had a large house and small farm, and Grandma and Grandpa had lived there a couple of times. They raised farm animals and gardens and did a little hunting and fishing and somehow got by. People can get by on a lot less than one might think. They didn't have electric bills, gas bills, car notes, phone bills, or house notes. There was no such thing as eating out or buying "heat-and-serve" foods. If people had kerosene, they had lights, and if they had a garden, milk cow, and canned fruit, they had food. There was no air conditioning or plumbing to worry about and no Wal-Mart with a million items to nickel-and-dime you to death.

Uncle Bennie, Grandma's youngest son, told the story about their moving from one farm to another. To transport the chickens, they would tie the chickens' legs together and load them on the ground slide to move them to their new home. The folk around there would tease Uncle Bennie and his brothers, saying, "Ya'll move so much, every time ya'll walk past the chicken house the chickens cross their legs." Sometimes, several of Grandma's grandkids would come out to visit. There would be Aunt Ruth King's kids: Janet, Jeanette, and Paul Vernon; and Uncle Lewis's kids: Maxine, Ruby, Charles Lewis (Pender), Walter Fred (Dubb), and Betty Idell. Walter Jr. and Kenny Lewis would also be there, and we all had a grand time. Grandma Love would use her riding whip to keep us kids in line when we would all be playing around there. This whip was about three feet in length, and it was four plait halfway from the stock and three plait to the end. She could swing that thing over her head and pop it like a rifle while she yelled out what she would do to our butts if we didn't mind her. I now know she would never have hit one of us with it, and she never did, but we didn't know that then, and we certainly didn't want to find out.

Every now and then, when we cousins see each other, somebody will mention those days and we wish we had spent more time playing together, but time means nothing to a kid, I guess. There is never a tomorrow. There were many other grandkids, of course, but they were either older or younger, and we didn't play together much, if at all. On one of my visits with Grandma Love when I was maybe eight or nine years old, I was down the driveway at Aunt Hazel's house. I was just playing around down there with my cousins Bobby and Irene, Aunt Hazel's children, and Aunt Hazel was cooking dinner. After a while, she said, "James, run up there and ask your grandma to come on down and have dinner with us."

I trotted up the drive, ran up on the porch, and yelled through the screen door to Grandma, "Hey, Grandma!" She answered, and I could see her inside, so I didn't bother to open the door. I just yelled through the screen, "Aunt Hazel wants you to come down and eat dinner. She has it ready." Grandma told me what to tell Aunt Hazel, but it didn't register in my mind.

The answer had been, "Okay, tell her I'll be down in a few minutes.

I skipped off the porch, hopped down the steps, and started on down the driveway toward Aunt Hazel's house. About halfway down the driveway, I suddenly stopped, turned around, and wondered why Grandma wasn't coming. I thought, *She did say she was coming on, didn't she? Maybe not. What exactly did she say?* I continued pondering in my mind, trying to figure it out. Since I couldn't remember, I would just have to go back up there and ask her again, but it was a long way back up there. *What will I do?* I thought, *Awh, it doesn't matter, I'll just make up something.* I trotted on up the steps, across the porch, and into Aunt Hazel's dining room.

"Is your grandma coming, James?" she asked.

I had to say something, and I didn't want to sound stupid and say,

'I *do not have a clue as to what she said, Aunt Hazel.*' So I just did what I usually did in cases like that. I lied. "Grandma said she didn't want any of your ole dinner." I don't know why I couldn't have been a little more tactful than that. I could have said, 'She said she wasn't hungry right now.' I didn't look up at Aunt Hazel when I spoke, because I was lying. If I had been looking, I might have noticed the hurt in her eyes and changed my story a little, but I wasn't looking so I just didn't realize the seriousness of the moment. Just about the time we had the food served on our plates, we heard footsteps on the front porch. *Oh, my God, that's Grandma!!!* I was embarrassed and ashamed of myself. I also knew if Aunt Hazel told Grandma what I had said, Grandma would kill me. She had never hit me, but she had threatened us with that whip many times. This little act could very well cause her to do exactly what she had promised she would do: bring that whip across my little butt a few licks. As she came through the front door and started across the living room, I jumped up and ran out the back door and around the house. I kept running up the driveway and up onto the front porch at Grandma's house. Later, after Grandma had finished eating and visiting with Aunt Hazel for a while, she decided to attend to me. When I saw her coming up the driveway, I was thinking maybe Aunt Hazel didn't mention it, but she probably did for she would want to know exactly what Grandma did say.

I decided to just wait there on the porch and face the music. Whatever happened would just have to happen, and after all, I could outrun Grandma if she came at me with that whip. "Young man, what do you mean telling a lie like that to your aunt Hazel?!!" Grandma was shouting from the front yard gate. She was pointing that finger at me, which meant she was furious with me. I didn't answer, for I was trying to think up a good answer. As Grandma walked on up the front walk, she blasted at me again, "I ought to wear your little butt out."

Ought to? I thought. *That must mean she's not going to wear my butt out.* Whew, I felt greatly relieved. "I'm sorry, Grandma. I didn't remember what you had said, so I just made up something," I told her.

"Well, you just march your little smart aleck self back down there, I mean right now, and tell your aunt Hazel you just made up that lie!" She was pointing first at me then down toward Aunt Hazel's house. She had fire in her eyes. I had seen that before and knew I had better move and right now.

"Yes, ma'am," I stated very nervously and ran off the porch and back down the driveway to Aunt Hazel's house, but I didn't go in. There was no way I could go in and face Aunt Hazel, so I just played around outside for a while. Aunt Hazel often remembers that little incident, and she will mention it to me sometimes, even today. She always laughs when she is telling it. I know it wasn't funny or cute to her at all, until she found out that I had made it up. Of course she knew I had made it up the moment Grandma's footsteps were heard that day on the front porch.

I would be visiting Grandma Love, and on weekends, Uncle Walter and his family would come out from Natchez to visit her and help with whatever she needed. Uncle Walter had two sons, Walter Junior and Kenneth Lewis. Walter Junior was one year older than I was and Kenny was about three years younger. We had many fun times playing around that farm. Uncle Johnny lived a few hundred yards down the driveway, and I guess he actually owned most of the farm. We never were concerned about that too much.

Walter Junior brought a large tricycle out there once, and it broke, so they just left it. I would try to ride it even though it was broken, but it was no use. One day, Uncle Johnny saw me trying to ride that thing. He came over, got some makeshift parts, and fixed that tricycle as good as new. He will never know how much I appreciated that, and I was too young to tell him. Even now, I think about that somewhat small favor and remember how much Uncle Johnny means to me, for one reason, because of him helping with my toy.

One time, just Pender (my cousin Charles Lewis Beesley) and I were staying with Grandma Love. She was going to Texas with Uncle Walter to visit some kinfolk. It was sometime in the morning when they picked her up and left me and Pender there by ourselves. Grandma was used to living alone; this was before she had let Grandpa move back in. If she wanted to go someplace, she didn't have any kids to worry about. Therefore, she had not thought about leaving us anything to eat. Daddy was working in Natchez, and the plan was for him to stop by and pick us up and carry us out to our house. That would not happen until four o'clock that afternoon, and Pender and I probably hadn't wanted to get up in time for Grandma to cook us breakfast, so by noon or so, we were getting pretty hungry. There were no potato chips or snack foods around the house in those days, so if a kid didn't have anybody to cook for him, he was in a hungry way. Pender, being a few years older, maybe fourteen or so, had a little pocket change, and I think I had a few cents. He thought it would be a good idea to walk over to Stampley Forks about a mile or so through the woods where there was a little store and we could buy some food. I remember it like it was yesterday. We got a half pint of mayonnaise, a few slices of salami, a loaf of bread, and some ice cream spoons to spread the mayo. We didn't have enough money for a Coke or anything to drink. We just walked out the door and back down the path stopping under a shade tree. There, we tore that bag open, making a tablecloth, and spread out our feast. We hadn't had any food up until that time of the day, and we had just walked a mile or more. We spread that mayo on thick, and that fresh sliced salami was smelling ever so fine. We ate it all, however many sandwiches it made. Until this very day, a salami sandwich is my favorite, and I never eat one, I mean never, unless I think about that day.

Grandma had a double-barrel rifle, it was about a .45 caliber on one side and .22 caliber on the other. If she heard a strange noise in the night, she would fire that thing in the air off the porch and yell out where the next bullet would go if she saw anybody sneaking around out there. She had chickens in the coop and thought somebody might want to steal one. I don't think any were ever missing, but she was going to make sure nobody stole one. One night, just the two of us were there. We heard a loud rumble on the roof. Being a small kid, I was frightened by the noise. In the still of the night, it sounded like the house was coming apart. I said, "Get your gun, Grandma! Somebody is breaking in!"

She just laughed and said, "Nobody is breaking in. That's just a rat running across this old tin roof."

I said, "Well, if that's what it was, that sucker must have weighed a hundred pounds."

She couldn't stop laughing at me. Until this day, I don't know how that rat got on that tin roof and managed to run across it.

Uncle Bennie was in the army in those days, and he had left behind a flattop guitar. Grandma and I would try to play it, but we weren't very good. We would strum and sing some old Hank Williams songs which were popular at the time, and she knew several gospel songs. On warm summer days, we would sit on the front porch and try to outdo each other picking and singing.

In the old house, in Grandma's kitchen, there was a hand-operated water pump that sat on the kitchen counter and was connected to a pipe that ran into the cistern in the backyard. I loved pumping water into buckets or the dish pan in the kitchen. She didn't have a bathtub. We used the washtub for bathing. The washtub was about three feet in diameter and eighteen inches in depth. One would wash one's hair first before getting into the tub. Then you got in and finished bathing. In the wintertime, we would place the tub by the fireplace. Everybody had to leave the room so the bather could have privacy. Bath time was no time to linger; others were waiting to get back to the fire.

She and Grandpa Pearl didn't get along very well most of the time, and that was why they finally separated in the mid-1930s. After this, he had worn out his welcome living from house to house with different kinfolk, so he came to Uncle Johnny. Uncle Johnny didn't have the room since he and Aunt Hazel had three children, but he had to somehow provide for his father. Uncle Johnny told Grandpa he would clean out the barn and he would fix it up for Grandpa to live there.

Uncle Johnny lived just down the driveway from Grandma, and she knew what was going on. She said, "As much as I don't want to live with him, I can't see him live in a barn, so he can move in with me." That was the type of woman she was, and as they say, "Love has many faces." She read her Bible everyday and frequently quoted the scriptures. I'm pretty sure it was some passage of the Bible that helped her make that decision.

Uncle Bennie had built Grandma a new house with three bedrooms, a kitchen, a dining room, a living room, and a bath. The house had gas heat and a gas stove—all the comforts of modern housing in those days—and she lived there by herself for the most part. Uncle Bennie and Aunt Rita lived in two rooms of the house they had added after they were married. Before Grandma would let Grandpa move in, she laid down a few stipulations that would be very strict. Grandpa could have the front bedroom and all his belongings would be kept in that one room. He would of course have to cook his own meals and not even be allowed to ask her for anything. He was strictly a guest there and on his own. He had better stay out of her way at all times and not give her any back talk. Another very important rule was he could use the kitchen to cook his meals, but he could only use the two left burners on the stove. She would use the two right burners which would allow her to go into the kitchen at anytime and have two burners available for herself.

Stories would get out every now and then about how she would catch him with a pot on one of her burners and she would knock it off on the floor. She would yell at him, and he would yell back, and they would get into this big argument. Mama used to say they weren't happy unless they were arguing with each other. I believe Mama was right; they would get bored and find something to fuss about for entertainment. One time, Grandpa had bought some bacon, and Grandma thought she would be nice and fry them both some bacon.

He shouted at her, "Are you going to fry all my bacon?"

This didn't sit well with Grandma, and they got started. She said, "You will know the next time I cook you something!"

They must have really loved each other.

Grandpa watched the weather every night on channel 3 out of Jackson. The weatherman was Woodie Assaf. Grandma would admit that she could aggravate Grandpa by telling him Woodie Assaf didn't know what he was talking about most of the time. She would tell Grandpa that if he had any sense, he wouldn't pay any attention to him. She told us she knew that would make him mad because he thought a lot of Woodie. Things like that kept them going.

When the word got out that they had gotten back together, different ones who had known them for many years would make fun of the situation. Bessie Lea Dickerson shouted from her yard to Mama who had stopped to talk to Mrs. Bailey, "Annie Mae, I'm ready to die now. I have seen it all. Pearl and Love have gone back together!" Then she and Mama would have a good laugh and talk about how they were doing.

Mr. Cash Garrett told us boys, "Ya'll tell Ms. Love she better watch out for Pearl. He might get to sleepwalking one night and stumble into her room." Then he let out a big belly laugh.

We couldn't wait to tell Grandma what Mr. Cash had said. She responded with, "Yeah, you just let him come stumbling into my room, and I'll knock him back in his room! He better not try to mess with me, and he knows it!"

We would make up little things and tell her we had heard "so and so." She would get started, and we would get tickled. I know now Grandma knew we kids were picking with her, and she would play along just for the fun of it. She liked to make kids laugh, because she loved us and enjoyed our visits.

Grandma always had a beautiful vegetable garden. I can't remember all the vegetables she raised, but I remember the onions. Her onions were very large, as big as the ones in the grocery store. The garden was just across the driveway and could be seen from the front porch. Grandma was famous for speaking her mind. She was very honest and open with people. I remember one of those honest and open remarks like it was yesterday. Ruthie and I were visiting at my parents' house one weekend when Ruthie was pregnant with Jim. This being her first child, she was somewhat nervous about the whole thing, especially the delivery part.

Well, on this visit, Grandma Love happened to be visiting also, and we began to talk about having babies. Knowing Grandma had had eleven kids at home and without an anesthetic, I thought she would be the right one to talk to Ruthie about having children. I said, "It's not all that much to having a baby, is it, Grandma?"

"Naw," she replied. "I had eleven of 'em."

Ruthie asked about the pain, and Grandma said, "Yeah, there is gonna be a little pain, but it's not all that bad. You will have several different pains kind of spaced apart, you know." Then her eyes got wide, and raising her voice a mite, she added, "But when that right one hits you, you're gonna to know it!!" It was funny in a way, but I could see Ruthie flinch from across the room.

Grandma Love and Grandpa Pearl lived together until he passed away. I am very proud of that. They were both wonderful grandparents even though they never had material things to give us grandkids. They had something more valuable. They gave love and caring and interacted with us. We knew we were loved and appreciated. What more is there?

Grandma Love passed away on February 15, 1976, while living with my parents. She had broken her arm, but the bone would not mend because of her age. If she had lived, the doctors would have emplaced steel plates to hold the bone together. She was very weak, and they were waiting for her to gain more strength before performing surgery. Aunt Hazel was there with Mama that day. They heard a slight noise coming from her bedroom. They went in there to see what was going on. They found Grandma had passed away, very quietly and without pain or suffering. She is buried in the Singletery Cemetery next to Grandpa Pearl and her children who preceded her in death.

Pearl and Love Beesley
My Maternal Grandparents
circa. 1930

7

Grandpa Pearl

Grandpa Pearl Beesley, my mother's father, was born January 18, 1881. He was born in Copiah County somewhere around Barlow, Mississippi, I think, but I'm not positive. His father was George Washington Beesley, who was born January 9, 1833, in Hazlehurst, Mississippi, and passed away August 25, 1902. His mother was Ophelia Jane Butler Beesley, who was born September 11, 1850, somewhere in Georgia, and died August 15, 1903. Great-Grandpa George was a soldier for the Confederate States of America. He is buried in the Nevels Cemetery beside Great-Grandma Beesley on Lucky Hollow Road in Jefferson County, Mississippi. He has a military stone.

Grandpa Pearl came to live with us sometime around 1948. I would have been about four or five years of age at that time. One thing I do clearly remember upon hearing the news is asking, "Where will he sleep?" The answer from one of my parents was, "With you." That made me very happy, because in our three-bedroom house, J. P. and William slept in one bedroom and Mama and Daddy in another, and I was all alone in the back bedroom. Boy, oh boy, I could hardly believe I would have a roommate.

When I heard the car coming down the driveway—I can remember it like it was yesterday—I ran out on the front porch and waited. The car stopped, and Grandpa Pearl stepped out carrying a little brown tin suitcase. Everything that man had accumulated out of sixty seven years of living was in that little brown tin suitcase, except the clothes he was wearing. He was never down and out about it and never mentioned a word about it. He was well satisfied to live one day at a time. He was always happy and very satisfied.

I knew it was true now, and I remember yelling, "Grandpa, I have somebody to sleep with now!" He set down the suitcase and held out his arms. I went running to him, and he picked me up and gave me a big hug. Grandpa had a crippled arm. I think it was his left. He had had surgery on either part of the muscle or a leader, and there was a bad scar between his elbow and shoulder. His hand hung freely at the wrist. He could grip with the hand, but he could not lift it. He would grab an ax or hoe with his good arm and sling the bad arm up, and the hand would flop upward. He would let the hand fall on the handle of the tool and grasp it. He could lift the arm, but the hand was limp. He could then use a tool as good as anyone. Grandpa chewed Bloodhound chewing tobacco, and I would beg him for a chew. If my parents weren't around, he would let me have a little pinch. It tasted awful, but I would spit like he did, and he would laugh and tell me not to swallow the juice. He didn't have to worry; there was no way I was going to swallow that nasty mess, but I did feel all grown up, chewing and spitting like Grandpa.

We got up early, my Grandpa and I. Some winter mornings, we would even beat William and J. P. out of bed. They got up early to go to school. I failed to realize how I should have taken advantage of those mornings until I had to get up and go to school myself. Anyway, Mama and Daddy got up before that, because Daddy left for work about 5:30 AM. They would have a big fire going in the wood heater in the front room. Grandpa and I would run out of our cold bedroom into the front room where it was nice and toasty. Grandpa would turn the radio on. It was an old AM radio; this was before FM radio or television. He wanted to hear Lowell Thomas broadcasting the news. After that, we listened to the "Hip Cats." That was what I was waiting for. They were a group of black singers, and they had a very good beat. The Mills Brothers would be on too, and Grandpa would pat his feet and get me to dancing all over that living room. I tell you we had a real good time. Being wintertime, it was too cold to be outside, so that was part of our entertainment. We also played checkers, both kinds, Chinese and regular checkers. We would play cards, and I had a puzzle of the

United States, in which each state was a puzzle piece. All those things were a lot of fun, and I will always cherish the memories of those dead-of-winter mornings in the living room by the old wood-burning heater with Grandpa Pearl.

I can barely remember one word of what Lowell Thomas had to say, but I can still hear him as plain as today saying, "Now let's go to the news from behind the Iron Curtain." I did not know what he meant, but I can still see the image in my mind of an iron curtain someplace in the world. Grandpa would have explained it to me, but I never knew to ask. In my mind, he was going to tell us what was happening behind that iron curtain. One winter, they kept talking about snow. We would go to bed, and Grandpa would say, "I'll bet it is going to be snowing in the morning!" He knew that would get me excited. I remember I had never seen snow, but somehow, I knew what it would look like. I had seen pictures in those storybooks Grandpa would read to me sometimes. Maybe it was just his telling me what it looked like. I would think about it every morning and jump up and look out the window, but there would be no snow.

One morning, I woke up and did not even think to look out. Grandpa was already awake and dressed. He said, "You better jump out of that bed and look out the window!" I did and saw the ground was covered with snow. How beautiful it was! Everything was white, I mean, the top side of everything—the tops of tree limbs, the top side of the clothesline, the top of the smokehouse, the top of the barn, the top of the cistern, the top of the slats on the gate, the top of the fence wire, the top of the fence post. Out across the cow lot, I could see the cow salt block which was set on a sharpened post, and there was snow on top of the salt block. I mean everything was white on top. It was unbelievable. I was standing there on my tiptoes in my pajamas with my little nose just above the windowsill telling Grandpa every where the snow was.

J. P. and William didn't go to school that day, and we had quite a time playing in the snow. We made a snowman and snowballs, and, of course, snow ice cream. We slid down hills on some kind of homemade sled. We had a big time playing in the snow. It snowed the winter of 1950–51. Not only did it snow, there was also a famous freeze. The rain fell, and the temperature was below 32 degrees so the water froze on the tree limbs. The limbs would break and fall on the power lines. Everybody was without electricity, and the limbs were falling in the roads, blocking traffic. This freeze lasted several days, and we were running out of food and had to get to town. Daddy, Mama, J. P., and I headed for Fayette. Daddy stopped to see about Grandpa John and Grandma Annie. Uncle Jack was there, and he wanted to go with us to help if we got into trouble. We had axes, saws, and gunnysacks in the trunk of our 1949 Pontiac. They would stop and chop trees out of the road, and when the car came to a hill and started spinning, they would lay the gunnysacks down in front of the rear wheels to give them traction.

We did very well until we got to Cole's Creek. There was a low water bridge across that creek. A low water bridge means the bridge is just high enough to clear the crest of the water when the creek is not overflowing. The road was graded down to the bridge from both sides so the traffic could drive down the creek bank and up the opposite creek bank. This was a common way to build bridges in those days on small county roads. They were much cheaper than building a bridge on pilings up even with the grade of the road. When we got to the bridge, we found that several cars were stuck partway up the grades on both sides. We got past them going down, crossed the bridge, and started up the other side. Our car wheels started losing traction and started to spin. Uncle Jack got on one side of the car, and J. P. on the other side. Uncle Jack told Daddy to spin the wheels slowly while he and J. P. held on to one end of their gunnysacks and whipped the gunnysacks between the frozen ground and in front of the spinning wheels. The spinning wheels would pull the sack under the wheel, and the wheel would gain traction so the car would move forward over the sacks. Then they would sling the sack back around in front of the wheel. They would whip the sacks around in front of the wheels over and over until the car reached the top of the grade. Then they walked back down and helped the other cars up to the top.

That freeze was very hard on the cattle and other animals as well as the people, but I also remember how beautiful it was. When the sun would come out and shine through the icy limbs, they would glisten, and it was ever so beautiful. I was about six years old and had never seen anything like that. Signs of that freeze could still be seen for many years after 1951. Trees that had bent over and then straightened up were left crooked. Treetops would be broken out, and the tree sprouted out around the break. I remember people talking about the millions of dollars of damage from trees crashing into houses and broken power lines and poles and of course the damage to the timber industry.

Grandpa Pearl told me a story about the time when my brother William was a small boy. William was playing with a rubber strap from an old automobile inner tube and was standing on the concrete hearth of the fireplace in the old house they later tore down. He was holding the string of rubber in the fire. After the end would catch fire, it would burn slowly so he would pull it out of the fire and hold it up in front of him and watch it burn. What he had not considered was that as the strap burned, the melted rubber would drip off. He was barefoot, and a drop of melted rubber hit the top of his toe. It was burning, and since the rubber was melted, it stuck to his toe so he could not knock it off. This caused him to scream and dance around. Grandpa Pearl happened to be sitting in the room at the time and started clapping his hands and saying, "Look at 'em dance," as he was laughing. William himself laughed about it after he finally got that burning rubber off his toe and probably still remembers that incident.

One day, Mama and Daddy were going somewhere. I don't remember just where they were going, but I was pitching a little fit to go with them. I was about four or five years old, I think. Being the third child, I usually got my way, but I wasn't going to get my way that day. I was yelling and crying, following them out to the car. Grandpa Pearl came out, picked me up, and was trying to console me. He stopped on the front porch and sat in the rocker with me in his lap. Daddy backed around and started pulling off. I yelled to them, "Well, just go on without me then, you blankety-blank-blank!" I had yelled louder than I expected. Daddy heard me; he stopped that car and came back stepping fast, while pulling off his belt. Grandpa started begging for me, telling Daddy that I didn't mean it. He reminded him that I was just a little fellow and anything else he could think of, I guess. This was too serious. Grandpa couldn't protect me this time, as he had done many times in the past. Daddy wasn't going to spare the rod or belt this day. Daddy was steadily stepping up that front walk to the porch. By the time he got on the porch, he had his belt off and doubled. He pulled me out of Grandpa's lap and gave me a few hard licks across my little buttocks with that leather belt. That was the first time he had spanked me without a warning. I never asked but figured cursing him and Mama was over the line. It didn't require a second warning. It certainly would never happen again. I would never have cursed them in the first place, if I had thought they might hear me. I had heard all that kind of talk from my older brothers.

One day, Grandpa Pearl and J.P. were going up to Grandpa Smith's for something, and I wanted to go with them. J. P. didn't want me to go for some reason. I had probably done something he didn't like. This was in 1955. I remember that, because he had that new 1955 Ford. He had graduated from school and had a job. He had bought that car but was still living at home. William had had an old pilot's type cap, when he was smaller. It was dark brown leather and fit tight on my head, and it had earflaps that folded up over the head and snapped in that position. The earflaps could be unsnapped and pulled down over the ears and under the chin and snapped in that position. A pair of goggles came with it. They snapped to the front over the eyes. I was wearing that old cap that day with the earflaps snapped under my chin and the goggles in place over my eyes. That cap was more or less a toy that William had outgrown and I had inherited. I wasn't even thinking about all that. I just ran out to the car when J. P. wasn't looking and hid in the back seat. I was crouched down behind the driver's seat, so I couldn't be seen. He got in, cranked the car, and away we went. When we got down the road far enough that I didn't figure he would turn around and take me back, I raised up behind him. He saw me in the rearview mirror and didn't recognize me, because of the cap and goggles. He slammed on the brakes and turned around in a split second, then realized it was me. He had just been startled, due to the unexpected view in his mirror. He had thought some evil person was in the car with him. He didn't take me back but fussed all the way to Grandpa's house.

Grandpa Pearl had a way of cheering kids up when they were crying. I remember several times when I would get a spanking or just be crying because I did not get my way. Grandpa would tell me that I sounded like a log truck changing gears. What he was talking about was when a kid cries and lets out a long wail, it sounds like a motor winding down. Then he takes a breath, and the sucking sound sounds like gears grinding, then he wails out again. As I would cry and he would say that, I would start to notice what he was talking about. This would get me tickled, and it is very hard to laugh and cry at the same time; besides, it is no fun crying when you are getting no sympathy. Somehow, he knew how to do those things, and he was good at it.

Grandpa had a way of removing warts from a person's body. He would rub the wart with his thumb or finger, and a few days later, after you had forgotten about it, the wart would be gone. I don't blame anyone for being skeptical about believing this and maybe have other theories about how it worked. All I can say is I saw him perform this miracle many times. He removed more than one from me. It didn't work every time on everybody, but it worked most of the time. So far as I know, he never revealed to anyone how he did that.

Grandpa moved out of our house. I don't remember the year. He was going to live with Uncle Johnny, but Uncle Johnny didn't have room in his house. So Uncle Johnny was going to fix up his barn for Grandpa to live in, but Grandma Love just couldn't stand to see him live in a barn, especially since she lived in a house large enough to accommodate them comfortably. They had separated several years before that time. Grandma Love and Grandpa Pearl moved back together, and we were all very pleased with that. They lived together until he passed away. I am very proud of that.

Grandpa Pearl passed away on October 4, 1969, in the Jefferson County Hospital. He had had a long illness, something to do with his lungs. All his life he had a cough that usually came about when he laughed. Doctors could never help him. During his later years, he was too weak to cough it up and was put in the hospital. He lay there sedated and didn't know he or anybody else was in the world. I stopped in to see him a few days before he passed away. He never knew I was there, but I was glad to see he wasn't suffering.

Grandpa Pearl is buried beside Grandma Love in the Singletary Cemetery on Block Foster Road in Jefferson County, Mississippi.

George W. Beesley
My maternal Great-Grandfather
circa. 1885

8

Great-Grandpa George Washington (Wash) Beesley

Great-Grandpa George (Wash) Beesley was born January 9, 1833, in Hazlehurst, Mississippi, and died March 25, 1909, in Union Church, Mississippi. He married Ophelia Jane Butler on December 18, 1867. Grandma Ophelia's parents came from Paris, France, or there about. She was born September 11, 1850, in Georgia and died August 25, 1903, in Jefferson County. From this union were born ten children, the first one was stillborn. The other nine lived to adulthood. The children were Willie, Mary Annie, James (Jim), Henry, Pearl (my grandfather), Lewis McQuere, Wiley, Nannie Mae, and Walter.

For easy reference to the characters in this story, I will refer to these grandparents by their first names to help avoid confusion over just whom I'm talking about.

Great-Great-Grandfather, Wash's father, was James or (Jimmy) Beesley, he was born in Wales, I think on January 8, 1800, and came to Georgia from Wales. His wife, Wash's mother, was Annie Gustairs, and she came from Ireland.

So, the Beesley part of our family is Irish and Welsh. Our Paternal Grandma Matildia Rogillio (Ro'heal-ya) came from Spain or Mexico and that makes us part Spanish. Then there are the Klars who came from Germany. I don't have much information about the Smiths and very little beyond the preceding. I'm just mentioning this to point out that we are very well melted into the American melting pot of citizens; that is, we descend from an influx of immigrants from several countries.

Grandpa Wash was a Confederate soldier in the Civil War. He mustered into the Confederate Army as a private in Company G, 36th Regiment, Mississippi Infantry, in Copiah County, Mississippi, probably in Hazlehurst soon after the war started. His parents owned a farm in Barlow, Mississippi, another town in Copiah County. All this information is from family remembrances that have been handed down through the years. We also researched some of this ourselves.

We are pretty sure that Grandpa's first battle was in Shiloh, Tennessee. We do know he was in the battle of Shiloh, because his name is listed on the Civil War Web site as being there. We think he was also in the battle of Port Gibson, Mississippi. His brother Henry was killed in Port Gibson along with about seven hundred other Confederate soldiers. After losing the battle in Port Gibson, we think Grandpa might have gone to Vicksburg. He might have been in battles in Raymond, Jackson, Champion Hill, and Big Black River. Those were possibilities, because the Confederate general Pemberton was trying to hold ground in Vicksburg. General Grant was trying to attack Vicksburg from the rear, because he wanted to take out enemy troops from Jackson, Mississippi. Grant crossed the Mississippi River in Bruinsburg, Mississippi, just south of Port Gibson. Grandpa's army was trying to stop Grant at Port Gibson and failed. Grant went on to the other places mentioned approaching Vicksburg from the land side.

We do know for certain, as certain as we can be, that is, that he was wounded in Vicksburg. He was wounded in his right jaw, and it was bad enough that he was hospitalized and was in the hospital when Vicksburg fell to the Union forces. General Grant didn't imprison the Confederate soldiers after taking over Vicksburg. He made them swear they would go home and not fight any longer. Grandpa Beesley gave his word, and being a man of his word, he was bound to keep it. I'm sure he wanted to be home worse than Grant wanted him home. Grandpa didn't keep his word, though; after all, he had given it to a darn Yankee and that didn't count for very much according by his standards.

He managed to keep fighting for the South and went to Nashville, Tennessee, and other places. I'm not sure just where all he served. We are pretty sure that he was captured in Nashville, Tennessee. The Union was winning the battle in which Grandpa was fighting in Nashville. Grandpa's unit retreated then turned and made a stand. After repeating this maneuver three different times, he figured they were all going to be killed and there was no point in just keeping on with the battle. He finally stood and put his knapsack on the ground on one side, laid his rifle on the other side, and held both hands in the air. A Union officer came by and told him to go to the rear. He did and was sent to a Union prison someplace in Ohio.

He spent the rest of the war in that prison. They released all the prisoners at the end of the war and gave each one two pounds of fatback (pork meat) and two loaves of bread. His friend couldn't eat the pork, so he traded Grandpa his two pounds of pork for Grandpa's two loaves of bread. That food was all they had for the trip from Ohio to Barlow, Mississippi. They were so starved that they ate the food in a short period of time. It didn't near about last until they got home. Once they were across the Mason-Dixon Line, they were among friends and got some help getting home. They jumped on wagons and trains and any transportation south. He got home, and the only problem he had from the war was a lump on his right jaw caused by the bullet wound he got in Vicksburg. Grandpa grew a beard to cover the scar, and unless you know it's there, you can't tell it in the picture.

I can state with the utmost accuracy that Grandpa Wash didn't enter the war to fight for slavery. Grandpa Pearl used to say his father was fighting for "states' rights" and that was dubbed the "cause." None of Grandpa's relatives owned any slaves in the first place. Only wealthy planters owned slaves, and the slaves were competition against any farm boy who was searching for a job on a plantation. No planter was going to pay for labor when he could have slave labor to do the job. Anyway, slavery didn't become an issue until the Civil War had been going on for at least one year. The war started at Fort Sumter, just off the coast of South Carolina in April 1861.

Grandpa joined the Confederate Army sometime after April 1861. The Emancipation Proclamation, a law to free slaves, wasn't passed until September 22, 1862, one year and five months after the war had begun. Grandpa and many others, maybe all other Southern men, were led by Senator Jefferson Davis, who later became president of the Confederacy. Senator Davis, who was from Mississippi, mentioned in the following excerpt from his speech to the United States Congress, that states had the right to secede from the Union. He delivered this speech during his resignation from the Senate on January 21, 1861.

> *It is known to Senators who have served with me here that I have for many years advocated, as an essential attribute of State sovereignty, the right of a State to secede from the Union. Therefore, if I had thought that Mississippi was acting without sufficient provocation, or without an existing necessity, I should still, under my theory of the Government, because of my allegiance to the State of which I am a citizen, have been bound by her action. I, however, may be permitted to say that I do think she has justifiable cause, and I approve of her act. I conferred with her people before that act was taken, counseled them then that, if the state of things which they apprehended should exist when their Convention met, they should take the action which they have now adopted.*

Jefferson Davis also stated at some point, "We are not fighting for slavery. We are fighting for Independence, and that, or extermination."

It gives me great pleasure to be able to say, based on my research, that my forefathers who joined the Confederacy did not do so because of slavery. Our great-grandparents, Great-Grandpa Phillip Barnes Trevillion, who died from pneumonia during the war, and Great-Grandpa James Monroe Smith and Great-Grandpa George W. Beesley, did not fight for slavery. They fought for states' rights and more than likely just wanted to remain free men. After a year of battle, they were still fighting for the "cause" along with other soldiers. The cause was the rights of their states. I can say with conviction that I for one am glad they lost. We are much better off, in my way of thinking, because we have one union. No matter the thoughts or opinions, when they took part in the Civil War, their cause had nothing to do with slavery.

There were many problems that I'm not sure about. One problem was that most of the farming in the country was in the Southern states. These states needed farm implements, and most farm implements were manufactured in the Northern states. The Southern states were importing implements from foreign countries. In order to force Southern farmers to buy their implements from American factories, a tariff was placed on foreign goods. That had to be one of our Grandpa's issues, due to the fact that all their families were row-crop farmers.

After Great-Grandpa Beesley returned home and married Grandma Ophelia, he and his wife moved to Hubbard, Texas, just a little south of Dallas. They moved over there along with his brother-in-law, a man whose last name was Vardaman. Mr. Vardaman was the husband of Grandma Butler's sister. They moved early in 1873 by loading the farm implements on a flatbed wagon pulled by oxen. They loaded the furniture and other household goods in a covered wagon, which was pulled by horses, and headed out for Texas. They made the trip and settled down in the row-crop farming business and were out there a few years. Grandpa Wash's father, James, was ill and sent word to Grandpa Wash that if he would come back to Mississippi and help him manage the farm, he would inherit the farm at his father's death.

Great-Grandpa Wash came back to Mississippi and lived out his life in Copiah and Jefferson counties. At one time while living in Texas, he came home for a visit without the family. He rode a horse with his dog following him. That dog had gone to Texas with Grandpa Wash and his family and had been out there a few years when Grandpa came home for the visit. When Grandpa reached the Mississippi River, the ferry charged extra to bring an animal across. Grandpa Wash didn't have enough money to pay for the dog, so he reluctantly left his dog on the Louisiana side of the river. After Grandpa reached home a few days later, the dog came running into the yard. Grandpa never knew how his beloved dog got across that river. Maybe someone felt sorry for him and brought him across or maybe he swam, but he still had to be a smart dog to find his way home from Vicksburg. I'm not sure just where Grandpa crossed, but it could have been Vicksburg, Bruinsburg, Natchez, or another place. The dog had to travel at least forty miles from the river to home.

If Grandpa Wash had not moved back to Mississippi, we would all be Texans. I sometimes wonder if life would have been different growing up in Texas. You know, I wonder if I would have been an oilman or cowboy or something. I have my kin in Texas to compare life with. They are mostly Great Uncle Jim's family, and as far as I know, they seem to be much like us Mississippi Beesley descendants.

Grandpa John Hiram Smith
My paternal grandfather
Circa: 1903

9

Grandpa Smith

Grandpa John Hiram Smith, my father's father, was my Grandpa John. He was born in Pike County or maybe Franklin County in April 1875. His parents were James Monroe Smith, born 1845 in the state of Georgia, and Nancy Courtney Serman Smith, born in 1841. Grandpa was a very kind and gentle man, and I know without a doubt my father inherited that personality. Grandpa came down with a crippling type of arthritis, and it put him in bed for a long time. He finally regained some of his mobility, but he had to use two walking canes for support when he walked. This disease was common in his family. Two of his brothers had the disease, and one, Uncle Willis, was confined to a wheelchair from about the age of sixty or so until his death. Uncle Willis had a son with the disease.

There was a lot of difference between Grandpa John and Grandpa Pearl. Grandpa Pearl was happy just lying on the porch with his head propped up against the wall. Grandpa John, however, was busy working around the farm doing something all the time, before he became ill. Before Grandpa John became ill, in about 1951, he was still running his blacksmith shop. He also had a corn mill and cane syrup mill. To power this mill, he had a one-cylinder open-radiator six-horsepower engine. He would start that thing, and the engine didn't have a governor to control the speed. It had a spindle with two steel balls that spun around on the end of a perpendicular shaft. The spinning motion caused centrifugal force to sling the two balls out which broke the power to the sparkplug and cut off the spark to the sparkplug killing the engine for a few seconds. That caused the engine to slow down, and the balls would fall switching the spark back on, then the engine would hit again. There were two large steel flywheels on the sides of the engine that provided torque. This torque would cause the engine to coast, and depending on the amount of load, the engine would make a few revolutions. It would be slowing down all the time until the two balls came together again, closing the electrical circuit and firing the plug. The engine might hit two, three, or more times in succession until the speed picked up again and caused the whirling balls to sling out and switch the spark off. I can still hear that old engine running, and sometimes, it would backfire. It would hit, pop-pop-pop, shut off, then pop once, shut off, pop-pop, then shut off again. It was a beautiful beat.

Grandpa would put the corn into the hopper and crank the old engine by spinning the flywheel. After the engine started turning the belt and got the mill going, Grandpa would run to a post in the mill house where there was a homemade wooden knob with a rope tied to it. I don't know what the rope did, but turning that knob adjusted something concerning the mill. I had watched him do that routine on several occasions. One day, he started the engine and was just standing there watching the engine run for a few seconds. I ran over to him and tugged on his shirt sleeve. He looked down, and I pointed to the knob on the post. I must have been about five years old, and he ran laughing over to the knob and gave it a turn or two. Later when we were back at the house, he was telling everybody that I knew how to run that gristmill. Then he told them how I had reminded him to turn whatever it was, and they all thought it was cute for a little boy to notice that. It made me very proud, and I told my folks about it when I got home. Maybe that is why I remember the occasion.

After Grandpa became immobile, he sold the equipment out of the mill, but he never sold that old engine. It stayed there for about twenty or so more years, and my cousin Johnny Harold hauled it out to his house. It is still sitting there today. I talked to someone who belonged to a one-cylinder club; they restored those old engines. Johnny Harold and I considered having it done, but it was in such bad repair that it would cost more than we wanted to spend on that project.

In his younger days, Grandpa would meet other farmers for a log rolling. A farmer would have trees cut on a piece of land that he wanted to clear for a field to grow crops. He would have the trees cut down and tops cut off. The logs would still be waiting there to be removed from the field. The farmer would invite his neighbors over one day for a log rolling. They would bring their teams and hook them to the logs and drag them out of the field. Some would be rolled with a cantilever tool. This was called a "can hook" by loggers. It was a long wooden pole with a steel point on the end and a hook about a foot from the end. The hook was shaped like one side of a pair of tongs. It had a sharp point on the end. The point on the end of the can hook, would be jabbed into the log and the hook lapped over the log and the point on the end of the hook jabbed into the log, making a solid grip. The pole was then pulled over causing the log to roll. With two or three men pulling can hooks alternately, the log could be rolled out of the field. The only cost for this service was a fine meal with plenty of desserts. The ladies would come along with the men to help with the cooking. After the day was done, everybody would sit around, visit, and drink. Oh, yes, did I mention that whiskey was one of the perks that had to be furnished by the landowner? The landowner also had to take his turn at some of the other farms when they had a log rolling. They were helping each other with heavy farmwork and at the same time enjoying the entertainment with their neighbors. Getting together for whatever the reason was an enjoyable outing in those days.

In the last years of Grandpa's life, during the winter months, he sat by the fireplace, but during the summer months, he mostly sat around the house on either the front porch or back porch smoking Prince Albert tobacco in "roll-your-own" cigarettes. He would sit there in his rocker and talk about things to me or whomever he would be visiting with, and roll those Prince Albert's. He would buy his tobacco in half-gallon cans, and the can would be sitting beside his rocker. His walking sticks would be hooked over one arm of the chair. He would pick up that can of Prince Albert, put it in his lap, and tell you a story as he snapped off the lid. This could take maybe fifteen minutes or longer. He would reach into his shirt pocket, pull out a book of cigarette papers, and blow on the edges so the thin papers would fly up; then he would hook a thumb under the top leaf and tear it out of the book. With the book of papers in one hand, the one paper in the other, and the can of tobacco in his lap, he would maybe turn his head around and ask, "How's your mama and daddy?" After he heard the answer, he might make a few comments while still holding the paper book in one hand and the paper in the other. Finally, he would fold the book closed and put it back into his pocket.

Grandpa John would then hold the paper in one hand between his fingers, with one finger in the middle of the paper making a gutter effect. He would then gouge his thumb and forefinger of the other hand into the open can of tobacco, pinching just the right amount and placing it in the middle of the guttered paper. "That was a good rain we had yesterday, wasn't it?" he would ask or something similar. We would then talk about the rain, how much we needed it, and how dry it had been for awhile. He would look down at the paper waiting in his hand, maybe pick up the lid and snap it back on the can. He would then set the can back down on the floor. The cigarette would still be waiting to be rolled. He would even out the tobacco in the paper taking all the time he wanted, and he usually took at least five minutes for that task. He might stop at that point and ask, "You been huntin' lately?"

"Yeah, I went the other day," might be the reply.

"Did you do any good?" he might ask. Then he would probably go into a hunting story from the late nineteenth century. How I wish I had a recording of some of those stories. He had been born around 1870 so the story might date to 1885 or so. Grandpa would go into details like it was yesterday, all the time holding that paper full of tobacco steady. Finally, he would roll the paper around the tobacco and run the edge across his tongue to moisten it so it would stick together. After he pressed it together, there in his hand would be a "roll-your-own" that looked like it came out of a cigarette pack ("ready roll"). One end would be carefully wedged into the corner of his mouth. The cigarette may not leave his mouth for maybe an hour or so. He would reach into the other shirt pocket, pull out a kitchen match, and enter into a little more conversation; then when he was reaching the end of the story, he would strike the match on the arm of the chair.

The match would be burning as he finished his story. I would think he was going to burn his finger before he touched the flame to the cigarette. It never happened. I watched this scene play out more times than I can count. He would light that cigarette and flick the remains of the burning stick into the yard just as the flame was about to burn his fingers. He then would pull a long draw, suck it down deep, and blow the smoke out, with that cigarette hanging out the corner of his mouth. He continued to talk about whatever with his guest. That cigarette would burn up to his lip and usually go out with about a quarter of inch of cigarette left. I don't think he even knew it was there sometimes, but he didn't look like Grandpa if he didn't have a portion of a cigarette in the corner of his mouth.

Grandpa always churned the butter. Grandma Annie would get out the old crock churn, which was about twenty-six inches tall and ten inches in diameter at the bottom and smaller at the top. It had a wooden lid with a hole in the middle. A dasher was made from a wooden stick, about the size of a mop handle. It had two one-inch-wide slats nailed to the end of the stick, that made a cross at the end. The stick was set into the churn and reached to the bottom. The dasher handle then protruded out the top of the churn through a hole in the center of the lid. I don't know for sure, but I just know Grandpa made that dasher and churn lid, just like he made most of the furniture. Grandma Annie would pour cream into the churn. The cream came off the top of the milk in the safe. The cows were milked every morning and/or afternoon and the milk brought into the house and strained through a piece of fine-meshed cheesecloth folded double. The milk was strained into the large crock that held a little more than a gallon. The crock was set in the safe, and after about twelve hours, cream would be forming on top of the milk. The cream would be skimmed off, placed in a bowl, and kept in the refrigerator. After another day or so, the milk would clabber, and the remaining cream would be skimmed again. The cream was placed on the table at mealtime, dipped out with a spoon, and poured over a hot biscuit with preserves, jelly, or syrup on top. This was very good with bacon or sausage. After enough cream was collected in the bowl, Grandma would pour that in the churn and add a certain amount of clabber. She would set the churn by Grandpa's chair, and he would work the dasher up and down, up and down, churning the clabber and cream. After a while, he would have butter and would call out, "Annie, I think this butter's ready."

She would dip the butter out into a small crock, and that would be kept in the refrigerator and placed on the table at mealtime. Of course, it was used to make cakes and other foods as well. The remainder of the liquid in the churn was poured into jars and stored in the refrigerator. That was called buttermilk. I never could decide which I liked the best, cornbread and buttermilk or cornbread and clabber with cream added. I can plainly remember cornbread and buttermilk or clabber and a slice of ham with green onions on the side. A coffee grinder hung on the wall in the kitchen near the window. Grandpa John would buy green coffee beans in a cotton sack. He would pour some of the beans into a pan about one foot wide and two feet long. He would place the pan of beans into the oven and bring his chair up close to the oven door. With a long wooden spoon, he would stir the beans every few minutes until they were roasted to perfection. I can still smell those beans roasting. After they were roasted, he would pour them into the old coffee grinder on the wall, turn the wheel, and catch freshly ground coffee in a can which had a lid for sealing the can air tight. He liked his coffee strong and that required about half a cup of freshly ground coffee to about a quart of boiling water. The water was placed on the stove in a coffeepot with no lid. After the water reached a rolling boil, he would pour in the freshly ground coffee. The mixture would foam up, and he would turn the heat down a little, waiting until the foam settled some. He would add a little more coffee until he had all the coffee in the water. He would stand there until the coffee quit foaming, and it was ready. He then removed the pot away from the heat and waited while the coffee grounds settled to the bottom of the pot.

He would then turn to whoever happened to be there and ask, "Ya'll want some coffee?" He could not carry his coffee cup and walk on his sticks at the same time, so he would ask one of us kids, "How about bringing me a cup of this coffee out here?" Then he would slowly walk out of the kitchen and down the hall to the front porch in the summertime or to the front room by the fireplace in the winter. He never put anything in his coffee. He wanted it strong and black. I loved to visit my Smith grandparents especially when Uncle Willis, one of Grandpa's brothers was visiting there. Uncle Willis had a great sense of humor and loved kids. He had to be pushed in a wheelchair everywhere he went, and we kids loved to push him. He had the same disease that Grandpa had. That was a form of crippling arthritis, except his was much worse than Grandpa's. They would build a makeshift ramp from the yard up onto the front porch. I remember one day starting Uncle Willis down that ramp and I couldn't hold the wheelchair. Uncle Willis and the chair went rolling down that ramp. I was holding on to the back of the chair with my feet sliding, but I didn't have enough weight to give me much traction. I thought Uncle Willis was going to get after me for that, but he just laughed and said, "I wanted to go down that ramp, boy, but not quite that fast." I must have been seven or eight years old, and I doubled over laughing, partly because it was funny and partly because I was very happy he wasn't hurt.

Uncle Willis smoked a pipe all the time and filled it with Prince Albert. He and Grandpa would be sitting on the front porch, and Grandpa would have his roll-your-own going and Uncle Willis's pipe would be boiling smoke. If I only had a recording of their conversations, but I can hardly remember any of it. I do remember they would reminisce about the late eighteen hundreds when they were boys growing up and other good times they had. One story I remember about Uncle Willis was when he first came down with the crippling arthritis. They were getting him dressed to go to the doctor one day when Daddy stopped by to see him. Daddy, noticing he was getting ready to go somewhere, asked, "Where you going, Uncle Willis?"

As two of his daughters pulled his shirt on him, he said, "They taking me back to the doctor, Tom, but I done told them even if they get me well, I'm not going to hit another lick at work." How someone could keep a sense of humor at such trying times is amazing to me, but that was Uncle Willis. He was always joking, laughing, and just having a real good time.

Grandpa John passed away on November 20, 1956, at age eighty-one. He had been feeling bad that day and just stayed in bed. He died from a heart attack later in the day.

Grandma Annie Smith with her sister's Inez
to her right and Ressa to her left.
My paternal grandmother
circa: 1903

10

Grandma Smith

Annie Elizabeth Trevillion Smith, born February 11, 1883, was my father's mother. I remember her as an average-sized, gray-haired lady who was always busy around the house or working in her vegetable garden. Grandma loved flowers and shrubs. Her front yard was full of both. Grandma wore her hair in plaited pigtails coiled in a small bun on the top rear of her head. She never spent much time with us grandkids, but she very often wanted to know if we were hungry. If we were, she didn't have any chips or Cokes around the house, but she had a kitchen safe with leftover food stacked inside.

Her kitchen food safe had been made by Grandpa John himself. It had two or three shelves in the upper part with screen doors and two drawers below that. The bottom was closed in with two doors. Those shelves always had food sitting on them, mostly biscuits, bacon, and sausage. She liked to cook, and she cooked more than was required for every meal. The leftovers were placed in the safe, and if we were hungry, we would get a biscuit and punch a hole in it with our fingers. We then went to the table where syrup would be sitting in the center with the salt, pepper, and pepper sauce. We would pour that biscuit hole full of cane syrup and have that along with a sausage link or slice of bacon. Sometimes, there would be sliced ham in the safe and some green onions. We would open a slice of cornbread and place the ham inside and eat green onions along with that, and it was ever so good. Hog-head souses would be in her refrigerator most of the time. I never cared much for souse, sometimes called "head cheese," but many folk did, and Grandma kept it in a large crock.

She got her refrigerator before their house was wired for electricity. They had butane gas for heat, and the refrigerator ran on that as well. It worked very well, freezing unit and all, and it looked just like an electric one. In fact, she never got an electric refrigerator because the butane one was paid for and it worked just as well. I asked Daddy how they kept food from spoiling before the refrigerator, and he said they had a screened area outside the kitchen window. That was gone before my time, and I don't know all the details of how well it kept food from spoiling. The years before Grandma's house was wired for electricity, she washed clothes in a gasoline-powered washing machine that sat on the back porch. The thing had a one-cylinder gasoline engine similar to a lawn-mower engine. It had a long exhaust pipe which extended across the back porch with a ball on the end which served as a muffler.

Other than the gasoline engine, the machine looked about like any other wringer-type washing machine I had ever seen. She would pull that starting rope, and the little engine would start popping. The machine's agitator would start turning back and forth, sloshing the water around. Grandma would say, "Now, you young ones stay away from that exhaust pipe. It's poison." I often wondered why that exhaust was more poisonous than that of other gasoline engines. Finally, I figured out that a washing machine is usually closed in, like in a laundry room, so a user would be warned to extend the long muffler outside because of carbon monoxide fumes. Grandma probably knew that and just wanted to make sure we kids stayed away because the thing was very hot also.

My cousin Johnny and I helped Herbert, the local electrician, wire the house for electricity. This was sometime in the early fifties, and being as young as we were, I don't know how much help we offered. However, we did get it wired, and I don't remember any problems. In the late fifties, my grandparents had a telephone installed. It was a party line which meant three or four houses shared the same telephone line. The telephone system was designed to ring different customers with different rings so they could tell who was being called. We had the same phone system at our house also. One house would have one long ring like telephones today. The next house would have two short rings, the third would have three short rings, and the fourth would have four short rings. There were never more than four customers sharing the same line.

It was impolite to pick up and listen in on a neighbor's conversation, but it was often done. Sometimes, the phone would ring, and since everybody new the code for each household, they would eavesdrop on each other. It was very secret in the beginning, but it got to the point that if somebody's phone rang we would pick up and see what was going on. If it was somebody calling we knew, we might join in on the conversation. If we needed to use the phone, we would pick up the receiver, and if a neighbor had made an outgoing call, we would not know, because we had not heard the phone ring. We would hear the party talking, and if it wasn't anything interesting, we would hang up and wait a while, then try again. If you needed the phone for something very important and you picked up the phone and heard a conversation, you listened for a moment. If the conversation didn't sound as important as your business, you would speak up and ask, "May I use the phone a minute? I have to make a very important call." Everybody was very accommodating about sharing the telephone.

That phone system was upgraded sometime in the 1970s. Everybody was so glad that you could have a conversation without wondering if somebody was listening in. Somehow, the old system was missed though, because a neighborly bonding that had been enjoyed with the old party line was gone forever.

One Christmas, they made some eggnog at Grandma's house. All the family was there, and Uncle Jack and Aunt Lillie broke two dozen eggs into a large crock. The eggs were separated from the yoke, and only the white was put into the crock. That was beaten until it was white and foamy. Then the yellows were beaten, slowly poured into the crock, and stirred in with the whites. After that mixture was done, they added whiskey; then sugar and vanilla flavoring were added to taste. Somebody watching the event asked if they were going to eat those raw eggs. Uncle Jack's remark was, "Raw egg is good for you." Ha, ha, yeah right. Then Aunt Lillie explained that the whiskey was added to cook the eggs. I don't know about that, but they didn't look cooked to me. We all had a cup, and some had more than one cup. I didn't finish my cup, because the whiskey ruined the taste as far as I was concerned.

I wasn't more than ten years old or something like that. Mama wasn't too crazy about us kids drinking that eggnog that had whiskey in it, but none of us were too fond of it anyway. She allowed it, just to be sociable.

One Christmas long before I was born, the family was all there, and after some amount of time, the desserts were all about gone. My great-aunt Ressa, Grandma Smith's oldest sister, had hidden a special cake she had brought on a shelf in the crib out in the back of the house. She always thought she was a high-class lady and was always pulling special surprises for the homefolk. She had wanted to serve her special cake last, so it would stand out and not be just another cake on the table that no one would give a special notice to. She went out to the crib and came strutting back across the yard with her special cake high on the end of her fingers. Grandpa John was sitting on the back porch about half drunk from the spirits and smoking his self-rolled Prince Albert cigarette. As Aunt Ressa came up on the porch, she said to Grandpa, "I bet you wish you had a piece of my cake."

He replied in his drunken stupor, "I don't think I care for any of your ole ratty cake," referring to the fact that it had been in the crib among the rats. Aunt Ressa was just plain humiliated. At that point, the entire event became comical and worth mentioning for many years to come. Daddy had brought that story home to us. Aunt Ressa had two daughters and was living within the city limits of Fayette. That brought her a cut above the rest of the family, as she thought. Her husband, Uncle George Reynolds, was a bridge contractor as opposed to a redneck farmer. So, she had that to brag about, and being the oldest sister, she was, in her mind, real special. Since they had only two girls and no boys to help around the house, they invited Daddy to stay with them one school year and go to school in Fayette. Daddy liked that, because he didn't have as far to walk to school. He was building Aunt Ressa a chicken house when a nail flew back and hit him in the eye. Years later, he lost sight in that eye from that accident.

While he was staying with them, he was told not to use their indoor toilet, because he might make it stink. He had to use the outhouse. Many townfolk didn't have indoor plumbing in those days, so outhouses were still common, even in town. It hurt Daddy's feelings (something I'm sure Aunt Ressa hadn't thought about). Maybe she made Uncle George use the outhouse as well. It had been kept intact for some reason after the indoor toilet was added. Daddy was telling Grandpa about the incident, and Grandpa said, "Well, Tom, those people are so high class that they think their own **** don't stink."

Aunt Ressa was a dear sweet lady. I thought the world of her. She moved to Memphis with her girls after Uncle George died. She would bring us children presents when she came home with her family. She had been born cross-eyed; her left eye was pointed to the left. I remember when I was a small boy, she would be talking to me and looking across the room. I wouldn't be sure she was talking to me. She understood that and would mention my name to let me know she was talking to me. She tried to look directly at someone when her conversation started to get their attention, then she had to turn her head to focus. We felt so sorry for our dear sweet aunt. She lived into her nineties and is buried in Memphis. We thought she would want to come back to Mississippi and be buried in the Trevillion Cemetery next to Uncle George. But her daughters wanted her in Memphis, so they could visit and attend to her grave. We visited her daughters Blanche and Georgia and her husband Uncle Fred Owens when our children were small. We enjoyed them so very much. They served lamb and mint jelly. That was the first time I had been served that dish. I'm sure they knew that and wanted to be the ones to serve us such a high-class dish, inheriting the class action from their mother.

Grandma Annie enjoyed working in her vegetable garden. She would be hoeing and weeding and picking her vegetables a lot of the time when we were visiting her. I remember a quince tree that grew in her garden. This tree grew a golden or greenish-yellow apple-shaped fruit. This fruit was very hard, and the taste was very sour, but it was very tasty with salt. Grandma used them to make some very good preserves, but she would let us kids pick a few of those fruits and sell them at school for a nickel each to have a little extra spending money.

My very first ride in a wagon occurred at Grandma's house. Her brother-in-law, Uncle Bud Neal, who was her sister Inez's husband, had lived at one time just down the lane three or four hundred yards away in the next house. Uncle Bud had a team of two horses harnessed to a four-wheel wagon, and he came up to Grandma's for something. When he got ready to go, I asked, "Uncle Bud, can I ride in the wagon?"

Reaching down and picking me up, he said, "Why, sure, boy, get yourself up here in this wagon and drive these horses for me."

I must have been five years old or less, and the wagon had sides all around about three feet high. I can remember being just barely tall enough to see over the sides. Maybe the sides came up even with the top of my shoulders. Uncle Bud took hold of the leather wagon lines and told the horses to come up, and they started walking. He pulled on the left line, and they circled around. The wagon was extremely rough; it had no springs, and the wheels were made of wood with a steel rim around the outside. That wagon was rolling on gravel, and the wooden boards were loose from age. They rattled very loudly as the wagon rolled along.

After the horses were straight and headed down the lane, Uncle Bud handed the lines over to me saying, "Here, boy, drive these horses down to the house." The horses didn't need driving, of course; they were walking down the lane, but I thought I was keeping them straight. I don't know how I thought I was keeping them straight because it was all I could do to hold those heavy lines. I was reared back with one foot braced against the front of the wagon and standing on the other leg. This wagon didn't have a seat in it. When we got to Uncle Bud's house, he said, "Pull back on the lines and tell 'em to whoa."

I reared back, pulled with all I was worth, and yelled, "Whooooa!" They stopped, and I looked up at Uncle Bud and said, "That was fun!"

He smiled back and said, "Well, you can drive them back up there in a minute."

I don't remember what we were hauling, but when we walked in the house, Uncle Bud said to Aunt Inez, "You should have seen James driving those horses."

Aunt Inez laughingly replied, "I thought he must have been driving, because I heard him holler, 'Whoa!'"

I thought, *I must have yelled "Whoa!" pretty loud.* They must have been moving the last things out of the house for they had recently moved out to Highway 552, which was a short distance through the woods. Maybe they were just moving some things they didn't want up to Grandma's house. I can't remember any more than that, but I did drive the wagon back to Grandma's house after Uncle Bud got it headed back up the lane.

Grandma and Grandpa Smith were married to each other for over fifty years, and neither was ever married to anyone else. Grandma passed away in September 1962. She had suffered a long illness. She had lived with Aunt Lillie for the last few years and was totally bedridden. I was in Fort Leonard Wood, Missouri. She had a bad day and finally just passed on later in the day. She is buried in the Trevillion Cemetery next to Grandpa Smith.

11

Larry and Me

Larry Cook was one of my very best friends. He lived across the road about a quarter of a mile west of our house on his grandpa Mason Humphrey's farm from about 1954 until about 1956. He was three years younger than me, and his parents were sharecroppers with his grandpa Humphrey. I was always over there or he was at my house. Larry's brother Jerry had built a camp house using small pine trees for logs. Larry and I wanted a camp house like that, but we were too young to handle an ax like Jerry who was four years older than I was and seven years older than Larry. Larry and I wanted to build our camp house over behind our house in the pasture. We needed those logs in Jerry's house since we could not cut our own. So, we hooked our horse Shorty to the ground slide. A ground slide is a wagon without wheels. It slides on skids like a snow sled. We had Shorty pull the slide over into Mr. Humphrey's pasture where Jerry's camp house was. We tore down a few logs and loaded them onto the slide. After tying them down with a plow line (small cotton rope used for horse reins when plowing), we headed back across the road to our pasture. The chain would pull out of the fastenings on the slide, and we would have to fix it with nails and wire staples or whatever. The slide slid off into a deep cow path and turned over, and we had a time. We would talk about what Jerry was going to do to us when he found out we had torn down his camp house, and we would laugh until we hurt. Jerry either never found out who did it or he didn't really care—probably didn't care because building something was more fun than actually using it anyway, and I don't think Larry and I tore down very many logs.

After Larry and I were grown and hadn't seen each other in ten or more years, the very first thing we thought about when we ran into each other was the day we hooked Shorty to the slide and stole Jerry's camp-house logs. We had another good laugh about it that day.

For Christmas one year, I got cap pistols, two pistols complete with double holsters just like Roy Rogers. Larry would come up, and I would give him one pistol and I would use the other. After a few days or so, one hammer thumb grip broke off one pistol, and we would argue over who would use the good pistol. Then the other pistol broke, and the used-to-be-bad pistol became the good pistol. We played cowboys in those woods and hollows until both pistols were completely worn-out.

On rainy days, we would play under the house. The house was raised about three feet on one end, and, of course, no grass grew under there. It was just plain loose dirt. We would take an old hoe with the handle broken out and scrape the loose dirt down to the hard dirt in one hoe-width lane. Those were our roads. We would make curves, parking lots, etc. Most of the time, we made our own trucks by using a two-inch-by-four-inch piece of lumber about twelve inches long. A short piece of the same wood about four inches long was nailed on top of one end and that was the truck cab. Then roofing nails were nailed into the ends for headlights and taillights. We would nail a small piece of wood under another piece of board for the rear wheels of a trailer. We would then drive a nail through that piece of wood for a trailer hitch. A hole would be made into the rear of the truck so the trailer could be hitched to the truck. We would pile whatever on the trailer and slide the toy along the roads. Sometimes we would be going to Fayette, Natchez, Vicksburg, or even Jackson. The truck would turn over, and we would have another piece of wood that would be the tractor to pull the truck back up on its wheels. Sometimes, we had real toy tractors we had gotten for Christmas, but making those toys and seeing them work was more fun than having store-bought toys.

When we got hungry, we would hurry out from under the house, brush the dust off our clothes, run into the kitchen, and grab the light bread and mayonnaise jar and make mayonnaise sandwiches. Light bread was in the house to make Daddy's lunch, because he brown-bagged a lunch to work. We couldn't eat all of the bread. We had to save enough for one more lunch for Daddy just in case he didn't bring home a loaf. He brought a loaf home when Mama told him to stop by the store and pick up some bread.

Larry and I didn't want anything between that light bread but mayonnaise. Sometimes, just for fun, we would mayonnaise one piece of bread and place another piece of bread on that and mayonnaise that one and place another piece of bread on that and have a triple-decker mayonnaise sandwich. Mayonnaise sandwiches and milk made a complete hardy and fun meal. Larry asked me not too long ago if I still ate mayonnaise sandwiches, and I laughed and told him, "Not in the presence of company."

Larry later came to live with his grandmother Kate after his grandfather passed away. He came by the house one night—this must have been about 1961—and asked me if I would help him herd some cattle the next day. "Whose cattle are we going to herd?" I laughingly asked. He told me Aunt Maggie's cattle had roamed off down to Gerald Smith's farm, and he and Gerald had penned them down there until he could drive them through the woods back to Aunt Maggie's.

Larry and I were no kin, but Aunt Maggie was his mother Catherine's sister. She was Uncle Jack's wife. Most of the people around there were related in some way. I told him I would be glad to help and asked about the details on how we would get the horses to Gerald's. He said, "We can get Lee to drive us over there in the pickup hauling the horses, and he can bring the truck back." We then worked out the details about when we would get started which was about daybreak, or first light, as they say. I was afraid Larry was going to say early, but I didn't expect to get started quite that early. I didn't argue with him though, because I knew it would take time to saddle and load the horses and we had to go pick up Lee, then drive to Gerald's, and who could know how long it would take to drive the cattle back through those woods?

We pulled up at Gerald's farm, unloaded and mounted the horses, and started the cattle toward Aunt Maggie's. Those cows went pretty well for about fifty feet, then they scattered all over the woods. The woods were too thick to round them back up, and Larry said, "These [few choice words] can stay in these woods until hell freezes over if they are waiting for me to drive them to the house." Cattle are smarter than the average person gives them credit for being. Aunt Maggie's cattle roamed around in what we called Crosby Woods. Crosby was a timber company, and they owned thousands of acres south of Aunt Maggie's. She, along with other people, would let the cattle roam in those woods and keep up with the cows by feeding them in the winter in the cow lot behind the house. They would also come to salt, even in the summer. Aunt Maggie would call the cows and have either feed or salt for them when they came up. She named all the cows by their color markings or some distinct marking on their hide. If one didn't come when they were called, she would know it. However, there wasn't a lot she could do if a cow was missing. There were thousands of acres of wooded land to search.

She had several acres fenced in to pasture cattle. If a cow came up with a calf, she would put the cow and calf in the pasture until the calf was weaned. Then she would put the calves in a smaller pen and feed them to around three or four hundred pounds, maybe larger. I don't remember the size exactly. After the calves reached a certain size, she would call the sale barn in Fayette to send a truck and haul them to the sale. Many times, I heard her talking about buying the kids' school clothes or clothes for some special occasion. She would mention that she was going to sell come calves to raise the money.

Her cattle would sometimes scatter off to better grass on someone else's farm when they could get through the fence of the farm as these had done. Gerald knew there were only a few people who let their cattle roam in the Crosby Woods, so he didn't have much trouble getting the word to whomever they belonged to. He might have to describe them a little bit as he had done when he called Aunt Maggie. Cattle will mostly herd together with each other as a family. Deer and turkey will do the same thing. Very seldom will a farmer have to notify anybody about just one cow getting in his pasture. But it happened occasionally, I'm sure.

After getting the cattle started and losing them immediately, Larry said, "Let's go to the house. Which way is it?"

I said, "Larry, I don't quite know how to tell you this, but darned if I know. I don't remember ever being in these woods before." That was an understatement. I knew I had never been in that part of those woods before. The only experience I had with the forest was hunting. I had never hunted in that section of the Crosby Woods, so I was lost.

"Well, let's just ride until we get to where I can recognize something," Larry said. We rode for a little while down a fire lane, and what did we see? Some of the cattle standing in the fire lane up ahead. A fire lane is a dirt road about ten feet wide. The road is cut by the timber company to allow passage for fire trucks to fight forest fires.

I shouted, "Look-a there, Cook! There's the cattle!" We started after them very easily trying not to spook them. After the horses took a few steps toward the cows, they scattered through the woods again.

"Let's don't chase them and get even more lost than we are," I suggested.

With that thought, Larry stopped his horse, looked at me, and asked laughing, "So, you think we can get more lost than completely lost?"

I told him, "Listen, I think I hear a power saw." It was a gasoline-powered saw, and we headed in that direction. Maybe somebody could tell us where we were.

After riding a while, we got to the power saw, and it was David Abbott, a logger whom we both knew. We asked David if he knew how to get to Aunt Maggie's house, and he said, "Why, sure, ya'll are going in the right direction. Just stay on this road to the top of a tall hill around there a piece." He studied a minute and continued, "There ought to be a little fire lane to your right. Take that and that will bring you out at the sand cut." He stopped talking and started fiddling with his saw. There was a moment of silence. Larry and I were waiting to hear directions to the next turn, but I guess David thought everybody knew how to get anywhere they wanted to go once they reached the sand cut.

"Ah, what is the sand cut?" I asked.

David looked up kind of puzzled and said, "Why, that's a deep washout ... uh, that's a sandy hill and the water drains down it and cuts a real deep gully there."

I replied, "Oh, yeah, I think I'll recognize that. Which way do we go from there?"

David set his saw down and said, "Boy, ya'll really are lost, ain't you?" He continued with the directions, "Just stay on that road and keep heading northeast. Don't make any turns, and you will come out at the red sand pit. You do know where that is, don't you?"

"You mean that red sand pit down the road from Aunt Maggie's?"

"Yeah," he said, "That's the one."

Larry and I thanked him and started riding down the fire lane. When we reached the top of the hill, we saw those cows again. Larry said, "You know, I think these cows are going home."

I told him, "I think you are right. All we had to do was get them started."

We rode on and yelled cow language like, "Souck, souck, souck, and huheee." I don't know if it was necessary, but we could see a cow up ahead every now and then. When we rode up to Aunt Maggie's lot about noon, the cows were all there.

Larry explained to Aunt Maggie, "We lost them when we got started, Aunt Maggie, but they came on to the house anyway."

Aunt Maggie said, "Oh yeah, baby, all you had to do was get them started. They would come on to the lot."

Larry and I ate lunch with Aunt Maggie, then bid her farewell and started back through the woods toward home. As we rode off, she yelled, "Thank ya'll for bringing these ole cows home!"

We yelled back, "Wasn't any trouble! We were glad to help you! We enjoyed lunch."

Larry said, "If we had known those cows would come on home with a start, I could have started them on foot yesterday evening."

I said, "Yeah, Cook, you could have, but I don't know about you, but I have enjoyed the day."

He looked at me and grinned, saying, "And if we hadn't been on this cattle drive, we would still be the only ones who don't know where that ole sand cut is."

I laughed out loud, "Yeah, we now know these woods same as the old-timers."

12

Picking Wild Plums and Berries

Many wild berries grew in the pastures and in the woods around the country. The most popular was the blackberry. Blackberries grew on briars and in patches. Birds ate the berries and spread the seeds around the pastures. Cattle grazed the grass around the berry plants but didn't like the plants because of the briars. Therefore, once the briar started and the seeds fell around the plant, more plants grew and there was soon a blackberry patch.

In the spring of the year, the patches would turn snow white with blooms. Later, the blooms would turn into green berries, then large juicy blackberries. The berries finally get ripe in the very hot summertime. That would be about the time we would hear Mama ask us to get a bucket to go pick a few blackberries. After all the griping was done, we would head out into the pasture and start picking blackberries. Mama canned those berries in quart jars, and we had blackberries all winter long. During the summer, we just ate freshly picked berries. Daddy would go out early on Saturday mornings with the foot tub. He wouldn't get back to the house until after lunchtime. He would be wringing wet with sweat, and his foot tub would be rounded off over the top of the rim with big blackberries.

Another tasty berry we all loved to pick was the huckleberry. Huckleberries grew on bushes and in the woods. There were many huckleberry bushes around the house, but the most I have ever seen were just south of Union Church, Mississippi. Mama would write her sister, Aunt Ruth King, and let her know when the huckleberries were getting ripe.

Aunt Ruth would load up some of her kids—Janet, Jeanette, Paul Vernon, and Faye—and they would all come over to pick huckleberries. We would pull mattresses off beds and make pallets all over the house. We kids would have fun playing, and during the day, we would all go huckleberry picking. A large huckleberry is probably about one-quarter inch in diameter; most were smaller than that. We could pick for a long time before we covered the bottom of a syrup bucket. Somehow, with everybody picking and talking and laughing, we eventually filled enough buckets to cause Mama and Aunt Ruth to want to go back to the house. Mama told me once that she and Aunt Ruth canned eighty quarts one year, and Aunt Ruth took half of them home for her family.

We were off in those woods one year picking berries when my sister Bessie was about three or four years old. They were all about ready to go, and Bessie was thirsty or hungry or just plain tired. Aunt Ruth told her daughter Faye and me to carry Bessie to the car and take some full buckets of berries with us. Faye was about seventeen or eighteen, and I was probably twelve or thirteen years old at that time. Faye loaded Bessie on her back, and I picked up about four buckets of berries as we started up a wooded ridge toward the road where the cars were parked. We couldn't see the road from where we started out, but we knew it wasn't very far. After walking a little while, we began to ask each other if we were lost. At first, we didn't agree, but finally, we both decided we didn't have any idea how to get back to the road.

I took a turn carrying Bessie, and Faye carried the berries for a while. It was blistering hot, and sweat was pouring off both of us. We stopped to rest and talked about leaving the berries but decided against that; they were too hard to pick. We decided to hang the buckets in a tree so they could be seen from a distance, but we were afraid we wouldn't be able to find them again. After awhile, we finally heard Daddy blowing the car horn and followed the sound to the road. That was quite an ordeal and one that will never be forgotten.

Faye later married a military man and moved out of the country to Germany and other places. Quite a few years had passed since I had last seen her. We ran into each other, and both reminisced about the day we got lost picking huckleberries. Faye laughingly told me, "James, we were both embarrassed about getting lost, but we can be very proud to say we didn't loose or leave the first one of those wonderful huckleberries." We both had a good laugh over that.

I said, "Yeah, we considered leaving them a few times, but as you said, Faye, we never left a one of those mighty huckleberries."

She said, "Mama and Aunt Annie Mae would have killed both of us for sure!"

We then talked about how good those berries were over hot buttered biscuits, a little sweet cream spread over that, with a few slices of bacon along and a glass of milk. We talked on, and neither one could remember when we last had had a huckleberry. I said, "Well, Faye, I'll start watching for 'em, and if you'll give me your number, when they get ready, I'll call you."

Faye said, "Never mind, James, I'll just live with my memories." She continued, "The taste of store-bought blueberries is good enough for me."

There were three species of plums growing wild in the country in those days. One was a very juicy and sweet plum about three-quarters of an inch in diameter. There were mostly red plums, but a fair amount of yellow plums also. These two plums tasted about the same. These plum bushes grew in patches, or thickets, as we called them. Some plum thickets were a few feet across, and others were maybe a half acre or more. I think they ripened in June or early July. They made very delicious jellies and preserves. The one thing I enjoyed the most was crawling into a plum thicket and picking the ripest plums off the ground where they had fallen off the bush and eating them right there. I just swallowed the juice and spit out the seed and peeling. It is very hard to find plum bushes anymore because the deer bite off the sprouts as they come up out of the ground. We didn't have many deer when I was a kid, so that wasn't a problem.

One time, Daddy, Mama, Aunt Pearlie, Uncle Archie, and I all went to the Marlar place where Uncle Bill had told us there was a large plum thicket. And large it was. That thicket must have been two acres or more. We carried buckets to pick in and a washtub in the trunk of the car to haul the plums back. That washtub was full of plums.

Mama and Aunt Pearlie canned plums and made jelly, plum butter, and preserves for a couple of days around there.

The third species of plum was the wild plum. It was a hard, less juicy, and very sour plum. Actually, all the plums were wild, just growing on their own without any cultivation or care. So, I'm not sure why we only called that one wild. That was the name it was given, so that was the name we used to distinguish that plum from the other ones. Wild plums made great jelly, but the tree would grow alone, and they weren't very plentiful. Wild plums ripened in the early fall of the year. I would run across one while squirrel hunting and fill my squirrel sack with plums. Mama would cook them down and make wild plum jelly to go with my fried squirrels and hot buttered biscuits.

13

Summer Jobs in the Country

A country boy, like almost any kid, likes to have a little extra cash when he can get it. We had several ways to make extra money around the different farms. We would connect a two-wheeled trailer behind the Model B John Deere Tractor to haul firewood, the disk, or whatever else needed hauling. I would sometimes attach the trailer, load the disk, drive down the road to some other farmer's place, and disk his field. The charge was three dollars per hour including the driver's pay. Daddy, of course, let us kids keep all the money. We didn't owe him one penny. He let us use the tractor for free. The other farmer would furnish the gas for the tractor and lunch for the driver. Most farmers had a gas storage tank and had their gas delivered by local gasoline companies. This gas was set aside for farm use, and farmers didn't have to pay road tax on the gas. The road tax was several cents per gallon, I'm not sure just how much, but it was quite a savings. A ten-hour day was the norm.

Work was easy to come by in the country, if a kid knew how to drive a tractor. I, for one, was always looking for a way to earn a few bucks. When I was seventeen, I drove a tractor for Mr. Guy Kelly. I was clipping the weeds in his pasture with a Barintine pasture clipper. Since he furnished his tractor and mower, the pay was fifty cents per hour and lunch. This was a ten-hour-per-day job, fifty hours a week, but no taxes were held out, so the take-home pay was twenty-five dollars every Friday evening. Twenty-five dollars in my pocket and an old 1952 model Plymouth automobile, which was a hand-me-down from my older brother William, made me a very happy lad.

I had the old Plymouth repaired by Mr. Hiram Norton and didn't have quite enough money to pay him. To keep from having to ask Daddy for the money, I worked a deal with Mr. Hiram to cut him some firewood for the wood heater in his shop. I cut the tree off his place with a gas-fueled chainsaw. I had to split some of it and load it onto a pickup truck, haul it, and stack it behind his shop. I couldn't tell how much wood the tree would produce, but it looked like enough to settle the bill. It was more than two pickup loads of wood and made a pretty large stack behind his shop. I was hoping that would satisfy Mr. Hiram, and it did. He said, "Boy, you didn't have to cut all that much wood. I won't burn all that this whole winter." I was glad to hear him say that, and I told him if he considered it extra, or more than enough, that would be fine with me, because it was nice of him to let me work out the debt instead of having to pay the bill. I don't remember the amount, but it couldn't have been much, because I wouldn't have had the work done if the estimate had been very expensive.

Another job I landed once was driving a tractor for Mr. Bud Short. He had a few acres of corn and a little Ford tractor. I cultivated his corn with that tractor. It took all day, and he paid me five dollars and lunch. When he hired me, he didn't specify an hourly amount. He just told me that he could do that job in a day, and he would give me five dollars. I immediately agreed, because I didn't think Mr. Bud would have worked more than ten hours in one day. That was about a dollar per day more than the other farmers were paying, and I didn't know why Mr. Bud was so generous, but I certainly told him how much I appreciated it. I had earned five dollars working for Mr. Guy Kelly, but I had to put in ten hours, because the Kelly job was by the hour. Mr. Bud's job wasn't a real long day.

One year, the Mississippi Forestry Service was opening a pine tree nursery near McNair, Mississippi, and needed green pine cones. They were going to let the cones dry, then retrieve the seeds, plant them, and grow plant seedlings. They would then grow pine trees and crossbreed with the pollen to end up with a trophy pine tree. They were paying three dollars for a peach basket full of green pine cones, about a half bushel. My brother J. P. and I were climbing pine trees and picking pine cones. My uncle Jack found out about this venture, and we told him if he helped, we would split the profits three ways. He agreed, and we were off. After a short period of time, Uncle Jack got a brilliant idea. He said, "Boys, why don't we just get the ax and cut the limbs off and let them pile up on the ground, so we can pick the cones real easy."

What a grand idea! Just leave it to Uncle Jack, he would always come up with a simple solution to a complicated problem. One of his friends once said, "Jack Smith was a smart man. If he had had an education, he might have been president."

We, of course, wanted to know if cutting the limbs off would kill the tree, and he assured us the tree would not know the difference. I don't know how he knew that, but he knew a lot of things that you wouldn't expect him to know. I tell you, we picked more pine cones than anybody else in just a few days. As we turned the cones in, the forester asked us how we got so many so quick. We were too smart to give our secret away. We just told him we worked real hard. In fact, we had probably worked less than any of the other pickers and retrieved more cones than anybody else. We never saw anybody picking in our neck of the woods, so they didn't catch on to our method. I can't remember how much money we made, but it was quite a lot. We were anxious for the next season, but they had all the cones they needed to start the nursery, so that job never came around again.

One time, I collected scrap iron and sold it to a salvage junkyard in Port Gibson. They paid one cent per pound for steel and iron and more for aluminum, but I never found any aluminum to sell. They paid several cents per pound for copper and brass, and there was plenty of that. Daddy and I had collected quite a few worn-out faucets doing plumbing work in houses. A lot of the faucets weren't just worn-out, they had burst due to freezing. Most faucets are made of brass and brass had a very good scrap value in those days. I can remember I had enough money to buy a brand-new hunting suit. It must have been thirty or so dollars. It made me feel real worthwhile to think of a way to make money and see my ideas materialize. I just felt better owning something that I had purchased with my own money, rather than handouts from my parents. I had been using old clothes for hunting. I had to wear several shirts over each other to keep warm. All the shirts were pretty well worn-out or they wouldn't have been used for hunting.

I looked real sharp in that new green hunting coat, new hunting shirt, and matching pants.

During the fall of 1960, the sixteenth year of my life, Mr. Guy Kelly asked me to bring our Model B John Deere and our pulverizing disk over to his farm and help him plant his winter wheat. The rate of pay was the usual three dollars per hour, lunch for the tractor driver, and gas for the tractor. I, of course, could keep all three dollars for myself. Daddy would furnish the tractor for nothing.

Mrs. Stella Kelly, Mr. Guy's wife, was a very nice lady and a very good cook, and she believed in preparing very hearty meals for the farmhands. Terry, my good friend, had one of his father's tractors down there, and we enjoyed working together. He was the same age as me, and we went to school together. We really enjoyed those fine lunches of fried chicken, potato salad, field peas, sliced tomatoes, cornbread, and ice-cold tea. Mrs. Kelly always had a big vegetable garden, and we had collard and/or mustard greens at different meals. I grew up loving vegetables, and she had a nice selection in her garden.

There would be sliced cucumbers and green onions on the side. She made a very good sweet potato casserole, and there was always a dessert, like maybe a peach or apple cobbler, a chocolate or lemon pie, banana pudding, etc. There were many more dishes on that table at different times, and only the flour, salt, pepper, tea, sugar, bananas, and lemons came from town.

In those days, people didn't depend on the government to take care of them. They might be lacking in some things, but food was real easy to grow on a farm. Of course, it takes a little getting up off your behind and attending to your garden. Today, folk complain about not getting enough food stamps, but if you go over to their house, you won't find a garden, pig pen, or milk cow, and I mean the ones in the rural areas where they have land for such things. They just depend on the government.

The evening before I was to arrive at Mr. Kelly's farm, I greased the tractor and disk. I then filled the tractor with gas; this was a custom because you didn't want to arrive at the customer's farm with an empty tank. It was just a custom, especially if you wanted to fill up when leaving the customer's farm. After checking the oil and water in the old B, I hooked the disk to the tractor and pulled it up to the loading bank to be loaded on the trailer. Then after unhooking the disk, I hooked up the trailer and backed it up to the bank in front of the disk, loaded it, and chained it down. I had learned this entire job by helping Daddy and my brothers. You might say, I just grew into it, and I felt a sense of accomplishment about my abilities. This, in my opinion, is a real part of growing up. A young person doesn't know what their abilities are. This gave me a chance to prove myself to myself.

I arose early the next morning well before daylight. Mr. Guy had said he wanted to get started at first light, and I had to cover about six miles at about ten miles per hour. This trip would take about thirty minutes, but of course maybe less, counting the speed I would pick up coasting down the grades. I, of course, coasted down Clanton Hill. It was just customary to do that. However, with the trailer behind, I didn't let it go as fast as it would have. I braked a little on that hill. There was another good downhill grade at Blue Hill, but I would have to brake a little going down Blue Hill also, because of the curve about halfway down. Mama got up and prepared breakfast. I could have done it, but Mama knew I would need a good breakfast, because starting that early, it would be a long time on the tractor seat before dinner. While she cooked breakfast, I put some ice in a glass jug and sacked it in three or four brown paper bags for insulation. We didn't have a water jug as such.

After breakfast, I started out the door, and Mama said, "Now you be careful out there on that tractor. It's still dark, and that thing only has one headlight."

Walking out the door, I replied, "I will, but don't worry, there ain't much traffic this time of day."

A lot of traffic would have meant maybe meeting and being passed by maybe two different vehicles, so "not much traffic" actually meant "no traffic."

I fired up the old B, put her in sixth gear, and pushed the throttle wide open which was a little more than recommended by the manufacturer. You see, we had screwed that little bolt that stops the throttle in slightly tighter to give the tractor a little more speed. That was the stop to keep the throttle from going in past a certain point. This added a little RPM to the engine which added a little speed to the tractor, and we loved speed.

After the gear was in the number-six slot and the throttle was pushed as far forward as it would go, I eased in on the hand clutch. You could jam the clutch too fast, and that would cause the engine to stall before the tractor started rolling and the flywheel started spinning to give the engine torque. After the tractor started moving very well, the clutch was pressed all the way forward. It had a catch that would engage to hold it in place. I had a smile on my face, I'm sure, because it was fun driving that tractor. Being a kid and doing something worthwhile was especially gratifying. I would be singing songs along with the clucking of that ole two-cylinder tractor. All that, plus the money I was going to earn, gave me a special happy feeling. There would be another downhill grade at Mr. Tanksley's farm and also at Ann Baker Hill, but I would have to brake on Ann Baker Hill as well, because of the speed but also because there was a sharp curve at the bottom. I never thought of timing that trip from home to Mr. Kelly's, but I'm sure it could have been done in less than thirty minutes.

My tractor and I traveled up the driveway and out onto Lucky Hollow Road, and we were on our way to work. I coasted down Clanton Hill and on down the road to the Lucky Hollow and Highway 552 intersection. Pulling out and heading west on the graveled Highway 552, I was feeling real good. There was a stillness in the dark and no traffic. The one dim headlamp on the tractor barely lit the road enough to see, but the sun was on the rise and the traveling was easy. The tractor clucked on up Blue Hill and down the other side. I was very careful to slow down before reaching the curve in the downgrade about halfway to the bottom.

After a few minutes, I passed Ely's (or Snow's) house, and I could smell the aroma of bacon frying. They still cooked on a wood-fired stove as we did, and that aroma would travel out the stovepipe with the smoke. I figured Snow was probably getting ready to do a little plowing himself or maybe take his mule over to somebody's place and work their fall garden or something. It was good to know I wasn't the only one getting an early start to work that morning. As the tractor topped the hill just before Nesler's store, there was an eastward opening to his pasture. The sky was just turning red over the treetops. I rounded the curve in front of Mr. Hiram Norton's mechanic shop, and it was just light enough to see him pushing the doors open on his shop, getting ready for the day. We waved at each other as I passed on by. There was a slight early fall chill in the air that morning, but the leaves were not moving in the early breaking dawn. Mr. Kelly's farm was about a mile ahead now, and I knew I would arrive in the expected time. It has always been important to me to be on time, especially if someone was expecting me to be at a certain place at a certain time.

Mr. Guy, as we all called him, was out beside his house where his farm equipment was parked, and he had a cigarette in his mouth. He used a cigarette holder which was almost out of fashion by those days. I heard somebody ask him one day, "Mr. Guy, why do you use a cigarette holder? You don't see those much anymore."

Mr. Guy smiled and replied, "My doctor told me to stay away from cigarettes, so I'm taking his advice!" He probably thought it was nobody's business, and he just liked to smoke that way. Mr. Guy passed away many years later from throat cancer, when he was maybe in his mid-seventies.

When I pulled up and idled the tractor's engine, he said, "Come on, boy, let's get that thing unloaded and get to the field. Do you need a bank?" He was talking about the disk and a bank on which to unload it.

I yelled over the idling tractor engine, "No, sir, I can unload it here." With that, I opened the throttle and looked around for an open space. After I picked out a spot, I pulled the tractor around and backed up to the space. I dismounted the tractor, and took the binder and chain off the disk. I asked one of the farmhands to help me push the disk toward the rear of the trailer.

When I saw the trailer tongue rise against the tractor's drawbar, I knew the trailer was weighted to the rear. As I lifted the pin that attached the trailer to the drawbar, I told my helper to step back. Putting one foot on the trailer tongue and bracing my back on the tractor wheel, I pushed the tongue sideways, dislodging it from the drawbar. The tongue raised up, and the disk rolled off the rear of the trailer and out onto the ground. I knew to jump out from behind the tractor at the right moment, because that trailer was built heavy on the front, and with the weight of the disk running off onto the ground, it was coming down hard.

With this accomplished, we shoved the trailer out of the way and backed the tractor up to the disk. My helper hooked the u-bolt through the disk tongue and dropped the pin through the u-bolt and the drawbar. With the tractor still idling, I walked over to where Mr. Guy was working with his equipment, and looking at my watch, I said, "I'm ready to go, which way is the field?" Seeing me look at my watch, he pulled his pocket watch, which hung on a gold chain from his belt loop, out of his watch pocket. We both were checking the time to be sure each agreed on the starting time. He said, "Yeah, it's six thirty (or whatever time it was)."

And I said, "That's what I have." Checking time was important. He had to keep up with the time and make every minute count. He was planting winter wheat for grazing his cattle to help with the winter cow feed. All his hands and tractors were being paid by the hour——well, at least the tractors, the hands might have been working by the day.

There were a certain number of acres to plant, and it all had to be planted as quickly as possible to cut down on expenses. He had to get the seed in the ground before the rain. He had watched the weather reports, as all farmers did when planning a project such as this, and he knew he had plenty of time, but he also knew weathermen did make mistakes. I'm sure he had gotten very wet during one of those "20 percent" chance of rain days. If it did rain before he planted, he had to wait for the ground to dry again and hope for enough time between showers to plant the fields. If he got a rain, then a dry spell, and after that, another rain, the ground he had flat broken would be too packed for the pulverizing disk to break up. This meant he would have to run the flat-breaking disk or plows again and all the progress thus far would be wasted. He told me once a farmer was either praying for rain or praying for a dry spell.

He said, "We're ready to pull out to the field now. Just follow us, and I'll show ya'll what to do when we get there." We all caravanned the tractors and equipment down the lane to the field across a little creek. This flat piece of ground was about seventy-five acres or so, and he had already finished the flat breaking, and part of the field was pulverized. He had his old Farmall steel-wheel tractor pulling a pulverizing disk about six feet wide. This tractor had pulverized the day before, so Mr. Guy would have some ground ready to immediately start planting this day. The steel-wheel driver started disking where he had left off the day before. Mr. Guy had another modern John Deere MT. He was using it to pull the fertilizer spreader. His steel wheel was pulverizing, and my job was to pull a pulverizing disk to cover the wheat seed.

Mr. Guy told me, "You set your disk so it won't cut too deep and you can cover up the seed and fertilizer."

I said, "I'll put it in the fourth notch, and that ought to be about right."

He didn't trust this young kid to know just how to cover wheat. It can be covered too deep, making it take longer to grow out of the ground. If it's deep enough, it won't come up at all. It will just rot in the ground. He replied, "You set it and start down the field a ways and stop. I'll check and see if it is cutting right."

After pulling and checking and resetting the disk, he finally decided on a setting, and I was off. Four tractors in the same field did in twice the time a task that one tractor could do today. None of those tractors had more than thirty horsepower, and they were considered large tractors at the time. John Deere did make more powerful tractors although it wasn't anywhere near the power of tractors nowadays.

Mr. Guy had a long-wheelbase black pickup load of wheat seed and fertilizer. His MT John Deere was hooked to a fertilizer distributor, and Terry's Ford tractor was hooked to the grain spreader. They loaded the fertilizer in the distributor and filled the spreader with wheat. The fertilizer distributor started spreading fertilizer around over the field, and Terry came along behind him spreading the seed. We got the job done, and Mr. Guy was proud of the work we had done.

Another job I had around the place was picking cotton. That is all explained in the "Picking Cotton" chapter.

14

Picking Cotton

The Sheltons, our neighbors, grew cotton every year, and they hired people to pick it by hand. When I came in from school a little after 4:00 PM, I would go to the barn and find a gunnysack. A gunnysack is a bag made of burlap. Cow feed was packaged in those bags, and after they were empty, they were very handy around the farm. By tying a hay string to each end of the opening at the top of the sack and using the hay string as a strap, I would have a cotton sack. A gunnysack would hold probably about twenty pounds of cotton, I don't know because I never came close to filling one. A regular cotton sack was about ten feet long and tarred on one side of the bottom so it could be dragged down the row without damaging the cloth. This kept the picker from having to carry the weight. I don't think my little sack dragged, but that wasn't a problem because it never had much weight in it. The cotton pickers would laugh when I came running into the field with my little homemade cotton sack. They would make little remarks like, "James, if you fill that sack up a couple of times, you could make you a pillow," or "I don't think this field is big enough for that sack." They would all join in the laughter, and I would go, "Ha, ha, ha." My good friend Lee Dee would be there, and he would take up for me. He told me not to pay them any mind and to come on over to his row and I could pick there. He would let me go ahead of him and pick the best and biggest bolls. While we picked, we would visit and we would enjoy each other's company. Sometimes if I was riding my horse around on weekends and found them picking cotton, I would go out and help Lee fill his cotton sack. I guess he remembered those times and was kind of repaying me for my friendly gesture. That might happen on other farms, too. I only picked for myself on Mr. Clint's farm.

Walter Trevillion (Souck), who worked as a handyman on Mr. Clint's farm, would come to the field with a tractor and trailer a little while before dark and collect the cotton sacks and us pickers. We would ride to the cotton house, and Mr. Shelton or his son would be there with cotton scales to weigh in the cotton. My little sack would not be heavy enough to weigh so they would give me a dime and sometimes fifteen cents. Pickers got four cents per pound, and it took a good picker to get very much over one hundred pounds in one day in that part of the state. Up north in the Mississippi Delta, they could easily pick two to three hundred pounds per ten or twelve-hour day. That was up around Greenwood, where they bragged about being the cotton capital of the world. Farmers around our neck of the woods thought they had a good crop if they harvested one bale per acre. The folks around Greenwood thought they didn't do too well if they made anything less than three bales per acre.

The next day at school, I would have maybe fifteen or twenty cents. I would be a very happy schoolboy. My usual allowance was a nickel per day plus the ten or fifteen cents I earned picking cotton. Mr. Henry Spencer ran a store in Red Lick near the United Vocational School where we went to school until 1958. Red Lick is about five miles east of Lorman, Mississippi, on Highway 552. Mr. Henry Spencer had hundreds of items in that store that sold for a nickel: double-dipped ice cream cones, candy bars, packs of gum, ten lemon cookies, five pieces of bubble gum, soft drinks, a box of Cracker Jacks with a prize inside every box, and more than I can remember. With my nickel, I had to make a decision. I could afford only one item. If I chose a soft drink, I couldn't get a bag of potato chips. It had to be one or the other and no ice cream. After a day in the field picking cotton—or a couple hours would be more like it—I could get a soft drink, potato chips, a candy bar, and ice cream. I felt rich ... Well, I *was* rich.

15

Hauling Hay

It was the summer of 1960, and Daddy had bought some hay from Mr. Geoghegan. This was Bermuda grass hay that does not have to be cured before it is baled. It was mowed by a mower that cut it off even with the ground; then it was raked into rows and baled. Mr. Geoghegan didn't haul the hay, so Daddy sent me to Mr. Goza's farm to hire him to haul the hay. Mr. Goza was too busy, and all his hands were busy since it was hay season. Mr. Goza had a very good-sized hay operation himself.

Mr. Goza told me he was baling hay that didn't have to be hauled the next day and we could use one of his trucks, but we would have to furnish a driver. I told him I didn't know who we could get to drive the truck. He said, "Why don't you drive it?"

I couldn't believe my ears. Why, I was a sixteen-year-old kid. That thing had five gears forward on the floor and more gears in the rear-end deferential. It would haul a hundred bales of hay, and that was a big load that would require shifting gears on hills. If I missed a gear, it might run backward down the hill, and I didn't know what all might happen.

I asked, "Are you serious?"

He said, "Of course I'm serious. You might as well learn how to drive it; other people have learned."

"I don't know if I can work all those gears, especially with the truck loaded."

Mr. Goza said, "I can show you how to change gears. Come on out here."

We went out to where the truck was parked, and he got in the passenger seat and told me to get under the steering wheel. He told me to clutch, then he showed me how to shift the gears. The five on the floor were simple enough. Then he taught me how to shift the gears in the rear end. There was a little red button on the side of the shift lever for shifting the rear-end dog gear. He explained the clutching procedures required to shift the dog. First, press the clutch, then press the red button, let out on the clutch, and the deferential would be in low or dog gear.

Mr. Goza got out, and I started home in the truck. When I got there, Daddy wanted to know why I was driving the truck, and I explained that Mr. Goza had taught me how to drive it. I told him that I would be hauling the hay myself. I don't know if I could have let my sixteen-year-old son drive a truck that size, but Daddy had a lot of confidence in us kids and didn't figure I would have a wreck. I told him the truck would haul a hundred bales and asked how many loads he wanted. He said three.

The Geoghegan farm was about twenty miles from our house, and as I lay in bed that night, I was counting the hills between our house and that farm. There was Ann Baker Hill, Blue Hill, Clanton Hill, and the hill at Sander's farm that I could think of at the time. Daddy had hired a black man for my helper. His name was Eli, but he was nicknamed Snow. I got to Snow's house the next morning about the break of day. Eli had been nicknamed Snow all his life, and evidently, he was okay with the name, because he never asked to be called anything else. He smiled at me as he climbed into the truck and moaned, "Mornin'." Then he added, "Ain't this Mr. Goza's truck?"

"Yeah, it is, and we got to make three trips from the other side of Fayette to our house today with a hundred bales on each load." I started the truck down the road as I finished, "And I ain't never drove a truck like this until today." I cut my eyes over at Snow to see how he was bearing the news.

Snow was in his sixties then, and he just smiled and said, "If you can hold it between the ditches, maybe we will make it all right."

Snow and I talked on as we drove down the winding gravel country road. I was reminded about the time he came over to our farm to plow our garden. He had ridden his mule over and hooked him to our plow and plowed all day. The garden was too small an area for the tractor; that was why he used his mule. That afternoon, when he got ready to leave, he and I were out near the woodpile and he was trying to get on his mule to ride him home. He couldn't jump up on him, so he led him up near a large block of wood, stood on the block, and got on the mule. He said to me as he reined his mule around, "James, I used to jump on a mule or horse wherever he stood. Now I have to get on a high place to mount one, just like I had to do when I was a little boy." He let out a chuckle and continued, "James, we are once a man, but twice a child." He rode on down the driveway, and I just stared in his direction for several minutes thinking of those words of wisdom I had just heard from that knowledgeable old man.

We continued to talk in the truck that morning about how some people make mistakes that cost them money. Snow said, "James, bought sense is the best sense a man can learn." Well, there he went again, giving me some common sense that I still remember. We pulled into Mr. Geoghegan's hay field, and his hands were waiting under the shade tree. It was barely past seven o'clock, but the day was heating up. They started the tractors, with one mowing the grass, the next one raking the hay into rows, and the final tractor pulling the baler. I drove the truck along beside the bales, and one threw the bales up into the truck where Snow stacked it nice and neat. Once we had on a hundred bales, Snow got in the cab, and we pulled out of the field and headed home with the first load. I had to get this load over those hills and to the barn using gears on the truck that I had never used before. Snow had never learned to drive, so it was all up to me.

The road was paved from Geoghegan's to Harriston, Mississippi, and the truck didn't need the dog gear in the rear end for extra power. When we got to Sanders' Hill, I had a very good run and made it over without the dog. Ann Baker Hill was another matter; the road crossed a little creek and ran straight for about a quarter of a mile, then there was a sharp curve at the bottom of the steep grade. One couldn't get a run at the hill, because it wasn't possible to safely turn that sharp curve at the bottom very fast. Mr. Guy Kelly's farm was about a mile from the hill, and along about there, I told Snow, "Ann Baker Hill is coming

131

up, and because of the sharp curve at the bottom, I'll have to slow down which means I'm probably going to need the dog, and I might get this thing out of gear and roll back down." I then added, "If you want to get out and walk to the top of the hill, I'll wait for you once I'm up there." Snow was having no part of that. He told me not to worry about changing gears, that I would make it all right. That was some more of his encouragement that I needed. Snow said something like I would never know if I could make it or not unless I tried. I had heard that before from my father.

I had all the confidence I needed to shift a Ford differential on a steep hill, and I was going to prove to myself that I could do it. I slowed the truck to about fifteen or so miles per hour in the curve, clutched it, dropped a gear, then floorboarded the accelerator, then let off, clutched again, and pressed the infamous red button on the shift lever. There was a grinding sound coming from the rear, I had missed the dog somehow. The truck was slowing; the differential was out of gear. I got scared and just stopped the thing. I later learned the proper procedure was to just press the clutch again, and it would have shifted. I didn't know that at the time, so I just stopped. The load pressed the rear down since the truck was slanted up the grade. In that position, the rear was pressed downward which caused the front to rise. The front wheels didn't come off the ground, but I thought they were going to. Since I had no experience in driving loaded trucks and had no way of knowing what was normal and what was not, I just had to wait and see what all would happen. Everything leveled out, nothing came off the ground, and the brakes held the truck in place on the road.

There we sat. Snow was laughing, and I started laughing too, not that it was all that funny, but the brakes were holding and we weren't rolling backward. I shifted the transmission into double low, the lowest gear on there. Since the truck had stopped and the differential gears weren't turning, the dog dropped into low also. I let out on the clutch while pressing the accelerator, and we started up the hill from a standstill. I up shifted once I was on top of the hill, and on down the road, we went. I began to breathe normally again. I asked Snow if he was worried, and he told me he wasn't worried a bit. He knew I could do it. I never thought he really did think that, but it sounded good to hear him say it.

The next hill was ole Blue, and I was worried more than ever now, but I now knew the truck would pull off from a standstill, even on an uphill grade. That thought made me feel better about things. As we approached Blue Hill, I thought about Daddy telling me about Grandpa and the oxen pulling a load over that blue clay hill and Daddy and the T-Model Fords trying to get over with everybody out pushing. Now here I was, another generation trying to get a load over that ole hill. The more things change, the more they stay the same, I had once heard. If they could do it, why couldn't I? How would I fare with my turn at the hill? We were about to find out. That hill had a short grade then a curve, then a steeper grade, then another sharp curve, and I would be over the top. We would be going down the other side with two sharp curves along the way.

I had a pretty good start at the lower grade. I went for that mean dog gear first. With it out of the way, I could probably shift the other gears properly. I pressed the clutch and then the red button and didn't hear any grinding noise. How about that? I had shifted to dog successfully! Now, I had only the transmission gears to worry about. I shifted to lower gears each time the truck slowed, and finally, we cruised over the crest of the Mighty Blue. We were over with a load, just like my father, my grandfather, and my great-grandfather had done. I felt good; it was a beautiful day in the sun. Intrepid nerves and utter boldness had overcome fear and frustration. I had let myself try, given myself a chance, and proven to myself that I could do it.

Snow and I finished those three loads of hay that day before dark, and I carried the truck back to Mr. Goza. He asked me how I did, and I just told him I didn't have any trouble. I didn't go into any details. I didn't figure he wanted to hear about me grinding the dog gear, and I knew he wasn't interested in my personal stories about Blue Hill. As the sun went down on that day, I knew I had learned how to drive a truck and learned even more about myself. It was a good day, one that I obviously still remember and still treasure as one of my better days.

16

The Blue Goose

There is a small creek called the Blue Goose Creek that begins a mile or so southwest of our farm and ran all the way across the farm. That's right, this stream actually ran northeast. I haven't a clue as to how that stream of water got its name. I don't know if I have ever seen a goose that was blue, but I sometimes think maybe somebody saw a blue goose on the creek and named the creek after the goose. Maybe it was a regular goose and the person was color blind, but the creek ran under Lucky Hollow Road about one-half mile south of our driveway. After flowing another one-quarter mile from there, it flowed across our farm. Then it curved back and forth, coming a few hundred yards behind our barn and down through the woods then out across our pasture, and ran off our farm on the northeast side and flowed onto the old Bailey farm.

The Blue Goose wouldn't be much of a creek to most people, but it was a mighty majestic stream to me when I was a small farm boy. Since the Blue Goose crossed our farm completely, the cattle would never be far from a cool drink. On a hot summer day, the cows would wade out into a long, deep hole until the water was up to their bellies. We would go swimming in the Blue Goose until we discovered James Cole's swimming hole. The Blue Goose isn't fed with springs like the Clark, so the water wasn't as cool as the Clark except shortly after a rainfall.

One time, J. P., William, and I were swimming in a long hole of water about waist deep. I had not learned how to swim and somehow fell backward. I was flopping around like a big fish and was too panicked to simply stand up. My brothers were watching me. William was the first one there and pulled me up. I tell him now and then that he saved my life once, but he hasn't done much for me lately. I was probably about five years old at the time, and it was my first experience with deep water. We would go down there after a big rain sometimes and watch the swift water. I think every time we saw that creek flooded, somebody would start talking about how we should make a raft sometime and see how far we could float. I do sincerely believe a raft would float to the Mississippi River and out into the gulf. We never got serious about making a raft, and that was a good thing; we probably would have drowned our fool selves.

The creek came in handy many times; for example, when the tractor needed water while plowing the field, the creek wasn't far away. If we were riding our horses, no matter where we were on the place, watering them was never a problem. The creek was handy if we needed a drink ourselves. When Daddy built the new house, he used the existing blocks for pillars to support the house. The pillars (blocks as we called them) started to rot after a few years, and Daddy hired Uncle Jack to replace them. Uncle Jack measured the height of each block, bought a load of dry concrete mix, and went down to the creek to set up what you might call a concrete factory. He sawed some one-by-twelve-inch lumber into the proper lengths and used them for concrete forms. We kids helped him shovel sand and gravel from the creek bed into his wooden mixing vat. The dry cement mix was poured into the vat on top of the sand and gravel. That was mixed together until Uncle Jack said, "That'll do, boys." We then carried water from the creek, poured it into the vat, and stirred that with a shovel and hoe until we had concrete. Then Uncle Jack had us pour the concrete into his forms, and after about a day, we had concrete blocks. He had some old fencing net wire rolled up inside the forms that ended up in the core of the concrete block for reinforcement. We backed the tractor and trailer up to the blocks, loaded them, and hauled them to the house where Uncle Jack put them in place.

That creek helped us catch our horses. They were very difficult to catch, so we had to outsmart them by building a trap. We constructed a trap where the Blue Goose made a wide turn toward Mr. Clint's farm leaving about twenty feet of ground between the line fence between our property line and the creek bank. The creek bank was high at that narrow location and that narrow passage made it ideal for a trap. We tied fence wire from a tree standing on the creek bank over to the line fence. When we started chasing the horses, they crossed the creek and headed down the line fence into our trap. Once these horses were hemmed in, they would stand so we could bridle them. The creek had served another purpose, and we were very proud of ourselves for having outsmarted those dumb animals. You might call that "ignorant bliss." We, however, failed to give the dumb animals credit for having any horse sense at all. The very next time we tried to catch them, they crossed the creek but ran in the opposite direction of our trap. They had remembered the trap. Now what would we do?

We then resorted to tying chains onto leather straps and leaving a piece of chain about three feet long dragging from the horse's hoof. Only one horse had to be chained, because after we caught one horse, we could ride him to catch the others. Watching cowboy shows taught me that horses were kept corralled all the time, so I decided to build me a corral. This was after J. P. and William were grown, and I had to catch my horse by myself. A corral would make my horse available at all times. Why hadn't I thought of that before? Since the horse would need grazing and water, I wanted my corral designed for those essentials. I tied some old barbed wire to the garden fence and ran my corral fence from there down to the creek where the bank was high on the opposite side of the creek. About a hundred or so feet down the creek, I set a post and ran my corral fence back up the hill and over to the pasture fence. This made a corral about two acres in size, which was not enough grazing for a horse, but with a bale of hay and some corn now and then, the horse would be all right and the creek would supply the water. The creek had come in handy again. There was just one flaw in that plan, hay and corn were in short supply in the summertime, because that feed was fed to the cattle in the winter. I remember buying some mixed feed, but the horse didn't stay corralled very much.

Fishing on the Blue Goose in the early spring is one of my fondest memories. The old cold winter had passed; the weather was warm, the trees were turning green, and the birds chirped all along the Blue

Goose. Honeysuckle vines were blooming and cool water babbling as it ran down the brook, as I had read in my storybooks. I was fishing on a babbling brook. I could throw a couple of dry chunks of wood together at the foot of a large beech or oak tree and sit there for a long period of time just listening to the quiet and musical sounds of the forest coming alive. If the fish were biting, that was okay, but the time didn't require any extra entertainment. I'm so proud to have lived near the Blue Goose, and I plan to go there this spring and revisit those fleeting moments of my childhood. We camped out on that creek now and then. We stuck cane fishing poles into the bank and caught many catfish. That was called *set hooks*.

There is a waterfall on the Blue Goose Creek that is mentioned in a separate chapter of this book, so I won't go into that here. Uncle Jack, Aunt Maggie, and their kids would come over, and we would all go fishing on the Blue Goose. We caught perch, catfish, and a bream now and then. We would be spaced around the creek at different deep holes of water. The ideal spots were just above a drift. A drift is caused by a tree or large chunk of driftwood wedged across the creek. It will trap trash drifting along the creek. The fish will be feeding under that trash.

Being spaced out along the creek, we would not always be in sight of each other. Somebody would yell out that they had caught a real big fish, but you didn't run down there to see it right then. If you did, some kid would yell out that he had caught a big fish and laugh at you when you ran down there to see his big fish. He would be lying, just to watch you run down there. My friend Lee Dee and I used to fish that stream a lot, and we talk about that every time I see him. We dressed all the fish we caught no matter the size. Usually, most of them were small. We didn't have a cord fish stringer, so we cut a small forked limb off a bush. We tried to find one that was two or three feet long before the fork. The forked branch was clipped off about three inches from the main branch. The long prong of the branch was slid through the fish's gill opening, and the three-inch forked piece would keep him from sliding off. We could then lay the fish in the shallow water so they could breathe and stay alive longer; that way, they wouldn't spoil. If you got thirsty, you could get a drink out of the Blue Goose. First, you found a "cowcumber tree," as we called them. (I did some research not long ago and found out the tree was a wild magnolia.) Anyway, it has very large leaves. They measure about twelve to eighteen inches long and six to eight inches wide. The lower limbs grow out of the trunk from just above the ground, so they are easy to reach. If you pull off a leaf and fold it just right, that makes a water dipper complete with a handle. Then you find a shallow, rocky-bottomed clear place in the stream and dip a leaf of water. Never dip from still water; it's not sanitary, and be sure there is no cow manure or dead animal lying in the creek upstream. There is no telling what might have been upstream that was a lot worse, sanitarily speaking. The water must have been sanitary, because I guess I saw most every member of the family including the relatives get a drink from that cool running stream on a hot summer day, and most of them lived long, healthy lives.

Honeysuckle grew all along the creek bank, both vines and honeysuckle trees. We kids liked to pull the blooms and suck the nectar from the ends. It had a sweet taste. Maybe that's where the honeysuckle got its name.

The Blue Goose will always remain in my memories. It ran into Clark's Creek, which ran across James and Janie Cole's farm a couple miles north of our farm. There is a waterfall about a quarter of a mile off the road in the Clark on their farm. Below that waterfall, there was a nice cool hole of water. I remember that pool of water was about a quarter or half acre in size. The creek had springs upstream, and the water ran pretty steady all the time. The hole was about six or seven feet deep, and some summers, it would be deeper. Sometimes we had a cable or rope tied to a limb high up in a willow tree that grew on the bank and leaned out over the swimming hole. It was a lot of fun to swing out on that rope and drop into the water.

When watermelons were in season, just about everybody had a watermelon patch. We would bring those watermelons down to the swimming hole and throw them into the water. They would cool down while we were swimming, and then we would eat cool watermelon on the creek bank. Many kids learned to swim in that swimming hole. That's where I learned to swim and dive. Sometimes, if there were only boys down there, we would just skinny-dip. More than once, some girls came down to swim unexpectedly when we were in there without swim trunks. We would stay in the water and ask the girls to throw our pants in, and we would put them on underwater. That was embarrassing, but at some point in time, we finally got swimsuits or shorts made of cut-off jeans, then we could go swimming in a crowd.

There were fun things to do at the swimming hole. We played a game called tag that meant chasing each other up and down the creek bank and in the swimming hole. If one was good enough, he could run down the creek bank, dive into the water, and tag somebody underwater. That took skill, but it could be done.

That is one of my favorite childhood memories, playing in that hole of water. We never had the nerve to dive off the high bank about twenty feet above the water. We talked about it many times and stood there wanting to do it, but no one ever had the nerve. After we were all grown, kids were coming from Port Gibson out there to swim even though they had a swimming pool in town. Some kid walked up to that bank for the first time and looked off in there and said, "I'm going to jump in from here!" They said he ran back a few steps, got a running start, and sailed off that bank. He didn't know how deep the water was or if there were boulders in there or what. He made it okay, and they all began to dive in from on top of that bank. I wish I could have been there to see that, but I still have never seen it done.

I was hunting along the Blue Goose one day and got a might thirsty. I found a place where the stream was running over rocks, lay down, and had a drink. I wandered on upstream, and as I rounded a bend, I saw a dead cow in the stream. She had been there for awhile. I'll spare the details. I started feeling rather badly, but got my mind back on hunting and got over it. Back at the house, I was telling my daddy all about it. I also told him I had learned a valuable lesson that day. He asked, "I hope you learned not to drink water out of that creek."

I said, "No, that's not what I learned. I learned that after you get a drink out of the creek, don't travel upstream."

17

My Broken Leg

It was the 20th day of May 1952, and I was down at Baybay's house. Baybay was a black kid who lived at the end of Grandma Love's driveway and across Highway 61. He was a few years older, and we played together quite often. This day, the red plums were just coming on the trees, and they were still green and firm. Baybay and I started throwing them at each other, running and dodging and having a good time.

The owners of that farm came along in a GMC pickup to build and install a wooden gate. They backed the pickup to the opening of the fence and started to work. Baybay and I were running around the pickup and into the back and over the side dodging each other's plums. I jumped up in the back of the truck and started out the other side by stepping on the rear truck fender. The body of the truck curved sharply out over the fender leaving about two or three inches of space between the body and the fender. My foot slipped into that space, and the slip caused me to fall out toward the outside of the truck bed. The foot was trapped, and the shin came over the fender. I heard a loud pop. I would later learn that loud pop was the big bone in my little eight-year-old leg. One of the men came running around to see what I was yelling about and lifted me down. They loaded me into the cab and carried me to Grandma Love. She didn't really know what to do, and she had no phone to call my parents. My parents didn't have a phone anyway, so she decided to doctor the leg herself.

She had some cow salve that was used to massage a cow's bag when it would swell. Since my leg was swelling, she thought the cow salve would be good for that. After greasing the leg real good, she wrapped it in an ace bandage that Uncle Bennie had left there. It was part of a soldier's first-aid kit. Grandma said, "If it don't get better in a day or so, we will have to take you to the doctor." Now there was an idea, let a doctor look at it; you never know, he might figure something out. It could happen.

Most of the time, doctors say, "If that doesn't get any better in a day or two, come back," but sometimes they do actually know what to do. Neither Grandma nor any of those Beesley's believed in doctors. They believed that after all the old home remedies were exhausted, if the patient was still alive, then it might be time to go to the doctor. They still might not do what the doctor ordered, and they might not take the medication. They kind of believed in, well, let the body heal itself, sort of.

After a day or so, Daddy came by to tell us that he had taken Mama to Claiborne County Hospital, and Bessie had been born on May 23, 1952. We explained why my leg was propped up and bandaged. After considering the situation, he and Grandma thought since he was in a hurry to get back to Mama and Bessie, we could wait a few days to see how the leg was going to fare.

Before leaving, he cut a couple of forked sticks and made me two makeshift crutches. So we bid Daddy farewell, and I went hobbling around the house on my new forked-stick homemade crutches. Grandma laughed and told me what a sight I was and all that, but I wouldn't have expected anything less out of Grandma Love. However, it was a shock to know I would have to do a little waiting on myself now that I was mobile.

Daddy came back, and the leg wasn't any better so we went to Doctor Greene over in Fayette. After x-raying the leg, Dr. Greene said to my father, "Mr. Smith, the big bone in that boy's leg is broken half in two."

Well, now, I thought, *that could explain that loud pop I had heard when the leg got hurt.*

Dr. Greene went on, "James is very lucky. The bone has started to mend, and it is mending straight." That was just what the Beesley family needed to hear. To them, this would confirm they knew almost as much about treating a patient as any doctor.

Grandma's cure was working, and if I had not gone to the doctor and if I had not accidentally put any pressure on the leg, it would have been as good as new in a few weeks. I'm telling you, if the doctors depended on the Beesley's for a living, they would starve to death. Grandma confirmed that analogy about my leg and was proud that she had known what to do. She then told a few stories about kids she had healed at one time or the other and began each story with, "When one of her kids was a baby ..." She did however say the leg was better off in a cast. The cast reached from my toes to about four inches above my knee. Daddy took me home and made me some real good-looking crutches, just like store-bought, only much stronger.

I somehow have managed to hang on to one of the crutches until this day. It hangs from a rafter in my boathouse where I can look up and be reminded of the care and love I received from my parents and Grandma Love. Many kids have played with the crutches, including nephews, nieces, and whatever kids might come by my parent's house over the years. I have picked them up from where the kids dropped them in Mama's yard after playing. After all that, this crutch is still better today than any you can buy. I don't know where the other one is, but one is enough to serve my present purpose.

The doctor had said the cast could come off in eight weeks. Eight weeks is a century for an active eight-year-old boy, when he cannot bend his leg and has to hobble around on crutches. Pearlie Victoria Beesley Smith, Aunt Pearlie, Mama's oldest sister, must have realized this when she came by one day and asked, "Annie Mae, why is that cast still on that young'un's leg. Ain't it been six weeks yet?"

"The doctor said he would leave it on for eight weeks," Mama explained.

"Eight weeks?!!" Aunt Pearlie shouted. "Well, I never heard of such! You don't leave a cast on for more than six weeks." That was that Beesley gene kicking in. "Doctors don't know what they are doing most of the time these days," she continued. I think if Aunt Pearlie had considered her words, she might have realized that she was implying that doctors did know what they were doing, at some point in time.

She continued, "We ought to cut that thing off that child's leg." She was pressing now.

"Pearlie, I don't know about that now. The doctor said eight weeks," Mama told her.

"Mama, Aunt Pearlie is right. I have never heard of over six weeks," I chimed in. "Let's go back down there and tell Dr. Greene to take it off. I'm tired of this thing," I begged.

"You don't need to go back to the doctor. We can cut the thing off," Aunt Pearlie said.

"Pearlie, you have to saw those things off. That thing is hard as a rock," Mama reasoned.

"Shoot, all you have to do is take a pair of scissors and cut the thing off; it won't take but just a minute or two," insisted Aunt Pearlie.

"I don't know now, Pearlie, the Doctor said eight weeks, and we better wait. That's not but a few more days," said Mama.

"No, Mama, me and Aunt Pearlie are going to cut this thing off my leg right now," I insisted.

Mama always let us kids have our way, and I knew it was left up to me. I knew if something happened, Mama would say, "I tried to tell you and your Aunt Pearlie to leave that thing alone, but noooo, nothing would do ya'll, but take it off, and now look what has happened."

I was willing to take the chance. I wanted it off that bad. Finally, Mama gave in and said, "Well, if ya'll think you can cut it off, go ahead, but I don't think scissors will cut that hard thing."

"Aw, sure they will, Annie. Go get the scissors, and I will show you," said Aunt Pearlie.

The scissors didn't work, so we got the tin snips, and they didn't work. Then we got the keyhole saw, the handsaw, the chisel, the hammer, the pliers, and any other tool Daddy had that would cut, tear, rip, chip, or bend. After quite some time, the cast was off and I was looking at a poor little leg with long hair on it. It was a pitiful sight and very tender to put weight on. Maybe Mama had been right; maybe the cast should have stayed on longer like the Doctor had prescribed.

"Naw, the leg hasn't had any weight on it in a long time," Dr. Pearlie Victoria Smith explained. "It will be all right in a day or two. You just take it easy on it for a while." Aunt Pearlie was right. In a few days, I couldn't tell my leg had ever been broken.

A couple of years went by before I had to go back to Dr. Greene, but while I was there, he was looking at my file and asked, "What ever happened to that cast we put on your leg?"

"Oh, my Aunt Pearlie said the cast didn't need to be on eight weeks, so we took it off at about six weeks," I told him.

"Is your aunt a nurse or something?" he wanted to know.

"No, she just knew that, I guess," I explained.

He just shook his head and didn't ask any more questions.

18

Tripping to Kentucky and Alabama

Uncle Archie Smith was Aunt Pearlie's (Mama's sister) husband, and he worked for the Illinois Central Railroad company in Vicksburg, Mississippi. He started working there as a steam engine mechanic, and when the diesel-powered engines came along, the railroad trained him to be a diesel mechanic. He carried me down to the station where he worked a couple of times. There were pits in the floor with railroad rails on each side, and the train engine would pull up over the pit so the mechanics could work under the train.

Uncle Archie wanted me to come down in the pit under the train and look at it from the bottom side. I must have been eight at the time, and I told him, "I ain't going under that big heavy train. That thing might fall down on us."

He laughed and tried to persuade me to come on down there with him. "We all work under here, James, every day." He continued, "These pits have been here since they built this place, and no train has fell on anybody yet."

I thought about it for a few seconds and started shaking my head and backing up. "I ain't going down under that train!" I insisted. Even for eight years old, that was pretty stupid, and I have wished many times I had gone under there with him.

I was servicing some equipment in a nursing home a few years ago, and I ran into a man who had worked in that shop with my uncle Archie. That old gentleman and I had a very interesting chat about

Uncle Archie and those trains. He told me Uncle Archie had wanted to be an engineer, but he never did get his chance. The railroads had started fading out after World War II, and there were not many new engineer jobs coming open.

This man talked quite a bit about the demise of the railroad. I could tell by the look on his face and the sound of his voice that it was a part of him that was dying. He pointed his finger at me and stated very firmly, "I'll tell you something, boy, those railroads will come back one of these days; you just wait and see." Although I agreed with what he had said, I really didn't believe him. To me, he was just a retired old railroad engine mechanic living out his last days in a nursing home and trying to hang on to what would inevitably be lost. I have since decided that man was right. There was a program on television awhile back that talked about just that: the waning of the railroad system. Railroad passenger service, as we know it, is definitely on the way out, but faster passenger rail service will probably become popular again. Cars are jamming the highways, and fast overhead railroads within the cities are the answer. Of course, standard railroads will work in the open country and we are seeing many of them rolling down the tracks.

This man in the Vicksburg nursing home, I think, was referring to the freight rail service. This TV show I mentioned was making the point that due to the large volume of freight that must be moved daily in this country, it is becoming too much for the highways. Highways are expensive to build and maintain. Many interstate highways need two triple lanes already. With many more freight trucks being added to the system every day, the highways will soon be unable to handle both the large trucks and passenger vehicles.

This is causing the freight to slow down, and the amount of money required to build and maintain the highway system to speed up the traffic will make it cost prohibitive. Railroads will be the answer. They are much cheaper to build and maintain. So, with the added savings in the amount of fuel and power required to move freight by rail, I believe that old man will be right one day within the next twenty years.

Now, getting back to my trip; it was Uncle Archie's vacation. He had two weeks, and they wanted to go to Horse Cave, Kentucky, to visit Aunt Pearlie's aunt (I can't remember her name) and Uncle Lewis Beesley. They of course were my great-aunt and uncle. Uncle Lewis was

Grandpa Pearl's brother. After visiting them for a few days, we were going on to Birmingham, Alabama, to visit Uncle Archie's brother and his family. At that time, I had only been out of the state of Mississippi once since I was old enough to remember. We had been to Louisiana to visit Aunt Ruth, and that was the only other state I'd been to.

This added to my excitement quite a bit. I told Aunt Pearlie, "After this trip, I can add three more states to my list of states that I have been in!"

She said, "That's right, and we are going inside caves in Kentucky. And you will see some iron mines in Alabama."

Boy, I tell you, I was wound up like an eight-day clock. They had been down to the house and picked me up on a weekend. I stayed in Vicksburg with them all week before we left. Uncle Archie's vacation didn't begin until that Friday at quitting time. As soon as he got home that Friday evening, we headed out.

Aunt Pearlie had packed sandwiches, ice water, and hot Postum. Postum was a black decaffeinated coffee. They were Mormons and didn't drink anything with a drug in it. Uncle Archie would drink an ice-cold Seven-Up on a hot day, but he said that was for medical purposes. It made him belch and relieved his gastritis condition.

She made a bed for me on the back seat. The bed was for me to take a nap when I got tired. I didn't think I was going to get sleepy with all this excitement. All the food was stored on the back floorboard. I also didn't know that Uncle Archie and Aunt Pearlie didn't spend money on motel rooms. They planned to stop only for gas, oil, and restrooms. One would sleep, and the other would drive. They drove all night long or until they reached their destination.

We traveled up Highway 61 through the Mississippi Delta country. I had never seen so much cotton or fields of that size. I looked out one window and the other until it was dark. After it was too dark to sightsee anymore and I was full of peanut-butter crackers, sandwiches, and Postum, I stretched out on the back seat and went to sleep. After a few stops during the night for gas and restrooms, the sun began to rise, and we finally reached Horse Cave, Kentucky, early the next morning. Aunt Pearlie had awakened me when we crossed the Tennessee line, so I could see Tennessee, but it was still night. When the sun came up, we were in Kentucky. We began to see tobacco fields. It was my first time to see tobacco, and I asked why it was green and not brown. They got a chuckle out of that.

Horse Cave was a small town, and we went through there going to Uncle Lewis' house. When we made it there, Uncle Lewis and his wife were sitting on the front porch. It was a large old home with large square columns across the front. It was built a few feet off the ground and was located at the base of a mountain. Inside the mountain about three hundred yards from the rear of the house was Horse Cave itself. Standing on the front porch, you could see acres and acres of tobacco and a couple of tobacco barns. On one side of the house was a small two or three-acre tobacco patch. That was all the tobacco Uncle Lewis grew. He was getting on in years and had spent many of his last years guiding tourists through Horse Cave. He had even retired from that by this time.

While they all visited and caught up on all the news with each other, I walked around and looked at the house then walked out into the tobacco patch to get a closer look at tobacco stalks. There was a garden out back and a small pasture, and across the fence, I could see cars and people. I went back around and asked Uncle Lewis what all those people were doing up the mountain in his pasture. He laughed and said, "They are on the other side of my pasture, son." He continued to explain, "That's Horse Cave, and all those people are tourists who are coming to go in the cave."

I asked, "Can we go in the cave?"

"Why, sure we will, anytime ya'll are ready," he said.

Later on that day, we walked out back and across the pasture to the cave site. After we got inside the cave, it got real spooky. I don't know what I had expected, but I felt like it might cave in with us in there. Uncle Archie was holding my hand, and I had decided to stay with them. The guide stopped and started telling his tourists all about the cave just inside the door. It was a large hole in the ground at that point with a high ceiling. All of a sudden, Aunt Pearlie started gasping for breath and shouting, "Oh, my Lord, I can't breathe! I got to get out of here!" and started toward the door. Aunt (what's her name) started out with her and helped her open the door. This really scared me, and I was afraid I might not be able to breathe in there either. I lit out toward the door. Uncle Archie was begging me to come back, but I didn't stop until I was outside with Aunt Pearlie.

After the tour, Uncle Archie came out telling us how beautiful it was way down in the cave. I started to get upset because I didn't stay with him. Uncle Lewis said, "Don't worry, James, we will come back again before ya'll leave, and I'll take you through the cave." However, for some reason, we never did come back. The next day, we did go to the Mammoth Cave National Park. There were many caves there, and we went to see Crystal Cave.

This was the cave where the famous Floyd Collins, the cave explorer, died. He got trapped inside the cave in 1925 for eighteen days and died there before he could be rescued. At this time, 1952, his casket was inside the cave, and the guide told us all about it. The tour was several yards away from the coffin. Some years after we were there, his body was stolen and recovered in a nearby field. A movie was made about the entire event, but I'm not sure just when it was filmed.

Just inside Crystal Cave, the guide stopped and started talking to us, and Aunt Pearlie pulled the same stunt, and out the door she went with Aunt (so and so) behind her. Uncle Archie squeezed my hand and said, "You're staying, aren't you, James?"

I said, "I sure am. I am going to see this cave."

He said, "Good boy, Uncle Archie is not going to let anything happen to you." He reaffirmed my excitement even further, "These caves are beautiful. You'll see."

That cave was very long and deep, and there were many crystal-like stones inside. The lights shined on them, and they were so beautiful. Deep down in the cave, the guide asked, "Is anybody afraid of the dark?" Nobody said anything, so he switched the lights off and asked, "Anybody ever seen it this dark before?"

Everybody moaned, "Noooo."

It was darker than I had ever seen it in my few short years anyway. One area was so deep, the ceiling was over a hundred feet high, and in other areas, the grown folk had to bend over to walk through the passage.

We came back out and started to tell Aunt Pearlie what she had missed, and she proclaimed, "I don't care what I missed! I can't breathe in them things, and I ain't going in another one!" And so far as I know, she never did.

Uncle Lewis took Uncle Archie and me over to his neighbor's tobacco barn and explained how they harvested and cured the tobacco. We toured around the country a little and finally bid them farewell. We headed out to Alabama. As we pulled out of the driveway, all our windows were down, and they yelled at us, "Tell all the folks back home we said hello and come to see us!"

We yelled back, "We will, and ya'll come when you can!"

I asked Aunt Pearlie, "What did they mean 'the folks back home'? They are home."

She laughed and said, "Your aunt (so and so) is home, but Uncle Lewis used to live where you live now." She explained how he had met her later in life, and they had married. She had inherited the house where they were living. It was a beautiful old home just sitting on the lower part of the mountain facing across the valley. I wish I had a picture, but Aunt Pearlie never carried a camera, so we just bought some postcards.

We bid our kin good-bye and traveled on toward Birmingham, Alabama, all that day and got to Uncle Archie's brother's house way up into the night. They were all in bed, and Uncle Archie knocked on the door until they got up. He had two kids. The oldest was a teenage daughter; the youngest was a boy just a few years older than I was. They were very nice kids, and I don't think I had seen a television at that time, so I was all excited that they had one. I wanted to watch TV immediately, but TV went off the air at midnight in those days. I was so disappointed that we couldn't watch this television that I had been hearing so much about.

We finally went to bed, and the next morning, I ran into the living room to watch television. Those two kids came in there with me and asked, "What do you want to watch?"

I replied, "It don't matter to me. I'll watch whatever is on there. I've never watched television before." They enjoyed watching me watch television more than watching it themselves. They had a radio in the room, and I asked, "Why do ya'll have a radio?"

They said, "We listen to it sometimes."

I said, "If I had a television to watch, I wouldn't need a radio." They laughed at this country boy.

Once I walked across the room while watching the television and some woman was talking on the screen. It was just a head shot, kind of like the news. I noticed as I walked across the room that her eyes watched me. Then I walked to different spots in the room, but no matter where I stopped, she would be talking directly to me. These kids were staring at me and probably wondering if I had lost my mind. I asked, "Can that woman see me?"

They said, "No. Why?"

I said, "Well, no matter where I stop in this room, she is still looking at me."

They didn't want to laugh at me, because they were nice kids, but this was a little too much. They covered their faces with their hands and just burst out laughing. The girl said, "Please excuse us, James, we don't mean to laugh at you, but that is the way a television screen works."

I replied, "Oh, I see."

We all went out driving to see the iron mines. However, as it turned out, we didn't actually see the mines themselves. We saw large piles of iron ore at the iron foundry. Mr. Smith said, "They melt this iron ore and make iron. Then they make steel out of the iron." I remember a lot of smoke coming out of that place. It was on this visit that Aunt Pearlie told me I was drinking water with iron in it.

When I got to school that year, I proudly announced to the teacher and class at Red Lick that I had drunk some water with iron in it. The teacher promptly replied, "The water here at the school has iron in it; that's what makes it red." The kids laughed, and I just shut up.

Uncle Archie's people took us to a tourist attraction called Little Jerusalem somewhere near Birmingham. This was a little miniature city with little buildings and streets. It also included other places from the Bible. We walked around a walkway, and many different things from the Bible were there: the temple, Calvary, the Tower of Babble, the River Nile, and many other places. We didn't need a guide, and I don't know if they had one, but Aunt Pearlie narrated every little detail. She and Uncle Archie got into a little argument over one or two of the places, and I saw his brother turning his head and laughing at them.

After two or three days with the Smiths, we headed back to

Vicksburg. I'll never forget that trip and Aunt Pearlie, and I would talk about it every now and then. I would tell her how much it meant to me. She would say, "James, we wish we had taken you kids with us more than we did." They went to Utah to be remarried in the Mormon Temple, but she didn't take me with her that time. They were never divorced or even separated; the temple marriage had something to do with their Mormon religion. I remember her talking about the two of them pulling off the road and sleeping in the car. I assume that was why she didn't want a kid along. There wouldn't be room in the car to sleep three. When we went to Kentucky and Alabama, it wasn't as long a trip as a trip to Utah.

19

Auto Accident

I had a very exciting experience the summer that I worked at Mr. Guy Kelly's farm helping him plant his winter wheat. We had plowed and planted two fields, taking about three days in all, if I remember correctly. When we finished and Mr. Guy told me I could go home, he sent one of the other hands with me to help load the disk. There was a bank down by the field that I thought was the right height from which to load the disk. I pulled the disk up to the bank, and we unhooked it from the tractor and started toward the house where the trailer was parked.

After hooking to the trailer, we started back down the lane. My assistant was standing on the right hub of the tractor and leaning against the seat. This was the usual riding place for passengers on this tractor. He was looking across the pasture toward the gravel road (Highway 552) and said kind of loudly over the noise of the tractor's engine, "I believe I saw a car turn over out there on the road." I pulled the clutch back, stopped the tractor, and idled the engine down as I turned toward the gravel road. There was a huge cloud of dust and dust in the air to the right of the cloud of dust and no dust at all to the left. This indicated that a car had been traveling from right to left and stopped at the cloud of dust.

The road was barely visible from where we were, but it was hidden by only the short trees and tall weeds that grew along the fence line. At the spot where the cloud of dust was, we both knew the road curved.

The curve was just past Mr. Guy's driveway, and the road slanted down from that driveway. A car traveling from the east going west would rise up the grade to his driveway and drop downward as it turned the curve. With this action, from vehicle after vehicle, the rocks had separated from the clay and sand. This caused a pile of loose rocks on the outside of the curve and along the edge of the road.

If a car came around that curve traveling very fast and the driver let the wheels run too far over to that pile of loose gravel, the driver could lose control. That was exactly what this car had done. The right front wheel had gouged into those loose rocks, and the front wheels had turned sharply left causing the car to spin out of control. As the car went sideways, it flipped on one side and came to rest on its side in the road ditch with the top lying against the road bank and the bottom of the car facing the road.

Thomas was the name of the person on the tractor with me, and I said, "Thomas, let's run over there and see if somebody wrecked." We jumped off the tractor and ran about one hundred and fifty or so yards across the pasture toward the cloud of dust. We jumped out into the road and heard screaming coming from inside the car. One child, who looked to be about six or seven years old, was standing in the road in front of the car and didn't appear to be hurt.

As we ran to the front of the car, the child said, "My sister is hung under the car!" About that time, a very frightened woman came crawling out of the car through the opening where the windshield had been. The car was a 1952 white Ford, and the lady was Mrs. Cecil Sullivan. I don't remember her first name, but I will never forget the look on her face when she saw us and screamed, "My child is in the car, and her arm is hung under the car. I can't get her out!"

I said, "Just stay in there with her, Ma'am, we have a tractor and chain just over there, and we will come pull the car off your little girl!"

She looked somewhat relieved, but not free from worry and shouted, "Please hurry! Please hurry!"

After we were over the fence and running across the pasture toward the tractor, Thomas shouted, "I hope that car don't catch fire!" I hadn't thought of that, and I silently wished he hadn't reminded me, because

I knew as bad as it would be for that little girl and that family, I could be right there hooking that chain when it blew up.

Somehow I knew that I would risk my life to save that child no matter what happened. When we reached the tractor, I told Thomas, "Go get Mr. Guy, and I'm going to unhook the trailer and go on over to the car." I added, "Tell 'em to hurry up. I will need some help." I ran the tractor as fast as it would go up the lane to the house, stopped, jumped off, unhooked the trailer, and hooked on the chain. As I did this, I was wondering why I hadn't done this while Thomas was still with me. Must have been panic, I thought.

I got the chain hooked and drove the tractor down the driveway and out in the road. I was very happy to see that Mr. W. L. Dickerson and his wife Mrs. Bessie Lea had stopped and were there to help. I backed the tractor around in position. Mr. Dickerson ran up to the rear, grabbed the chain, and hooked it to the frame of the car. He yelled, "Pull it easy, James. We don't want it to come over on its wheels with them in there!"

I eased up, tightening the chain, and wondered what that child's arm was going to look like after being pinned under that car. The mother was inside the car, and Mrs. Dickerson was comforting the other child. Mr. Dickerson was kneeling in front of the car peering through the opening where the windshield had been. He had one hand in the air batting it toward me signaling me to keep easing forward.

Finally, he brought his hand down sharply meaning stop. He reached into the car and helped the child out, and the mother climbed out afterward. I was happy for several things at that moment: the car had not caught fire, the child was standing on her feet, and there was no blood. Mr. Dickerson was looking at her arm. It was covered with dirt, but not bleeding. *Maybe it was only broken,* I thought. About that moment, that old black Chevrolet pickup truck came flying out in the road and bouncing sideways. Mr. Guy had arrived with everybody he had. I climbed down off the tractor to check on the little girl and to find out if anybody else was hurt. Everybody was all right, and both kids had stopped crying.

Mrs. Dickerson said, "I don't believe that child's arm is even broken."

After they took her to the doctor in Fayette, they found out it wasn't broken only bruised.

We all started laughing a little bit with the relief, and Mrs. Sullivan started thanking everybody and explained that the child had apparently reached up and grabbed the post to hold on as the car flipped over. She didn't need to mention that the windows were down, because very few cars around there had air conditioning. As the car came to rest in the ditch, her arm had gotten trapped under the post between the front and rear glass. There was enough soft dirt in the ditch to allow space for the arm to be trapped between the post and the ground without mashing it too badly. The side of the car below the window was resting on the road bed, and the top of the car was on the other side of the ditch. The arm was trapped just enough to keep her from pulling it out.

Mr. and Mrs. Dickerson said they would carry the family to the doctor in Fayette and then carry them home or whatever they wanted to do. After they pulled away, I told Thomas that I was going to back the tractor closer to the car, and if he would tie the chain, I would pull it over on its wheels. For some reason, I wasn't thinking about the thing catching fire. Mr. Guy shouted at us, "You boys will do no such thing! Ya'll let that thing back against that bank like you found it, and we will let Cecil Sullivan, (the owner of the car) decide what to do with it!"

That was good advice. The car didn't belong to us, so we had no business fooling around with it.

I got calmed down, went back to the field, finished loading the disk, tied it down, and came back up the lane to the house. I stopped, idled the tractor down, and went inside to tell Mrs. Kelly that I was leaving and how much I had enjoyed the meals. After the good-bye, she cautioned me to be careful, and I started on my way. I stopped at Nesler's Grocery with my pocket full of money (about thirty or maybe forty dollars) to buy a Coke, chips, and a candy bar. Mrs. Nesler was on duty that day, and as I walked in, she said, "Well, James, I heard you had a little excitement this afternoon." Mrs. Nesler was a very nice, well-mannered, attractive woman, and she was also my Sunday school teacher.

I was wondering how she could have gotten the news so quickly. As I opened the drink box and pulled out a nice cold Pepsi, I replied, "No, ma'am, I had a lot of excitement this afternoon."

We both laughed, and I asked, "Have you heard anything about the little girl?"

"Yes, Bessie Lea called Stella (Mrs. Kelly) and said to tell everybody the little girl was all right. She just had a badly bruised arm."

I guess Mrs. Kelly had gotten that news after I left or just didn't think to tell me.

"How do you know about it so soon?" I asked.

She said, "Oscar Rushing stopped by here and asked me who had wrecked in front of Guy Kelly's house. I called Stella, and she told me all about it and how you had pulled the car off the little girl."

"Oh, I see," I said. After a little more conversation, I walked out of Nesler's Grocery, got on my tractor, and headed on home.

At church Sunday, I asked Mr. Guy if Cecil Sullivan ever came to get his car. He said Cecil came that same day with a couple of people to help him. They just got on the bank and pushed the car over with their hands. He said, "Cecil got in that thing without a windshield and the top caved in, and he took off down the road as if nothing was wrong with that old Ford. One front wheel was cocked out of line, but with a stout hold on the steering wheel, he could keep it in the road," he continued.

20

Airplane Crash

One day, we heard an airplane roaring over the trees. We ran out into the yard to see what was going on, because it was unusual for airplanes to fly so low. It was a single-engine plane. I think it was a Piper Cub airplane or at least a plane about that size. It rolled over and disappeared below the trees, but it was still flying. It was flying lengthwise across a flat pasture on the Sheltons' farm. It rose up, circled around, and flew the same pasture in the opposite direction.

As my brothers and I were watching, our collective thoughts were that the pilot wanted to land in the Sheltons' pasture. That was what finally happened. We went back inside and talked about going over there to see the plane and find out who was flying it. Finally, to satisfy our curiosity, we got in the car and drove over there. The plane was sitting near the road by the fence, but no one was around. We figured somebody was probably coming to see the Sheltons since the pilot had landed in their field. We drove on down the road to the Sheltons' house. They didn't know any details about it but had also heard it land.

On the way back from the Shelton's, we saw Mr. Clint's pickup coming down the driveway from the Humphreys' farm. We stopped and flagged him to ask if he knew anything. It was Souck, one of Mr. Clint's hired hands, driving Mr. Clint's truck. He told us the pilot's name and that he had landed there to visit the Humphreys. Souck's house was located at the end of the pasture where the plane had landed. He had Mr. Clint's pickup there with him and had given the pilot a ride up to the Humphreys' home. He was on his way back, because the man was going to just walk back to his plane after he visited awhile. Later that afternoon, we heard the plane and ran outside to watch it take off. It went up and circled around and then started to dive. The pilot cut the engine. The plane went out of sight behind the trees. We heard the engine roar, then a loud banging noise, and the engine went dead.

We loaded in the car again to make a return trip to the pasture. We met Souck in Mr. Clint's truck. He had someone in there with him who was holding a cloth to his head. Souck seemed to be driving rather fast, so we assumed the worst: that it was the pilot and Souck was taking him to the doctor in Fayette about sixteen miles away. As it turned out, that was exactly what was going on. When we got to the pasture, we saw the plane nosed into the ditch of the road with the fuselage and tail jutting across the road.

The right wing had been damaged, and the plastic windshield was broken. The entire front end of the plane was all bashed in. Gasoline was leaking out of the plane and running down the road ditch. We decided to just leave it. There didn't seem to be anything we could do. If the thing caught fire, we didn't have any firefighting equipment, especially for a gasoline fire. Besides that, there was no danger of injury, since no one was around, and we were concerned about our own safety, so we just left.

Later, after we saw Souck come home, we talked with him to get some details on what had happened. The pilot had offered to take Souck up, since he had never been in an airplane before, but Souck had refused. The pilot had then told Souck he would put on a little air show for him, once he was airborne. He had started into that dive, and when the plane was close to the ground, he leveled the plane out. Then he gunned the engine to pull up into the air and noticed an electric power line right in front of him. The pilot tried to turn the plane to miss the line, but was too close to the ground, causing the right wing to come in contact with the ground. That tossed the plane's nose right into the road ditch. The pilot's head hit the plastic windshield, breaking it and cutting his head, but not very badly. The pilot might have been thrown through the windshield, but his seat belt had held him in the seat. Souck had delivered him to Dr. Harper's office in town. He only had a few stitches, so the injury wasn't too serious. The pilot had stayed in town and called someone to pick him up and someone to come for the plane.

The plane never did catch fire, and we were all proud of that. It was a very light two-passenger plane. The frame was aluminum, and the skin was a rubberized vinyl material. As the word got out that a plane had crashed, everyone in the country came to see it. People were taking pictures, and the crash made the *Fayette Chronicle* newspaper that week.

We were wondering how they would haul it away. It was blocking the road, so a two-by-four board was propped under the tail, so the traffic could pass. No one came for the wreckage until the next day. I don't know what we expected, but we were surprised that it was two men in a pickup. They simply took the wings off, loaded the main frame into the pickup, then laid the wings edgewise next to the fuselage and secured everything with a rope, and away they went.

We later found that the pilot was a crop duster from Vicksburg. He was akin to the Humphreys family and rented this plane to fly down for a visit. He continued flying, but I'm sure he checked for power lines before he tried any more stunts.

James Smith and one of his deer
circa: 1992

21

Hunting

When I was around four or five years of age, Grandpa Pearl carried me squirrel hunting. There were some woods a few hundred yards south of our house with large hollow beech trees and some oak trees. Squirrels liked to den up in the hollow beeches and feed on the acorns of the large oaks and on the beech mast. Beech mast is the fruit of the beech tree, which is sometimes called beech nuts.

Grandpa used Daddy's old single-barrel twelve-gauge shotgun and number-six shot shells. This gun had belonged to Grandpa John Smith and was passed to Daddy. Grandpa Smith repaired guns for a living, among other things, and someone had brought the gun there to be repaired and never came back. This gun was passed on to my father and then to me. I still have the gun, and it will belong to my son, Jim, one day.

Grandpa Pearl would let me follow him into the woods, and when he killed a squirrel, he would let me go get the squirrel. That was very exciting for me, so when my son, Jim, was about four or five, I carried him squirrel hunting. Jim used his BB gun, and I used my Remington automatic. I killed a squirrel and told Jim he could go pick him up. I expected him to be excited about that as I had been at his age. After retrieving two squirrels, Jim said, "Dad, why don't you pick up the ones you kill, and I will pick up the ones I kill."

I said, "All right then," thinking, *Things do change.*

After I was old enough to handle a gun by myself, at around twelve

165

or so, I would go into the woods down by Blue Goose Creek and Clark's Creek. I can very well remember the very first squirrel hunt I went on all by myself. That hunt was a very successful hunt on a Saturday morning in October. Squirrel season had just opened, and I got up at daybreak and went out across the pasture and across the Blue Goose Creek almost to Clark's Creek. There was a tall hickory tree just across the fence on Mr. Clint Shelton's place. There were some good hardwoods and some hollow beeches, and it was not far from the water of Clark's Creek.

I sat down on a stump as I had seen Grandpa Pearl do and waited for the squirrels to come to feed in the tall hickory. I only had three shells. I wasn't old enough to buy any shells, and we never bought a whole box at one time anyway. Daddy would tell us, "Ya'll don't need a bunch of shells to waste. If you don't have many shells, you'll have to make those shots count." He knew we kids would have fun shooting cans and bottles or something. He did have a point, as I later learned. After I was old enough to earn money and buy shells by the box, I would shoot at squirrels running and too far off. This morning, I had to make each shot count, and at the best, I could only get three squirrels.

Finally, about the time I figured the squirrels weren't hungry, one jumped out of a hollow beech and into the hickory. I remember how exciting it was and how I tried to control myself and pick a good shot. The squirrel ran all over the tree, and I had the hammer back and was aiming as he ran. He ran all the way to the top of tree. I was afraid I wouldn't hit him at that distance. I was also afraid if I didn't take the shot right then, he was going to get that hickory nut in his mouth and sail out to the top of the hollow beech from which he came and he might not come back.

While I was trying to make up my mind as to whether or not to shoot, another squirrel jumped into the hickory. My immediate thoughts were, *How am I going to shoot one squirrel, reload this single shot, and get the other one before he leaves?* Well, I didn't know, but I had to make up my mind and shoot one or the other. The second squirrel stopped on a bare part of the limb and not very far up the hickory. I decided to take the sure shot, and if I got the other one, that would be better, but I would at least have one squirrel. I aimed very carefully and blam! I got that one. I looked up immediately to the top of the tree and saw that the other squirrel was still feeding. I decided I'd better not go pick up the first squirrel just yet, because I might scare the other one off. I decided to try for the one in the top of the tree, and blam! I got that one and had only one shell left. Could I get a third squirrel? If I could, that would be three squirrels and three shots. I wasn't a seasoned hunter and that would be somewhat of a grand hunt. There was one slight problem; there were no squirrels in sight. I did hear one barking across the woods a ways and started over to where he was. As I got under the hickory, a squirrel came down a limb of another tree and stopped in an open spot, and I got him.

I had no more shells, and the squirrel was still barking. I got my third squirrel and headed back to the house. My parents were sitting in the kitchen drinking coffee when I came in. Mama said, "You didn't hunt long."

Very proudly holding my three squirrels up by their tails, I answered, "It doesn't take long when you know how to hunt!"

They gave me the usual praise, and I told them I might have gotten the limit if I hadn't run out of shells. Daddy asked, "How many shells did you shoot?"

Making the most out of the moment, I said, "Well, I got three squirrels, that must mean I shot three times."

He said something like, "I reckon I'll have to buy some more shells."

When I was about sixteen, Daddy, Johnny, Howard Goza, and I went squirrel hunting on Christmas morning. We left early in the morning and went down Lucky Hollow Road to hunt the Gupton and Tom Nevels places with a dog. We went in Howard's pickup and parked near the Nevels' cemetery. After hunting a few hours, we decided to head on home. As we started out of the woods, we got in a discussion about just which way was out.

Between the four of us, we pointed in at least three different directions. We decided since Daddy had been traveling around those woods all his life, we should listen to him. After walking for about an hour, Daddy said, "I think I messed up back there. These woods have grown a lot since I was in these parts."

Howard, Johnny, and I had been feeling pretty good up to that point. Howard said, "I didn't think it was this far to the truck. Mr. Tom, are you telling us we're lost?"

Daddy said with his usual lightness as in any situation, "No, Howard, we ain't exactly lost. We just don't know where we are."

Everybody chuckled kind of nervously, and Johnny said, "Uncle Tom, I believe we need to go back to that last hollow, and it ought to come out on the road," meaning Lucky Hollow Road. We walked a while longer in that direction, and then somebody suggested another direction, and we walked in another direction awhile.

We had started out of the woods a little after ten o'clock so we would be home in time for Christmas dinner. The time was now after twelve, and we still didn't know where we were. The day was overcast, and we couldn't get a bearing on the sun for directions. We started the usual mantra to determine directions like "moss grows on the north side of the tree." Problem was these trees didn't have any moss on either side. The old "water flows south" analogy didn't sit well with Daddy. He said, "Water flows downhill, and it don't make any difference which direction down is." He added, "Matter of a fact, the Blue Goose flows northeast as it crosses our farm." Actually, it didn't matter which way north, south, east, or west was, we still didn't know in which direction the truck was or Lucky Hollow Road for that matter.

There were many fire lanes, which were little roads cut by a bulldozer in those woods. These lanes made good walking, and if you stayed with one, sooner or later, you would come out somewhere. We decided to stay with one fire lane and follow it out of the woods. About three o'clock that afternoon, we walked out of the woods into a pasture. Way across the pasture, we could see cars going very fast. Somebody said, "That's the highway!"

Walking out into the pasture toward the highway, we could see a microwave tower. Somebody said, "That's that tower near Union Church!"

"Couldn't be that Union Church tower," somebody else said. "We have been walking in the opposite direction of Union Church."

Daddy said, "If somebody knew which way we were walking, I wish you would have said so before now." We all laughed real big, because we felt good that at least we were out of the woods. When we walked up to the highway, we had to discuss for a minute just which highway it was. We finally reasoned it was Highway 28 and that it was in fact the Union Church tower. It is strange how difficult it is to get your bearings when you are lost.

We got out on the shoulder of the highway and were about ten miles from the truck. It seemed nobody wanted to pick up four men with guns and a couple of dogs so we kept walking. We turned off Highway 28 onto old Highway 20 heading for Lucky Hollow Road. We kept looking back at each car hoping it would be a pickup that nobody would mind the dogs riding in, and hopefully, it would be somebody we knew. Finally, a man who knew Johnny stopped and gave us a ride. He was in a car, but he put the dogs in the trunk. I don't remember the man's name, but he wasn't somebody I knew. Being a holiday, the house was full of kinfolk, so we had to put up with a lot of ragging about getting lost in the woods. I know it embarrassed Daddy, because he had gotten lost in the woods he grew up in. Well, that happens, and it wasn't the first time I was lost and probably won't be the last.

One weekend, I went home with my friend Ronald from Red Lick School. It was during hunting season, so we went hunting Saturday morning. Ronald could hit the squirrels, and I was missing. I got frustrated as well as embarrassed. I knew I was a better shot, at least better than I was doing. On the way back to the house, I was saying, "It just doesn't make sense that I couldn't hit a squirrel this morning."

Ronald replied, "Oh, did I mention when using that gun, you have to hold it a little left of your target?"

I said very puzzled, "No, I don't remember you saying anything about that. Why do you have to hold it a little left of the target?"

He started laughing, and I knew I had been had. He said, "Well, that was Killingsworth's gun, and he somehow bent the barrel."

I said, "You are telling me you let me use a crooked-barrel gun?"

Ronald and I liked playing tricks on each other, and I told him I would get even if it took the rest of my life.

That afternoon, he wanted to use the crooked-barrel gun, but I was too proud to let him. I said, "No, I can hit a squirrel with this gun, now that I know to allow left windage." I did hit a couple that afternoon, and the challenge made it more fun than using an accurate gun. We both laughed about that, and every now and then until this day, we will think about it and have a good laugh about the time Ronald had me using a crooked-barrel gun.

I rode my horse up to see my friend John Bailey, who lived with his Uncle Buck and Aunt Velma. Mr. Buck said, "We are going deer hunting tomorrow, would you like to take a stand?" He meant a deer stand. When hunting deer, you stand in one spot until a deer comes by. If the hunter is hunting with dogs, he stands by a tree or some hidden place until the dogs chase a deer past the stand.

"Yes, sir, I certainly would, but I have never been deer hunting before!"

He said, "Well, stay all night with us and I'll put you on a ridge about daylight where a big ole buck has been crossing." He probably saw the excitement in my eyes, and he continued, "Ole Scrap …" This was his main most hunting dog. "… is raring to go, and he'll jump him up and drive him right up that ridge to you."

I rode my horse home and got Daddy's old single-barrel twelve-gauge shotgun and some more warm clothes. Mr. Buck gave me a couple of buckshot shells, because we didn't have any buckshot since we didn't hunt deer at that time. I was all set to go on my first deer hunt. Buckshot shells have very large lead shot, about a dozen or so quarter-inch-diameter lead pellets. There are different sizes and quantities of shot per shell.

When I got back to Mr. Buck's, John and I talked about deer hunting way into the night. I asked, "Why is Mr. Buck putting me on the stand where the deer are coming out?"

He laughed until he cried. "That's just Uncle Buck getting you charged up, because he knows you haven't been deer hunting before," John said. "He knows where those deer run. You can bet your boots on that." He continued, "And he also wants one of us to kill one, even more than he wants to shoot one himself. As good as he is, he still doesn't know where the deer are coming out or if ole Scrap will even jump one up," he continued explaining. "Uncle Buck knows deer better than any hunter I know and especially around these woods, because he has lived here and scouted for them all these years," he was saying, "If there is one in those woods, Uncle Buck and Scrap will put those other dogs on them. Now, Uncle Buck is putting you in a good place," he assured me, "but he can't be sure you'll see a deer."

I told him I understood. There was only Mr. Buck's grandson, his niece, John, and myself to take stands anyway. In later years, there would be more people than you could count in those woods during deer season as the word sifted out that deer were there.

There hadn't been many deer in the woods around Jefferson County, at least in the hill country, for many years. They were mostly in the extreme west end of the county in and around the Mississippi River swamps. Daddy said they were all killed out during the Depression. People hunted deer the entire year with no regards to seasons. People were just that hungry for meat. In the late years of the fifties and early sixties, some deer signs started showing up. I think the Mississippi Game and Fish Commission planted deer in the area—at least they did according to the rumors. I don't know for sure, because if they did, they kept it a secret, so people wouldn't hunt them before they got a herd started. Old hunters were very strict about shooting only bucks. Mr. Buck always stressed that very strongly. They wanted the deer population to increase and that meant you didn't shoot does.

Suddenly, there was a loud rapping on our bedroom door, and Mr. Buck's loud voice, "Ya'll better get up. Ole Scrap has jumped them." He opened the door enough to reach in and switch the light on and pull the door back shut.

He didn't have to call twice. I jumped clear out of bed, and standing there in my drawers, I said, "John, has he turned the dogs loose without waking us?!!"

It took John a few seconds to catch his breath from laughing at me standing there in that ice-cold room in my drawers thinking I had missed the deer hunt.

He finally said, "He must have. You better hurry up and get your clothes on. That ole buck will be coming up your ridge any minute!!" I could tell he wasn't serious, especially with all the laughing. In a jiffy, I had on every stitch I had with me, and my boots were tied in seconds. I was ready to hunt and went out into the kitchen where Mrs. Velma had eggs, grits, bacon, and biscuits smelling ever so good. I looked out, and it was still dark, but I wanted to have a good understanding of the situation. I asked, "Have you really turned the dogs loose yet, Mr. Buck?"

He set his coffee cup, which he had been sipping on, down, and he and Mrs. Velma chuckled. She reassured me, "Don't pay any attention to Charlie …" She always called him Charlie, but he was Mr. Buck to everyone else. "… He is just picking at you, James."

"I did get you out of bed and dressed. I believe that's the fastest I ever saw anybody put his clothes on," he said laughing as he cut his eyes over toward Mrs. Velma who was standing over the stove.

"How do you want your eggs, James?" she asked.

I was too exited to eat, but since she had cooked and assuming everybody else would eat breakfast, I responded, "Scrambled, please, ma'am."

John and Warren finally stumbled on into the kitchen, and we all ate and went on out to the dog pen with Mr. Buck. Margaret, whom Buck called by her nickname, Babe, came driving up. She was a very nice, short young woman about thirty at the time. Mr. Buck said, "John, ya'll help me get the chains on these dogs, and then ya'll walk on up toward the old Tom Nevels place and put James where I told you too. Warren, you go with Babe. She knows where ya'll need to be." He continued instructing as he hooked the leashes on his dogs. John was holding one, and I was holding another dog waiting for Mr. Buck to get them leashed.

After he had finished leashing the four dogs, Mr. Buck stood there with his two-hundred-and-thirty-pound or so frame dressed in brown hunting pants and matching brown coat and hunting cap. He held the stock portion of his Browning Arms, Co. twelve-gauge automatic, five-shot shotgun under one arm and draped over the same forearm. He had a cow horn that he had made into a blowing horn tied to a leather string he had looped over one shoulder and under the other, so it hung just above his waist on his side.

He would later blow the horn to signal his dogs to come back after the deer had run past all his standers. In his right hand, he held the leashes that were hooked to the collars of well-bred July-Walker canines. Mr. Buck liked the July breed for their nose, which could smell a deer scent better than any dog he knew about, and he liked the Walker breed for its size and ability to run fast for a long time. Therefore, he bred the July to the Walker and hence had what he called a July-Walker hunting dog.

The sun was coming up, and Mr. Buck stated, "It's getting light, so we better get going. Ya'll look here now," getting the undivided attention of his jumpy little, mostly green hunting party. "Ya'll don't get excited and shoot too quick now. Take your time and make that first shot count."

First shot indeed, I thought. *With this old single-barrel, after I make the first shot, I'll be so exited, it will take me until next deer season to get the shell hull ejected and another shell in the chamber.*

Then he added, "Don't come back to the house as soon as the dogs go out of hearing; those ole bucks will be slipping out after those dogs go through."

With those last words of hunting instructions, John and I walked for a good while up the lane to the Soda Field (a pasture nicknamed the Soda Field for some reason). The Soda Field was a forty or fifty-acre plot of ground (as I remember it) and lay flat from the woods on one side to the hillside to the south of the field. The sun was not in sight, but it was light enough to make the white frost on the dead grass glisten. When we reached the Soda Field fence, we turned west toward the creek. After crossing the creek, we hit a cow path, and John picked up the pace a little. "We have a good ways to go yet. We better step along a little faster, so we will be on our stand before Uncle Buck turns those dogs loose," he stated.

"You think we ought to run, then?" I excitedly panted.

He started laughing and couldn't wait to tell Uncle Buck and Babe about me wanting to run to my deer stand, so I would be sure and get there in time.

It wasn't far from Soda Branch (the spring-fed creek named for the Soda Field) to the Tom Nevels place. Mr. Tom Nevels had owned this patch of woods since sometime around the nineteen thirties. This had been his farm where he had raised cotton and cattle. When World War II started, Mr. Tom, along with many other small farmers in the area, had moved to the cities where there were more jobs than people to fill them. He had gone to work in the shipyards since he was too old for the army. His neglected farm had grown up in timber and become part of the deer habitat.

John and I finally reached the top of the ridge, and he started explaining my hunting area. "See these two hollows here?" he said as he pointed the barrel of his gun toward two ground depressions. "Those deer will run these hollows, and that will put them out right about here. Now I'm going over that way," he said as he pointed with his gun barrel. "A little ways out of the range of these guns. You sit right here by this big oak tree, so you can shoot either way," he instructed me. "The deer might come up either hollow. When you see him coming, wait until he is about fifty or sixty feet out before you shoot." Then he added as he walked off, "Hold it on 'em now!" meaning take time to aim and don't miss him.

I looked around and found a couple chunks of wood to make me a seat by the big oak. I sat down and leaned back against the tree and got comfortable. Then I raised the old single-barrel and aimed in all directions to my front, being sure I could aim from my position. The forest was just waking up, and the birds starting singing and chirping. A squirrel ran down a limb and jumped into a tree a little ways in front of me. That was a strange sensation; when hunting squirrels, I would have been very excited, but I was deer hunting now and that squirrel meant nothing. It was amusing to watch them playing around and not be interested in shooting one. The sun was gleaming through the woods now with an amber glow, and the frost was slowly dripping off the frozen leaves. Every now and again, a crash in the dry leaves could be heard. I would turn quickly in the direction of the sound thinking it might be a deer. I don't know what I would have done if it had been a deer; at that time, I had never seen a deer in the woods.

Why all the excitement? I had listened to the grown folks talk about deer hunting in the swamps and saw the deer heads with huge antlers mounted on den walls and over fireplaces. Several of my friends whose fathers belonged to hunting clubs talked about deer hunting. They would tell exciting tales about hunting the big game. All I had ever hunted were squirrels and rabbits. Maybe I had killed a quail or two by then and a few blackbirds, but nothing as mighty as a deer. *Well, I'm deer hunting this morning. Yeah, right now, I am actually deer hunting right now,* I thought. *This is what is meant by sitting on a deer stand. I'm sitting on my deer stand waiting for the dogs to run a deer out.*

No dog could be heard so I started thinking, *Maybe they won't jump a deer.* It was my first deer hunt, and I couldn't wait to tell all my deer-hunting buddies. They would be in their usual deer-hunting conversations at school Monday morning at recess, and I could chime in with my deer-hunting story. *What will I tell them?* I wondered. *Yeah, I went deer hunting this weekend and sat down by a big old oak tree for most of the morning, but the dogs didn't jump, and nothing happened.* Now, that would be a fine story to tell. That would get everybody asking questions about my exciting deer hunt, sure enough.

Then I started thinking, *I have to settle down and get control. Don't get excited when I see a deer, shoot too quick, and miss him. There will be a deer running up one of these draws anytime now. That's not just somebody down there running those dogs. That's Mr. Buck down there, and he is the best deer hunter that has ever popped a cap or yelled, "Hunt close in there!" to a dog. Would the best deer hunter of all times have a good-for-nothing dog? I think not. If any dog has hunted through one deer season and still can't run a deer, he sure wouldn't be eating Buck Shelton's dog feed one day past deer season.*

After a few minutes, a dog slowly yelped down the hollow from the direction of Mr. Buck's house. *Oh, boy, things are getting started now.* I would later learn that was ole Scrap "cold trailing" a deer. Mr. Buck had led the dogs to the area where he knew the deer had bedded down for the night. That was why he had wanted an early start; the deer would still be lying around and wouldn't have wandered off to feed. With them still lying down, the dogs would be closer when the deer jumped up to run. Scrap was the "jump dog," which meant he could trail the cold scent of the deer from the night before where they had walked into their bedding place. As Scrap trailed the cold scent, his slow bark every now and then kept his fellow hunting dogs close by waiting for him to get the deer started. Once the deer jumped up and started running away, the other dogs could follow the fresh scent or "hot tracks," as we hunters say.

The barks seemed to get a little closer together. Ole Scrap was getting closer to the bedding deer. Finally, he let out a louder bark and several barks close together; the other dogs joined, and we had a race in progress. They were coming straight up my hollow, my heart was in my throat, and the old twelve-gauge was shaking. I stood up. I couldn't sit down. I figured I'd probably shoot better standing anyway. The barking was waning a little which meant they were turning; they weren't coming up my hollow after all. *Well,* I thought, *just do what Mr. Buck said and sit down, be still, and wait for one to come slipping out.* Then the barking got louder; they were really burning him up, as deer hunters say, and from the sound, he seemed to be coming up the ridge instead of the hollow. I could tell from the sound they were going into the hollow, which was just what we had expected. This deer was coming by me after all, and I could picture a huge rack of horns on his head, as big a rack as I had ever seen on any wall, maybe even bigger. The barking of the dogs got louder. He had come out of the hollow over the next ridge and gone in a hollow over beyond where I was. Well, it looked like John would be the lucky one, but the dogs ran on by, and he never shot.

The dogs were going out of hearing, and I heard Mr. Buck's horn. He was trying to call them back. I would later learn those dogs couldn't be called back; they were having too much fun. Later in the day after they had gotten tired and lost the track, then they could be called back. Mr. Buck was blowing just in case they made an "out" (lost the track for some reason), but they didn't, and the woods got quiet again. My heart started beating normally, and I sat back down on my chunks and leaned back against the big oak.

It had been exciting, even if I hadn't seen the deer. The only chance now was to catch a big buck slipping out. That didn't happen, and after a while, John came walking down through the woods. When he came up to where I was, I asked, "Did you see a deer?"

"Yeah," he said with a little disappointment in his voice. "It was a big ole doe. I tried to catch the dogs, but they were too fired up." He continued, "I heard Uncle Buck blowing for them, but those dogs will run that deer into the next county before they quit." John brought his gun out from under his arm and laid it over one shoulder, kind of gazed up in the trees, and told me, "I'm about ready to head back to the house if you are."

I said, "You don't think we will see one slipping?"

He kind of grinned and said, "I believe he would have already slipped by now, if he was going to slip."

"All right then," I replied, thinking he knew a lot more about deer hunting than I did; after all, he had learned from the best.

As we walked along, I told him about the squirrels I had seen. He said, "You ought to have shot one; it would have been better than this deer hunt turned out."

I knew he was joking and replied, "If I hit them with these buckshot, there wouldn't be anything to pick up." We chuckled, and I asked, "Do you think Uncle Buck will want to go back this afternoon?"

He said very assuredly, "Oh, yes, he'll want to go back again if we can catch those dogs, but I doubt it we see the dogs before night." We walked up on the porch of the house, and John asked, "Aunt Velma, have you seen Uncle Buck?"

"Yes, Babe and Charlie have gone to look for the dogs," she replied.

Oh boy, oh boy, maybe they would catch them, and maybe we would have another hunt after lunch.

I don't remember much about that second hunt or if we even went back that day. I do remember going hunting with Mr. Buck many more times as the seasons passed. I killed one deer over the years out there, an eight-point, after I was grown and living in Baton Rouge, Louisiana. Sometime after that, Uncle Johnny Beesley, Frank, and myself all three got a six point. We three were standing there listening to the dogs run, and they were coming our way. This was on the road near Unity Church, and the deer came out across an open pasture. When he got into range, we all three shot at the same time. The other hunters said they counted thirteen shots. There were enough deer to run one almost every time we hunted, but there were too many acres of land and too many directions the deer could run for us to cut him off. It must have been sometime in the early seventies before the deer population grew enough and deer hunters gathered to harvest very many deer.

There were many exciting times hunting deer, and many stories to tell, but none compared to the hunts of my youth around the Blue Hill community. I don't remember the details of any other hunt the way I remember that first hunt with Mr. Buck Shelton and my good friend John Bailey. John passed away when he was in his early fifties; his death was caused by cancer. After moving back to Jefferson County, I would run into John once in a while, and we would talk about the old times. He told me, "James, I can still see you standing in the middle of that bedroom floor saying, 'Has Mr. Buck turned the deer dogs loose?'"

During deer season, our uncles Bennie and Johnny Beesley would come out to the house and take us kids deer hunting. In later years, Daddy would go too. Many mornings, Uncle Bennie would get up, load dogs, and drive from five miles south of Fayette another sixteen miles to our house, and we would still be in bed. He would have to wake us up then wait for us to get dressed and cook and eat breakfast. I know that had to bother Uncle Bennie, and I don't know how he had the patience to tolerate our laziness, but he did, and I appreciate him very much for putting up with it.

We would meet the other hunters someplace and decide where we were going to hunt that morning. Then the standers would get on different stands, and the dogs would be turned loose and driven by C. A. Shelton and Uncle Johnny most of the time. Other people drove the dogs some of the time. The dogs would jump and run in some direction around or through the line of standers and head on out through the woods. We had about ten to twenty people to stand thousands of acres of timberlands, so the deer very seldom had any problem getting by us. Once the deer were moving and past the standers, the fun would really begin. We would jump in pickup trucks and speed around the little country roads to a place where we thought the deer would cross the road. If we were right, we would jump out and try to shoot the deer as he ran past.

One morning, we were hunting the Farris place just north of Union Church, and the dogs had jumped and started north. I was riding with Uncle Bennie that morning, and I heard him start up the truck on his stand down the road. I could hear him spinning the wheels throwing gravel while turning around. I got on the right side of the road so I could jump in when he came by. I knew to be ready, because he didn't want to waste any time picking me up. He came flying down the road and slammed on the brakes. I jumped in before the truck had completely stopped. He pressed the accelerator, and rocks were flying out behind the truck. He said, "Where do you think they'll cross?"

I said, "Let's go to the Tom Abbott place!" About three miles down, the road forked. One road went past the Tom Abbott place, and the other went past the Roy Rankin catch pen; both were prime deer stands. He stopped and turned the engine off, and we both jumped out of the truck and listened for barking dogs. We heard them, and he said, "I believe we can cut them off at Roy Rankin's catch pen!"

I said, "All right, but we better hurry. They are really burning him up!"

Uncle Bennie fired up that old GMC, and we headed down the left fork toward old Roy Rankin's catch pen. After traveling about a mile or so, we stopped on top of Norton Hill and listened for the dogs again. He said, "I believe they are going to cross at the Tom Abbott place!"

I said, "Yeah, they sure are!" We jumped back in the truck. He turned it around, and we started back to the fork in the road then turned left down the road to the Tom Abbott place. He raced up to the point where the deer always crossed and stopped the engine, and we jumped out. The dogs were right there. They had just crossed, as had happened many times before. Hunters had arrived just seconds too late. We jumped back into the truck, turned around again, and headed back to the fork where the road turned down toward the Roy Rankin catch pen.

It was about one mile or less from the Tom Abbott crossing to the Roy Rankin catch pen through the woods, which was the route this deer was taking. Since this deer had been running straight for a considerable distance, it was probably a buck. Does run in circles, but this deer was running straight. When a big buck is in a hurry, he can cover probably thirty or forty miles in one hour on open ground. This buck was running through woods, and that would slow him a bit, but they will lay their horns on their back so the limbs won't hang their horns. They will usually be headed into the wind, so they can smell hunters without stopping. In this position and even in the woods, the deer could probably cover fifteen miles or so in one hour.

Using the aforementioned calculations and considering the deer had just crossed, it would be reasonable to assume the deer would pass the catch pen in about four minutes. Something else very important had to be considered: This buck was being pushed by well-bred July-Walker deer dogs. They had not been on the trail more than a few minutes; therefore, they were still fresh and were pushing that deer at top speed.

Uncle Bennie knew he had to make the Roy Rankin catch pen crossing, and we had just time enough to make it, maybe. If we missed the deer at the Roy Rankin catch pen, the next crossing would be the dipping vat on the little road to Mr. Buck's house. We couldn't depend on that being the next crossing, because there was a lot of territory between those two crossings, and the deer just might turn and cross at the top of the hill above the Segrests' house. We both knew choosing the right crossing after Roy Rankin's was a long shot at best. The little graveled road that passed by Tom Abbott's place was narrow, and the GMC was wound up. We rounded a curve, and here came Uncle Johnny moving just as fast in the opposite direction. Uncle Johnny had probably stopped at the fork to listen and made the same miscalculations that we had made. He thought he could cut them off at the Tom Abbott place, but just as we had been a little late, so was he.

Uncle Bennie and Uncle Johnny locked the brakes, and each got over as far as possible which meant they both had their wheels in the respective ditches. Uncle Johnny's ditch was deeper, so he was stuck. Uncle Bennie managed to spin out and back on the road. He stuck his head out the window and yelled, "We'll come back and pull you out in a minute!" I don't know if Uncle Johnny heard him or not, but I also know Uncle Johnny knew we would be back and that we were trying to cut a deer off. That took priority over anything else that could possibly be happening.

We went around the fork sideways, and he pushed it into second gear and pressed the accelerator to the floor. Down Block Foster Road we went around the crooked, narrow little road, over Norton Hill, over the bridge at Rainy Branch, past the Singletery Cemetery, and around the last curve before the straightaway to the catch pen. We topped the little hill, slid to a stop, and jumped out, and the dogs were not quite there. We had made it in time. Uncle Bennie ran to the pen and hid behind the boarded fence on one side where he waited. I was hiding on the opposite side, and we could hear the dogs across the pasture still in the woods.

The deer would be coming out any second, and he would have to cross the open pasture, just like he or some other buck had done many times before. The difference this time was no matter which side of the pen he came by, one of us could get him. After a few seconds, the dogs came out of the woods and across the pasture, but there was no deer. The dogs ran right by the catch pen, across the road, and into the woods on the opposite side of the road headed onto the Dee place.

Uncle Bennie and I gave each other a sad look and talked about what we should have done. I don't remember what we did do after that. We must not have continued on down the road, or I would remember it. We more than likely went back to check on Uncle Johnny. Even though we missed getting a shot at the deer, we had a really fun and exciting time chasing that deer. There had been many occasions like that as we hunted around Blue Hill, and I never had more fun deer hunting than I did there. Even though we very seldom killed a deer, we never had a dull hunt.

I quit hunting the Blue Hill area for deer before the deer population increased to a productive hunting level. Ruthie's grandfather, Robert Hynum, carried me to his hunting club south of Port Gibson on the old Greenwood and McGruder plantations. The deer were plentiful there, and many had big racks. I killed at least one buck with some sort of rack every year, and because of the population, we were allowed to harvest does. I mounted only one deer from down there, and he is a nice eight-point.

Ruthie's grandfather, Mr. Hynum, invited me to go hunting with him in the fall of 1970. As mentioned, he belonged to a hunting club just southwest of Port Gibson, which was located on a sixteen-hundred-acre forest of large oaks, beech, poplar, and cypress trees. It had wide, long hollows filled with switch cane. It was a real deer haven. The tract of land was called "Greenwood" and bordered Bayou Pierre river. Mr. Robert always had very good hunting dogs, and we killed many bucks in that club.

He and I would drive up to the gate at the entrance to the woods where we all met and gathered before the hunt each morning. Mr. Robert usually had a thing or two to say to the crowd about the way they had hunted the day before. He would say something like, "Hey, you all listen to me just a minute." When he had their attention, he would continue, "You all come out of those woods too soon yesterday morning; we still had dogs running." They would begin to grin and look at each other as though they were not taking him seriously. He would then state that famous line of his, "I ain't talking to one or two. I'm talking to the whole darn crew." Everybody would break into laughter, and he would laugh with them. Then we would all talk about something else.

Mr. Robert didn't believe in feeding a no-good dog. Every now and then, somebody would ask him, "Mr. Robert, is that old Walker there a pretty good dog?"

If he was a good dog, he would always be the best dog Robert Hynum had ever had, but if he wasn't a very good dog, he would say, "Heck naw, the only thing that dog is good for is to keep hot bread from coldin' and cold bread from moldin'."

They would then ask, "Well, what'cha keepin' 'em for?"

"Oh, I'm just waiting for somebody to come along and offer me fifty dollars for 'em," he would say with a big belly laugh.

When our son, Jim, was old enough to go hunting, I took him hunting with me down at Greenwood. He had never killed a deer at that time, and doe season was open. I thought he could kill a small deer better than a large one. We were on a stand, and a large doe and two small deer came out and stopped. They were in range, so I whispered to Jim, "Shoot one of the small ones."

He whispered back, "Why can't I shoot the big one?"

I whispered, "Well, go ahead and shoot the big one."

With this loss of time, the deer started to move, and he missed the deer. I have enjoyed telling that story to my deer-hunting friends, about Jim saying, "Why can't I shoot the big one?" There were a lot of kids Jim's age in that club, and they had a big time playing around the camp. When they were on the deer stand, they had to be quiet and still. Jim told me one day, "You know, Dad, I like everything about this deer hunting except that part where you sit on the deer stand."

I laughed and told all my buddies what he had said, and they got a kick out of it too.

I bought a 1947 model Willis Army Jeep for deer hunting, and it worked out quite well for about ten years. It didn't have a top when I bought it, so I went to the junkyard and bought some scrap aluminum and made a top complete with doors. It rattled when it rolled down the road, but it kept us dry and out of the cold wind. In 1973, we had a great flood, and the flood waters were pushing the deer out of the woods and into Bruinsburg Bottom. This bottom was a tract of land owned by Mr. James Beesley on his farm just west of the Greenwood tract. Our hunting camp house was on Mr. Beesley's place. The last day of the season that year, we decided to ring standers around the hill overlooking Bruinsburg Bottom. This is the same Bruinsburg where General Grant crossed the Mississippi River during the Civil War on his way to attack Vicksburg from the east. We then had the dog drivers carry the dogs to the opposite side of the bottom and run the deer toward us. There were over a hundred deer in that field, and when they came running up that hill, shotguns started blasting. There were more than one hundred and fifty shots fired, and only three or four deer killed. The hunters were so excited, they were missing the deer. Deer were coming from all sides and running fast. It's amazing how grown men can get more excited than kids when trying to kill a deer.

Colonel McGruder, United States Army retired, hunted with us for several years, and he really enjoyed hunting, of any kind. The colonel had hunted all over the world and had hunted game of many species. He admired Mr. Robert's Walker deer dogs and often commented on their size. They were long-legged, large-frame dogs. Every now and then, a pack of Beagles would run a deer onto our hunt, and being real small dogs, they were really dwarfed by the much larger Walkers.

Mr. Robert's dogs jumped a big buck one day and carried him down James Creek. Colonel McGruder was on a stand down there someplace. A pack of Beagles ran a small deer down through there a few minutes later. After the hunt that morning, we were all gathered back at the camp for lunch. Mr. Robert drove up and yelled, "Who was on that stand down by James Creek this morning?"

The colonel said, "I was, Robert."

Mr. Robert asked, "Did you see my Walkers running that big buck down there?"

The colonel answered, "No, Robert, I didn't see any dogs as big as yours or a big buck either. All I saw was ankle-high dogs running knee-high deer."

Everybody got a good laugh from that remark.

We had wild hog hunts in the early 1990s. Those woods were well-populated with Russian boar hogs. A man from Greenwood, Mississippi, had some crossbred Pit Bull/Catahoula hog dogs. He also had horses to ride, so he could keep up with the dogs as they ran the wild hogs. He and the dogs would chase the hogs through the woods, and we would drive around the stand roads trying to cut off the hogs. After he ran one down, the dogs would hold the hog until he could get in there and chain the hog's rear leg off the ground to a tree. He would pull the dogs back, tie them off, go back to the hog, and kill him with his knife. That took quite an amount of courage. These hogs have long tusks, and they can just about bite a human leg off with one chomp.

This man's name was Melvin. He had hunted all his life or ever since there have been Russian boars in this country. He explained why he was successful at this game. He said, "A hog can't bend like a dog; he has to run around to get to you." He went on, "If you hold onto that back leg, when the hog turns, he will pull you around with him."

Somebody asked, "What happens if his leg slips out of your hand?"

Melvin just laughed and said, "Well, the hog wins the battle, and you will probably lose a leg."

A friend of mine named Eric was riding with me one day, and the dogs had a hog going pretty good. We were running one road and then the other around the Greenwood tract, trying to cut off the hog. They finally bayed him down in a dry stream. A dry stream is a drainage ditch that only has water in it when it rains. We ran down there, and there were two dogs on each side of the hog. They had him trapped in the dry stream. There were banks on each side so the hog couldn't climb out. We waited for Melvin, but he was chasing another hog and wasn't coming our way. I thought I was pretty well armed with a twelve-gauge shotgun loaded with slugs. When the hog looked up in my direction, I took dead aim and shot him right between the eyes with that slug.

The hog's head was so hard that the slug didn't penetrate it. It didn't even knock him out. The dogs ran off when I shot, and the hog ran down the streambed. There were thick switch canes on the bank, and he went out of sight. I asked Eric, "What do we do now?"

Eric said, "Why don't we ease into those canes and see if he is dead in there?"

So, we started sneaking in there and looking for a wounded hog. These hogs are black and so are some old rotten logs. Everywhere we looked, we thought we saw a hog.

I said, "Eric, do we want this hog bad enough to take a chance on losing a leg?"

He said, "I don't think so."

"Well, I'm going to tip over here so I can look in that dry streambed, and if I don't see him, I'm leaving."

We eased over there, and the hog was lying on the opposite bank.

Eric killed him with his rifle. We got five hogs altogether that day. The meat is very white and tastes as good as any pork.

We had a hunting dog named Rip that was a very good yard dog. The only problem was he would not heel when we ordered him to heel. He bit a lady one day, and we almost put him away, but the lady didn't want the dog to be killed on her account. The neighbors didn't want that dog to come around their houses. He wasn't a bad dog at all unless somebody came to our house. He didn't understand; he was just protecting us. One day, he was running along in front of the tractor and I was driving. Some dogs came out from a tenant house and ran at him. He was running back toward the tractor and ran under the rear wheel before I could get the tractor stopped. It ran over him, and that was the end of Rip. I felt terrible, and it took me quite awhile to get over that. I was blaming myself for not being more careful. There was no way that could have been avoided, unless there had been someway I could have predicted what was going to happen. In a way, we were glad he was gone. We couldn't manage Rip, and the neighbors gave us a hard time about him. Now it was over.

When I was around twelve or so, we sometimes squirrel hunted in our neighbor's forest. One guy claimed he was hunting in that forest and had six squirrels up a tree, then ole Rip came down there and he didn't get any of them. That just didn't sit well with me. My respect for my elders kind of waned a bit, because I was tired of people putting Rip down all the time. I asked this man what kind of gun he was using that day. He looked kind of surprised at me asking, but told me it was his Browning automatic. I asked him if he was using his plug. He said he was, because a plug was required except for deer hunting. If you got caught by the game warden without a plugged gun, you were in a heap of trouble. A plug is a device that you place in the shell magazine, so you can't put in but two shells. One shell in the barrel of the gun and two spares in the magazine are all that one is allowed by law.

I asked him why he hadn't shot the squirrels when three came into the tree. He said he was waiting for more to come in, so he wouldn't scare any off. I asked him if his gun only shot three times without reloading, if he thought he had time to shoot three, then reload and shoot three more. I asked him if he was waiting for eight or ten. His face got red, and he had a sheepish grin on his face. I just stared at him waiting for an answer. He couldn't think of a good lie, so he asked me why I was asking all those questions. I told him I didn't like him saying bad things about my dog. I accused him of making it all up. He finally gave in and told me he was just kidding. I knew he wasn't kidding, but to tell someone you can shoot three squirrels that are running and jumping in a tree is rather stupid. One might shoot three birds flying through the air, but a squirrel is jumping from one limb to the next. He is sometimes out of sight in the leaves or other limbs as he is running. He is smart enough to get on the opposite side of the tree and stop. This guy knew that I knew that, and it was no use lying any further. Besides that, to claim you can shoot three, reload, and shoot three more before they are out of sight or out of range is just over the top. I just changed the subject and let it go, but that was how people felt about my dog. They made up lies in order to put him down. Rip was gone now, and I wouldn't have to put up with anymore of that foolishness.

22

Riding Horses

We had two horses, one named Candy and the other Shorty. Candy was a red bay mare and could outrun any other horse in the country. Shorty was a gray Welsh pony, which means he was a little bigger than a Shetland pony. Sometimes when we wanted to go to James Cole's swimming hole, we would go out in the pasture to catch the horses. They would run when they saw us coming, and we would chase them all over the pasture. By the time we corralled them, we could have run to the swimming hole and back more than once.

One time, a friend of mine named Billy and I were going to hook his horse Dan and my horse Candy in traces and snake logs for a logger who lived in Union Church. Grandpa John Smith had some harness for hooking two horses together. We asked him if we could borrow his harness, and he had long since quit farming so he didn't care if we tore them up or not. Billy was about sixteen, and I must have been thirteen. Grandpa John laughed at us kids and our unbroken horses going into the logging business. I can't remember exactly what happened, but we never got around to hooking up our horses. Son Smith was logging somewhere in our part of the country at the time and had moved on before we could get all our gear together. Grandpa's reins were leather wagon lines, and they hung in our barn for a long time after that. I don't know what became of those lines.

We had only one saddle for quite a few years, so when two people went riding, one horse was saddled with a couple of gunnysacks. This was comfortable enough for short rides, but if you rode very long, the horse's sweat would soak through the gunnysacks and through your jeans, and your bottom would be wet with horse sweat. If you rode much longer after that, your bottom would scald from the horse's sweat that was soaking through your jeans, and it was most uncomfortable.

I finally got my own saddle, so we then had two saddles. W. L. Dickerson had a riding saddle with no horn on it. I had never seen one before, and when I heard about it, I stopped by to take a look. He told me it was for sale, and he would take thirty-five dollars for the saddle and pad. I told Daddy about it, but I was told I didn't need a saddle because he never had one, and I should be glad I had a horse to ride in the first place.

After crying and begging for about half an hour, he gave me thirty-five dollars, and I bought that saddle. I was ever so proud of my new saddle—no more scalded butt. The next time I was in town, I bought some saddle soap. I took the best of care of my saddle. It wasn't just like the cowboys' saddles, but it did have everything except the horn. Other kids would tease me because I didn't have a horn. Uncle Jack heard them one day and said, "James, ask them what do you want a horn for? You don't plan to pass anybody." I used that line many times.

Uncle Bill Smith had a couple of horses and good saddles, because he bird hunted on horseback. Sometimes I would borrow his horse Doney, put the saddle on, and lead him up to Ruthie's, and we would go horseback riding.

Kenneth Lewis Beesley and I were riding one day, and we stopped in the pasture to give our horses a breather. We got ready to ride on. Kenny was riding Shorty, and when he stepped in the stirrup, the saddle slid off Shorty's back toward the side of the house he was climbing on and Kenny hit the ground. Shorty got spooked and started running away. The saddle slid under his belly, and he started bucking as he ran across the pasture. He didn't stop bucking until that saddle was torn to pieces. We gathered it up, and one day, it was put back together. We were all glad Kenny didn't get hurt in that ordeal.

My cousin John had a horse named Dora that was the best saddling horse I have ever seen. He and Dora and Candy and I made many miles together down the roads and in the woods around Blue Hill. Ray Brown had a horse named Frank, and we would go riding a lot. Frank was a smart, well-bred gaited horse, but he couldn't outrun ole Candy. I know Ray would take issue with that statement, but there wasn't a horse in the country that could out run ole Candy. She wasn't easy to ride, I mean, she had no gaits, except walk and lope, but she could outrun the wind.

When I was a teenager, Mr. Clint Shelton's son, C. A. Shelton, had a three-year-old that had never been ridden. I had broken a couple of horses before that, but they were two years old or about that. They didn't buck very much; they mostly just jumped around. They both had been easy to ride, so all I had to do was teach them to rein. This horse was a bit more spirited. William was there, along with C. A., Mr. Clint, and Mr. Clint's brother, Mr. Early Shelton. Mr. Early lived over in Claiborne County near Barlow, Mississippi. He dealt in horses and was interested in watching me ride. I knew I wasn't much of a cowboy, but I had been around horses all my life and was excited about the attention. Somebody wanted to see what I could do.

William and C. A. held the horse until I was in the saddle, and they let him go. It was flat ground, and since I was expecting a little action, I managed to stay on for a few yards across the barnyard. He finally tossed me off. I wasn't sure I wanted to remount, but there was a crowd of onlookers. I had to remount, no matter how I felt. They got him standing again, and I got back in the saddle. He bucked a couple of times then started kind of trotting a little bit. All I had to do then was teach him to rein. When a tamed horse is being ridden, a pull on either rein signals him which direction to turn. A horse that has never been ridden doesn't know what to do when the rider pulls on one rein. He feels the bit tighten in his mouth, and he will usually stop or turn his head and keep walking straight. It takes a little coaxing to teach that to a horse, depending on the intelligence of the horse.

I proudly rode him back over to the fence, where Misters Clint and Early were standing and asked if they wanted to ride. I told them the horse was now broken to ride. Mr. Early said, "Boy, you did a fine job. I want you to come over to my place and break my horses." I told him that I would be glad to, just let me know when. I didn't really want to break any more horses and hoped he wouldn't let me know. If he did call me to break a horse, I figured I could make up an excuse at that time. He never contacted me, and I certainly didn't call him. I worked with C. A.'s horse for a few days, and he became a pretty good riding horse. I don't remember if he had any gaits.

One time, when I was about seventeen, my friend James Richardson, who lived in Harriston, Mississippi, and I decided to go squirrel hunting on horses with dogs. We only had two shotguns at our house at that time. One was a single shot and the other was a double barrel. I wanted something that would shoot several times without having to stop and reload.

I went over to Clint Shelton's house and asked if I could use his Model 11 Winchester. This was a twelve-gauge, seven-shot pump gun, and there probably never has been a gun manufactured to this day that is any better. I know Clint didn't want to loan me his gun, because it had been in his family for years, but I guess it was easier for him to loan it to me than to say no. After I was older, I realized that I shouldn't have asked, but being a kid, I didn't think about how thoughtless I was.

For this adventure, I also borrowed Uncle Bill Smith's saddle, because it had a gun scabbard tied to it with leather straps. When I was a kid growing up in the country, all I had was a handful of "loan me" and a mouth full of "thank you." Uncle Bill liked to hunt quail off horseback, and that was why he had the scabbard. The problem was Uncle Bill used a Browning automatic twelve-gauge shotgun with a twenty-eight-inch modified barrel. The scabbard was designed for a gun that size. The Model 11 had a thirty-inch barrel, and being a pump gun, it was several inches longer than the scabbard. I didn't know this until I got to James's barn, saddled the horse, and placed the Model 11 in the scabbard. A lot of gun was sticking out the top end of the scabbard.

I examined the scabbard to see if some adjustments could be made. I found that the plug in the bottom end could be removed, letting the barrel run through and letting the gun slide farther down into the leather. I was afraid if I did that the gun barrel might hit the horse's rear leg if he took a long step or something. James advised against modifying borrowed equipment. He said, "I wouldn't take that thing apart, because we may not get it back together, and besides that, the horse's leg could hit the barrel and knock the gun out of the scabbard."

Then we decided I could watch the gun and maybe hold one hand on it if we started running the horses for some reason.

We went hunting on the Liddell place; it was located about two miles east of Harriston. James's family owned land up there that joined the Liddell property, and they also had the Liddell place rented for cattle farming. It was several hundred acres altogether with some forest and good hardwood timber on it. It was good hunting land, and we enjoyed the day very much. I don't remember killing any squirrels that day though. When you are squirrel hunting on horseback, you have to depend strictly on the dogs. These dogs either weren't very good squirrel dogs or they just didn't have their minds on hunting.

We rode up to the old Liddell house site, and James showed me several holes that had been dug into the ground around the yards. There must have been a dozen or more holes about ten feet deep or deeper at random spots all around the house site.

Liddell had owned a department store over in Fayette for many years and through the depression of the 1930s. During the economic depression, many banks closed, and anybody who had any money in the bank lost it. After that, many people didn't trust banks anymore, so they buried their money.

Through the 1920s and the 1930s, there were still a lot of gold pieces and silver money. Many people believed that the precious metal in those coins was the only value in money anymore. It was believed that for some reason, Liddell had brought money home from his store through the years and buried it somewhere around that house. It was rumored that Liddell saved his gold and silver pieces. He put them in a wooden nail keg, and the keg had been brought up to that house and buried in the yard. It was strange that someone would know it was buried in the yard, but not know where. The house set about a mile or so off the south side of Harriston Road and two miles east down the road from Harriston way back up into the woods. If anybody ever found any treasure on the Liddell property, it was kept a very good secret.

When we started back out of the woods to the public road, we came upon a fence with a wire gap that had to be opened. Since I got to the gap first, I dismounted and opened the gap to let James ride through on his horse. When I turned to close the gap, the bridle rein slipped out of my hand, and the horse turned to run. James's barn was about a mile or so down that road, and since this was James's horse, he knew where he was and knew where he wanted to go. That horse knew there was nothing between him and that barn but open road.

The horse was out in the road and past James, and in one leap, he was running top speed. James wheeled his horse around and started after him. I can still see the stock on that old Model 11 flopping back and forth. It looked like it was going to fly out of the scabbard and hit that asphalt at thirty miles per hour. My life flashed before my eyes. In that split second, I was thinking that no amount of money could replace that gun.

I yelled, "Catch him, James! Catch him! Clint will kill me if that gun gets broke!" I don't think James ever heard me, and he didn't need to anyway; he knew what he had to do. He was the only hope, and he knew he was on the fastest horse, but his horse had to carry him which gave the other horse an advantage. Besides that, the other horse was at full speed before James had gotten into the race. A little ways down the road, some kids were playing basketball in their yard. Seeing all the commotion and hearing the yelling, they ran out into the road and stopped the runaway steed. I returned the gun to Clint, and I never borrowed it again. I never even considered borrowing it again. That incident almost scared me out of my mind.

Well, I do remember borrowing a different gun from my friend Tommy Boyd, who in later years lived across Autumn Street from me in Jackson, Mississippi. I only had one shotgun at the time and it was in the shop. I asked Tommy how much it would cost me if I broke his gun, and he said, "Aw, just whatever it takes to fix it." He went on to say it was a cheap gun and didn't mean much to him. I wanted to make sure of that, and I told him the story about the day the horse ran away with Clint's Model 11.

I remember Tommy asking, "Somebody loaned you a Model 11 ... Winchester Model 11?" Then he added, "If I had a Model 11, you are nobody else could borrow it. My own brother couldn't borrow it." He made his point very well, and I told him that I had learned to be very particular about borrowing guns.

One day after Ruthie and I were married, I was riding one of my brother's horses at my parents' home. It had been quite awhile since either Ruthie or I had been on a horse. Ruthie wanted to take a turn on the horse, and she rode him up the driveway a little ways and back. She had let him walk down to the gate that went around the house to the barn. When she got to the gate, she tried to rein the horse back up into the front yard, so she could dismount. The horse was confused; he had been teased into thinking he was going to the barn. I guess he thought riding was over for the day. Ruthie was too easy with him. I had told her many times that if she was going to control a horse, she had to be meaner than the horse. I told her she needed to teach the horse who was boss. He wanted to go through that gate, and Ruthie was doing more talking than reining. He leaped over the gate, and Ruthie hung on like a real cowgirl until the horse hit the ground on the other side of the gate. When he hit the other side, she fell off. My brothers and whoever else was there started laughing. I ran down there, but she started getting up, and when I noticed she wasn't hurt, I started laughing with the crowd. Ruthie didn't like that one little bit, and as far as I can remember, she never got on another horse. Her cowgirl days were over for good.

We had just gotten to my parents' house one weekend in 1970. William had bought a new horse and had him in Daddy's barnyard. I wanted to check him out and went out to put the bridle on. He was a spirited horse, and I couldn't walk up to him. I got a rope and roped the lively animal. I got the bridle and saddle on and led him out into the pasture. He wasn't pleased with the way I had forced him to go riding. He was jumping around and wouldn't let me mount. I pulled the reins tight and wrapped them around the saddle horn. With that, he stood enough for me to get in the saddle. When I loosened the reins, he started bucking, and I was surprised at that action. He was headed downhill on a short ridge, and with that downhill motion and the bucking, I was over the front of the saddle and hit the ground hard. I hit on the ball of my left shoulder and broke my collarbone. I lay there balled up on the ground. I knew something was wrong, but I didn't know just what and didn't want to know right away. I was afraid to move, thinking that if something was broken, I needed to be real careful. Daddy had been in the barnyard watching this rodeo and came running down there yelling, "Are you all right?"

I had to get up, because I didn't want to upset him anymore than I already had. So, I got up telling him I was all right.

Once on my feet, I rubbed the shoulder and felt the broken collarbone. Ruthie drove me to Port Gibson to the hospital, and Dr. Segrest was on duty in the emergency room. Ruthie's grandpa Hynum was there, just visiting somebody. They did an x-ray, and while looking at the x-ray, Dr. Segrest and Grandpa Hynum, who were old friends, were visiting. Grandpa was telling Dr. Segrest all about his granddaughter and me. I asked Dr. Segrest for a shot for pain, because I was in quite a bit of pain. He said he would do that, and Grandpa kept telling him about our child, Jim, who was a few months old and had been left with my parents. I couldn't seem to get the doctor's attention or get him to stop visiting long enough to do anything for the pain. I told Ruthie, "Come on, let's go." I was going to Vicksburg to get something for this pain. As we got up, the doctor told the nurse to give me a pill.

He said, "I can't give you a vaccination unless you are going to stay in the hospital."

I thanked him for the pill, and we headed to Vicksburg. By the time we got there, I was feeling better, and we went on home to Jackson. I got an appointment with an orthopedic doctor, and he put a brace around my shoulders and told me I would just have to wait it out. The bone lapped over and healed just fine.

When the kids reached about eight and thirteen years of age, I bought two horses and two good saddles. Kim's horse was a Welsh pony that she named Dusty, and Jim's was a full-size horse he called Champ. Kim treated her horse like a puppy dog, and he did as he wished. We were crossing the creek one day, and instead of just simply walking on across the creek, he walked up the creek to where the water was deeper and lay down to wallow. Kim couldn't do anything with him, and I ran my horse up there to get her off before she got wet. I tried to teach her like I had tried to teach her mother—that is to get mean with the animal and he will learn to mind. She wasn't going to beat Dusty.

Another time—it might have been the same day—we had ridden up a trail through the woods, and Kim was ahead of me on Dusty. I turned around to head back toward the house and yelled at Kim to come on back. She turned ole Dusty around, and he started in a gallop. He knew he was headed home. I turned ole Champ around to stop him. She never did get to where she could manage the horse, but I think she might have if she had gotten in the right mood.

We kept the horses about a year and finally just sold them. I could hardly ever get the kids to go riding. They didn't want to get away from their video games and the air conditioning. I told Ruthie times were changing. Kids had other things they liked better than horseback riding, even in the country.

Ruthie and James Smith, May 23, 1965

23

Meeting and Marrying Ruthie

My horse and saddle came in handy before I inherited the old Plymouth car. I would ride to different farms and visit my friends and one very special friend after I turned sixteen. Up Highway 552 about three miles or so and only about two miles through the woods was a farm, and on that farm lived a girl named Ruthie. I would curry my horse and put on the saddle, then take a bath and put on my finest blue jeans and button-down collared shirt and ride through the woods and up the road to Mr. Bennie and Mrs. Earline Goza's farm where Ruthie lived. I had first met Ruthie on the school bus. Our school bus at one time had stopped at the Clantons' quite a ways from Ruthie's house, turned around, and went back up Highway 552 to Red Lick School.

Warren Shelton, who lived a mile or so up the road from the Clantons, started to school. Our bus then had to go up to the Sheltons to pick up Warren. The Union Church School had burned down the year before this, in the 1956 school year, and since the county had planned to build a new school in Fayette to consolidate Red Lick, Union Church, and Fayette, they saw no need to build a new school for Union Church, since it would only be needed for two years. When the new school was finished, they would bus the Union Church school kids to Fayette. Until then, they would just make room in the Fayette school for the Union Church kids.

Howard, Terry, and Linda Goza lived just up the hill from Warren, and they wanted to go to Red Lick School, because it was only eight months instead of the nine months required in Fayette. So, their daddy went to the superintendent of education's office in Fayette and asked them to allow his kids to go to Red Lick, instead of Fayette. He explained that the Red Lick bus was coming almost to his house, and it would be less than a quarter mile farther to pick up his kids. The superintendent was elected, so he liked to keep all the voters happy; therefore, he agreed.

Since the bus was coming to the top of the hill to pick up Mr. Goza's kids, it was only a few hundred yards on down the road to Ruthie and Julia's house, and they wanted to go to an eight-month school. So, Ruthie's mama got the bus to come to her house and get her kids. That was where I first saw Ruthie. She was such a cute little girl, just eleven years old. For some reason, I liked to pick on her. There was no love involved, but bus riding gets rather boring, and once the kids my age got off, there was no one else to keep me company. I liked teasing Ruthie, because she didn't take anything off me. She just let me have it. That was the fun of it.

Then she turned thirteen, and I was sixteen. Teasing wasn't fun anymore. I had grown up a bit and noticed Ruthie in a different light. She and her cousin Linda liked to sit together on the bus and sing whatever rock-and-roll song was popular at the time. I liked rock and roll, but I liked to sing country music myself and would join in sometimes. Ruthie liked to hear me sing certain songs and gave me compliments. That made me appreciate her ever so much.

We were never very big on birthdays around our house, so there were never any parties. I was probably thirty or forty years old before I ever knew when Mama's or Daddy's birthdays were. I knew the year, but the day was never special.

Ruthie asked me once about my birthday parties, and I told her I had never had one. So, she gave me a surprise birthday party at her house on my sixteenth birthday. All the neighborhood kids came. I blew out the candles and cut the cake. It was at night, and we built a fire and roasted hot dogs and marshmallows. She had a record player and a big stack of forty-five RPM records. We all danced to Elvis, Ricky, Conway, Buddy Holly, Chuck Berry, Fats Domino, Little Richard, Bobby Riddell, and many others. It was my best party ever, and I will never forget it.

The new school was finally finished in 1958, and the Clantons were no longer going to school. I think they had moved or something. The last kid in that direction was Margaret Abbot, and her dad wanted another school bus with a shorter route that was coming close to his house to pick up his kids. That school bus could pick up his kids, the Gozas, and the Sheltons with less travel than our bus. So, Ruthie and I wouldn't get to ride the bus together anymore. That caused me to miss her very much and look forward to seeing her at school. Anyway, I knew her very well, and we seemed to like each other.

Other kids and I would be gathered and want to go swimming or play baseball in the cow pasture, but Ruthie couldn't go with us until the eggs were gathered. She was just more or less one of the gang at that time. Our gang consisted of Howard, Terry, and Linda Goza; Barbara Norton; Pete Foster; and Ray and Burnie Brown.

Ruthie's parents had a three hundred acre cattle farm along with two commercial chicken houses. In those chicken houses were thousands of laying hens. They laid hundreds of eggs each day that had to be gathered mornings and afternoons, washed and crated. We all helped to make the job go faster, so Ruthie and Julia could play baseball, go swimming, or ride around or whatever with us.

We kids were expected to help each other with each other's chores to be fair. Howard and Terry had to feed the cattle in the wintertime. That was quite a job, because their farm was pretty large. They had a lot of cattle to feed. We helped them chop corn for the barnyard troughs for the cows with calves. Then we loaded bales onto a tractor and trailer and hauled it out to the pasture where we distributed it to those cows. We had fun running the hammer mill to chop the corn and adding molasses. We liked to drive the tractors and ride on the trailer with the hay. It was just something we didn't do every day, so it was something fun to do. Howard and Terry had to do it every winter day and were glad to get the help. They let us other kids drive the tractor and operate the hammer mill. A hammer mill is a machine with whirling blades. When corn is fed into the mill, it chops it and dispenses the corn into a gunnysack. We would do just whatever needed to be done, enjoying every bit, because it was new to us. Howard and Terry just stood by and watched. At our farm, there wasn't all that much feeding to do. We only had about thirty grown cows, and I had two brothers to feed the cows when I wasn't there. We just carried the bales to the barnyard fence and threw the hay over. There wasn't much corn to chop, because we used shoe-peg corn, and the cows with calves could eat the whole ear. We never got them used to molasses, so they didn't miss it.

When Ruthie was fifteen and I was eighteen, we were allowed to go out on dates in the 1952 Plymouth. Then the courtship really started and went on for years. On May 23, 1965, when Ruthie was eighteen and I twenty one, we married and are still together until this day. Five years after that, on February 22, 1970, Jim was born, and then on December 31, 1974, Kim was born. They have both finished college now and are living on their own. I can tell you that all seems to have happened about as fast as it took me to write it.

Our wedding was held in the Unity Baptist Church, and the church was filled with guests. I said "I Do" in the exact same spot where I had accepted the Lord as my savior thirteen years earlier. Mrs. Nina Allred was in charge of the wedding and had helped Ruthie's mother with the showers and planning of the wedding. Pastor Wayne Spencer performed the ceremony. Ruthie was escorted to the altar by her father, Mr. Bennie Goza. Ruthie's maid of honor was Joyce Richardson; her bridesmaids were her sister Julia and cousin Barbara Hynum and my best man was James Richardson. We left for the Mississippi Gulf Coast that day on our honeymoon and stayed at the Buena Vista Motel in Gulfport, Mississippi. It was located on the beach side of the highway. We moved across the road to a cheaper motel for the rest of the week. The Buena Vista was charging twenty-something dollars per night, and that was expensive in 1965. We got a room for about twelve dollars. It was a very nice room complete with a TV, and the hotel had a pool. Those were luxuries at the time even in a resort area. We sunbathed on the beach and swam in the gulf and motel swimming pool. We saw the popular singer Johnny Rivers live at the Gus Stevens nightclub. He was in his prime then; that was quite a big deal.

We left the coast and came home to a motel with a kitchenette in Pearl, Mississippi. We stayed there until our new house was finished. I had bought the house before we were married, and it was supposed to be finished, but it had been held up in construction. That was the height of the six-percent thirty-year mortgage era. Houses were popping up like mushrooms all over the place, and every carpenter was very busy.

The house was finished a few weeks after we got back to Pearl, and we moved in. The house cost ten thousand, seven hundred dollars with a two-hundred-and-fifty-dollar down payment. The monthly notes were sixty-five dollars. It had three bedrooms, a living room, a kitchen/dining room combination, and one bathroom. There was a central furnace for heating and an attic fan for cooling. The water bill was two dollars per month, and there was no meter. We could use all the water we wanted in a single month for two dollars. There was a sliding glass door for a patio, but the patio wasn't poured. Before we got around to pouring the patio, we moved to Baton Rouge, Louisiana, where I went to work for the Ethyl Corporation making tetraethyl lead that was used in gasoline. We had sold our house for two hundred and fifty dollars plus the buyer had to take up the notes.

We rented a house from James Richardson's uncle. It wasn't much of a house, but it was cheaper than an apartment. He didn't actually have the house for rent. He had moved into another house, and this one was just a vacant, run-down house. Ruthie and I thought we could put up with it for a short period. We planned to buy a house; we didn't like renting. I think it was about three or four weeks before we managed to buy a house. Down payments were extremely high in Baton Rouge. We finally settled on a house that had been financed by the Veteran's Administration and had been repossessed. The deal was there was no down payment; we just bid an amount and agreed to take the house as was. It was left in pretty good shape; about all it needed was a good cleaning. It was all electric, but the air conditioning didn't work. We agreed that they didn't have to repair the air conditioner, because it was getting to be wintertime anyway, and we figured we should be able to save enough to get it repaired by summertime.

Our realtor turned in our bid, and they turned it down. They didn't like the fact that I had only been working at Ethyl for about a month. The realtor told them, "These are the kind of people you want me to sell these old, run-down houses to, and I find one, then you tell me no." I didn't know just how to take that statement, but I didn't say anything, because I wanted that house. The VA allowed a new bid; there wasn't much to change. We only had the two hundred and fifty dollars we had gotten from selling the house in Pearl, but I thought by the time I had to make out the check, I would have another fifty dollars. We also put in all the things that were wrong with the house that we were willing to accept.

Our realtor made up a few things and said we would probably not get away with it. If they sent somebody out to check us out, he would just say he made a mistake. I figured he would just blame it on me, but with the three hundred dollars down, they accepted our bid and never came to look at the property. They had the pictures, of course, but I think they just wanted the house sold, and my bid looked better than the others. I don't think there were but about three of us trying to buy the house. The house was ours, and we loaded all our things into a small U-Haul truck and moved in.

After a few months, we put the house up for sale. All I wanted was my three hundred dollars back. We used the same realtor and told him we wanted the three hundred dollars back that we had paid for the down payment. He said, "I can get you a little more than that." He explained the down payments in Baton Rouge were a bit higher than in Pearl, Mississippi. He put the house up for sale for fifteen hundred dollars down. It sat there for longer than we wanted.

It was still for sale when we moved back to Jackson, Mississippi, into the Raymond Gardens apartment complex. After we had lived in Raymond Gardens for a few weeks, Ruthie recognized our old friend, Ronald Phillips in the complex. He and his wife, Shirley, lived just up the hill from our apartment. We had been friends for a long time. Ronald and I had graduated from Jefferson High together. We had been best friends since first grade. It was amazing running into him and finding we were sharing the same apartment complex.

We went around Jackson looking for a place to build a house. There were plenty of houses for sale, but we wanted to build our own house, selecting the paint, windows, doors, brick, and color of roof shingles. The fellow that I had worked with at Jackson Patrol Service lived in the Woodville Heights subdivision just south of Jackson. We went out there and decided on a vacant lot just below the Woodville Heights Elementary School. We had been married for more than a year and were thinking about having kids, so we needed a house close to a good school. Our rear fence and the school-yard fence were one and the same. We built a sixteen-hundred-square-foot house with a double carport, three bedrooms, a kitchen, a den, a living room, and two baths. It was cooled with an attic fan and heated with a furnace that was ducted throughout the house. Our address was 1056 Autumn Street, Jackson, Mississippi.

The patio was poured and had sliding glass doors, and the house had a fireplace. It cost six hundred dollars down with a twelve-thousand-eight-hundred-dollar mortgage for thirty-six years.

We didn't have the six hundred dollars down payment, but all we had to come up with immediately was the two hundred and fifty dollars earnest money. We desperately needed the money from the sale of our Baton Rouge house, but it would not be due for several months and then it would only be paid in monthly notes. We lived rather tight, but somehow managed to save the six hundred dollars.

We needed three hundred and fifty dollars to pay the balance of the down payment on the house in Woodville Heights or we would not get the house. We would lose our two hundred and fifty dollars earnest money. We had our rent to pay, plus the house note in Baton Rouge. That was quite a strain, but I don't remember paying but one house note in Baton Rouge before the house sold. The folks who were buying the house in Baton Rouge didn't have fifteen hundred dollars for the down payment. So they paid seven hundred dollars to the realtor for his fee then financed the eight hundred dollars that was our part. The realtor had the proper paperwork, so if they didn't pay our eight hundred, we could foreclose on the house. The eight hundred wasn't due for a year, so we had to wait for our money. I should have gotten the eight hundred first and made the realtor wait on his part. They paid the eight hundred and never were late with a penny that I remember.

We went over to the house site in Woodville Heights every day to check on the construction. It was slow, because the six percent mortgage money had the housing market booming. Construction workers were taking on more than they had labor for, but it was finally finished. We moved in December 16, 1968.

Our good friends Ronald and Shirley Phillips bought a house across the street, and we enjoyed living there, especially after that. We all lived there for several years, then Shirley and Ronald moved to Lahore, Pakistan. He was building power lines in that country.

Jim and Kim were born while we lived in Woodville Heights. We moved back to the country in Jefferson County to Route 2, Pattison,

Mississippi, in 1980 and built the country house. We still own the country house. After living there, we moved to 303 Noble Drive, Brookhaven, Mississippi, in 1997. We had moved the business to 1068 West Congress Street, Brookhaven, Mississippi, in 1996. I was satisfied with the commute from the country to town to work every day, but I had problems with driving home after work. It was about a forty-minute drive, and I had never had a long commute like that before.

After living in Brookhaven from 1997 until October 2003, we decided to move to 7325 Cedar Hill Cove, Olive Branch, Mississippi. Our wonderful daughter-in-law, Ashley, Jim's wife, had given birth to our first grandson, Jackson Parker, on May 3, 2002. We visited as often as possible, but it was a four-and-a-half-hour drive to Memphis, so the trips weren't very close together. When we did visit, he was walking and would come to the door, but instead of being proud to see us, he ran the other way, because we were strangers to him. During our drives home after a visit, we talked about moving closer to our grandchildren.

Our daughter and our wonderful son-in-law, Seth McCaskill, had also settled in the Memphis area. That was another reason to move closer to Memphis. All our moves up until that time had taken quite a bit of thought, and this one was no different. The business needed to stay in Brookhaven, because our employees lived around there and quite a lot of our customer base was located there. There were no options for relocating the business that were favorable. We had always run the business ourselves and just couldn't fathom the idea that the business could run without us.

We had two really good inside employees in 2003. We also had a qualified group of technicians in the business. With telephones, fax machines, e-mail, cell phones, and the Internet, we decided that it might just be possible to run the business from Olive Branch. We had a meeting with our two inside employees and told them what we were thinking and asked if they thought they could run the business without us there. They made a tongue-in-cheek remark, "We might be able to run it a lot better if ya'll weren't here."

We gave the move more thought and decided that if chain businesses could run without the owners being around all the time, why couldn't ours do the same? So, we put the house in Brookhaven up for sale and traveled to Olive Branch to look for a house. One thing was certain;

we weren't going to live in Memphis even though both our kids lived in Cordova, a Memphis suburb. We came up on the Thursday before Labor Day in 2003. We looked all over the Olive Branch area and either couldn't find a house we liked or couldn't afford a house we liked. We finally saw a house that fit our desires and called the realtor. The house was way more than we wanted to pay. This realtor asked us what we were looking for, and I told him the price range we expected. Then I told him we wanted it on a dead-end street, so the traffic wouldn't be too heavy, because we would have grandkids playing in the yard. I went further stating that we wanted an acre lot and two or three wouldn't be too large. We wanted a boathouse, because we had a boat that we didn't use much, but we would use it a lot when our grandkids were older. I told him we would like a pond, so we could teach our grandkids how to fish. Then I chuckled and said, "That's all."

I just thought I was being funny with the gentleman. He replied, "I think I have exactly what you are looking for."

After getting directions to the place, I hung up and told Ruthie, "This guy is a nut. He claims he has a place for sale that has all that." We both laughed at the stupid idea. When we pulled into the driveway at 7325 Cedar Hill Cove, we both almost lost our breath. It was exactly what I had described to the gentleman. During the phone conversation, I had gotten so excited about him saying he had what we were looking for, I had not asked the price.

No one was home; they were away for the holidays. We looked around and couldn't find any reason not to buy this house. There were lawn chairs in the shady backyard. We sat down as though we already lived there and in our imagination decided they were going to want way more than we wanted to pay. Before we called the realtor back to get the price, we had decided that it didn't make any difference what they wanted; we were buying this place. It would be thirty or forty minutes away from both our children and of course our grandchildren. We were going to buy this house, and that was it. I called the realtor, and low and behold, the house was well within our price range. It had been three days and one of those days included travel time up here, and we had found our dream house.

We had built a lake house in 1990. We could sell that, and along with the equity in the house in Brookhaven, purchasing the home would not be a problem. We moved to Olive Branch in October 2003. We have lived here ever since, and the business is running real well, even better than it was in 2002. I guess the employees were right; it might run better without us, but we are still staying in very close contact with the business.

24

Clothes

A kid could hardly wait until summertime to pull off shirt and shoes. We stripped down to blue jeans only. I don't know why we didn't wear shorts, but we only wore shorts while swimming. Our feet would be as tough as shoe soles. I could walk on rocks and in sticker patches on my bare feet. The normal wear was blue jeans with the cuffs turned up twice. The cuffs would be about two or three inches wide. The white underside of the jeans would show. We wore white socks and penny loafers.

A penny loafer was a shoe with a sewed-in tongue coming up toward the ankle and a strap across the tongue with a slot about a quarter-inch wide. Both girls and boys wore those shoes, and sometimes we put pennies in the slot across the tongue, hence the name, penny loafer. We would use a penny that was dated the year we were born. The date couldn't be seen, but it was something to talk about, I guess.

We wore button down casual shirts over white T-shirts and left two or so front buttons unbuttoned at the top of the shirt to allow the white T-shirt to show. After Elvis and James Dean were seen with turned-up collars, we turned our collars up in the rear of the neck and down on each end. We combed our hair with Wildroot Cream Oil or Vaseline hair tonic. We never wore a belt, and some kids even cut the belt loops off their jeans. These were the "dress-up and go see your girlfriend" clothes and school clothes.

Once when I was probably three or four years old, Mama bought me a real cute short set. If I remember right, the little short pants had suspenders that went over a little T-shirt. When she showed it to me, I shouted, "I'm not going to wear short pants!" She started trying to get me to try them on, and we argued, and I griped. Finally, she made me try the pants on, but I didn't like them, and I wasn't going to wear short pants.

I think my problem was none of the grown folk around there wore short pants in those days, and I always wanted to be like grown-ups. I especially wanted to be like my daddy, and he certainly never wore any short pants.

Aunt Lillie, Daddy's sister, lived in Vicksburg. One day, we were going up there for a visit to see her and Uncle Stowers Scott. Mama started on me about those short pants. "You will look so cute, James. Please try these on for Mama," she begged.

"No," I insisted. "I ain't wearing no short pants!"

After this went on for a while, she said, "I'll tell you what we'll do; put the short pants on, and we will take your long pants along with us and you can change later if you want to."

I agreed we could try that, but it wasn't going to work.

We all loaded up in the car and started up the drive toward the road. Daddy was driving with Mama in the passenger seat in front and J. P., William, and me in the back seat. About halfway up the drive, I started pulling off those short pants. William said, "Mama, he is already pulling off these pants."

Mama said, "Well, he can pull them off. I'm not worrying about it anymore. I paid good money for those cute little pants, and I guess I just wasted it." She went on, "You'll know the next time I buy you anything, young man."

I don't know why Daddy didn't say anything. All he had to do was gently tell me to leave the pants on, and they would have been left on, because we minded him with no back talk. I might have cried all the way to Vicksburg and back, but I would have worn those pants. He might have had to go so far as to tell me if I pulled them off, he would stop that car and tear my butt up, but that was all he would have had to do. We minded him that well. He would promise a spanking if you didn't mind him, and he always fulfilled those promises. That was why he only had to spank me three times in my entire childhood. I knew if

I didn't mind him, I was going to get a spanking. That left the spanking up to me, not him. All I had to do to avoid a spanking was do as he said. If I didn't, then it was the same as asking for a spanking.

When I was about sixteen, short pants really came into style. Everybody except me was wearing short pants, so I gave in and started wearing them. Mama pitched a fit. "I just should get a belt and wear you out for putting on short pants!" Then she reminded me of the time I pulled off that little short-pant suit in the car. Even after I was over fifty years old, when I would go around my mother wearing short pants, sometimes she would bring up that day. I don't think Mama ever got over that.

After my kids came along, I realized some of the things my parents had to endure with me. My mother wanted her little boy to be dressed real cute to visit Daddy's sister. If I could go back in time, I would wear those cute little short pants and suspenders just for my mother. That is a minimal amount of debt that I owe her.

Prom night was the real dress-up night of course. Most of us wore a white sport coat, bow tie, black trousers, and black shoes. The girls wore evening gowns knee high or floor length. The gowns spread out wide at the bottom. Every girl wore a corsage. When the boy showed up at the door to pick up his girl, the first thing he did was present her with the corsage. One year, we had a poor girl who could not afford an evening gown. She instead bought a real pretty slip and wore that with a slip underneath. I'm sure that no one had noticed that it was a slip, especially the boys. Somebody just had to tell our principal that there was a girl at the prom wearing a slip. He questioned her, and she told him her sad story. He was really under the gun. He couldn't allow her to stay at the prom, but on the other hand, he didn't have the heart to tell her she had to go home. Being a man of great intellect, he did the proper thing. He confronted her boyfriend when the girl wasn't looking and asked him if he knew his date was wearing a slip. The boy certainly had no idea, just as the principal had figured. He told the boy they would have to leave before everyone found out what was going on. He advised him to just make up an excuse and get her out of there. It worked. I don't know the details, but she was talking to friends at school about it. She was on to her boyfriend, because she had correctly suspected what had happened. Her friends consoled her by telling her they didn't see anything wrong with wearing a slip; no one could tell the difference—well, almost no one. Anyway, she was delighted that she had gotten to go the prom even if it was for just a short period of time.

J. C. Penny's department store marketed a line of shirts and pants once that was called "Penny's Foremost." I loved those shirts; they had a great look and fit just fine. Just below the collar, there was a loop sewn on for hanging the shirt. Girls liked to collect those loops; they would borrow a boy's pocket knife and cut the loop off the shirt. They could keep up with which boy's shirt it came off by the color of the material, so they claimed. They would have a little box or envelope in their purse to contain their loops. They would be in study hall or on the bus or at a ballgame, showing off their loops. They would want a loop off a certain boy's shirt, but he only had a few shirts. Soon, he wouldn't have any loops left for a girl to collect. I think some boys cut the loops off themselves, because no girl had asked for one and they didn't want it to be known that no girl wanted their loops.

There was another shirt made of nylon that was a see-through shirt. The first ones had large raised squares on them, about one-quarter inch. Then later on, the squares were real small. I wore a few of those shirts; you had to have a very good T-shirt on under it, because every hole or stain could be seen. The idea was the shirt looked like a summer shirt that was cool, but they were the opposite. They didn't breathe and were very hot.

Daddy wore thin nylon socks with no elastic in the tops. They would just fall down around your ankles. Those socks were designed to be worn with an elastic band that wrapped around the leg just above the calf. That band had hooks hanging on it that the top of the socks hooked onto to hold them up. Daddy always had trouble with those tight elastic bands; they bothered him. So, he just pulled the top of the sock out to one side and twisted it then doubled it back to the sock and rolled the sock down to just above the anklebone. I would roll my socks down the same way just to be like him. My socks had elastic, of course, like socks today, but I just rolled them down anyway.

Uncle Johnny had quite a few laying hens once, and the feed came in different colored sacks. The material was cotton, and Grandma Love would get those sacks and use the material to make clothes. The material made fine garments, and no one would know they were homemade, much less from feed sacks. She made shirts for me and other grandsons and dresses for her granddaughters. We liked the clothes very much. I would tell my friends that my grandma made me a particular shirt out of feed sacks. I wasn't ashamed. I was proud to have a nice shirt like that. Of course, I was less than ten years old.

25

My Car

My brother, William, had bought a car from Duncan Segrest for $350.00. The car probably cost around $ 1,800.00 when it was new. It had a flat-head six-cylinder engine, was light green, and ran real good. Duncan was a mechanic and apparently kept the car in top running condition.

I ran the old Plymouth on Billups brand tires that cost $20.00 and tax each. The Billups tire carried a one-year warranty, and if it blew out, which it did pretty quickly on those gravel roads, I could get a brand-new tire for one dollar for each month I had owned the tire. After I had owned a set for a few months, I was always replacing one, and by the time all four had been replaced, it was time to start over again. You often hear of somebody wrecking because a tire blew out, but I can tell you I blew out all four corners at one time or the other, never more than one at a time, and never lost control. Just lucky, I guess.

Ruthie, some friends and I would get in the old Plymouth and cruise around the country roads listening to rock and roll on WNOE out of New Orleans. That was a lot of fun, and sometimes the Plymouth would have mechanical problems and we would have to service it and get it going again. I had to take it to Hiram's mechanic shop down the road. I spent many dollars with Hiram on that old car, but I loved that thing. It had no air conditioning or cruise and was a standard shift, but that AM radio played very well. I thought it was a fine machine. I believe it was Thursday nights that you could get in the drive-in movie for one dollar per carload. That was a fun thing to do.

My then-girlfriend Ruthie, now my wife, and I were dating steady in those days, and there was a drive-in theater located on the left side of Highway 61 a couple miles north of Lorman, Mississippi. It never mattered what movie was playing, we would be there on Friday and Saturday evenings by sundown. They always showed a black-and-white low-budget movie first, then a couple of cartoons, then intermission, and then the main movie. The admission was thirty-five cents, I think. The concession stand served hamburgers, fries, popcorn, soft drinks, and other fast food. Large drinks were fifteen cents, hamburgers thirty-five cents, popcorn thirty cents, and fries must have been about a dime. I used my twenty-five dollars to buy this and a tank of gas at Nesler's store and that cost about thirty-two cents per gallon. After all that expense for a night out on Friday, I still had money in my pocket to spend for another night out on Saturday.

Sometimes the film would break and everybody would blow their car horn until the projectionist could get the thing going again. We blew our horns like that would hurry the repairs along. Finally, the film would be repaired and the movie would be going again. Sometimes it would start raining, and some people would run their windshield wipers. Others would just watch the movie through the water running down the windshield. We had a lot of fun at the drive-in.

26

Wrongdoing in the Neighborhood

We had an uncle who will remain nameless due to this embarrassing revelation. We will call him Dan for communication reasons. I never had an uncle named Dan.

This story occurred before my time, so I have it pieced together from stories I've heard from Uncle Dan, family members and other people that were living at that time. I have stated in the introduction that I did not change the names of family members, but I did this one time. The era was the 1920s, maybe early 1930s, and whiskey, along with other alcoholic beverages, was illegal. Manufacturing or selling alcoholic drinks for common consumption was prohibited. Folks in the country needed whiskey for parties and other entertainment as well as other personal uses. Uncle Dan, among other folks, saw a chance to make extra money making whiskey. They had to be very careful to dodge the law. If they were caught making whiskey, they would do major prison time.

Uncle Dan had a small dairy farm with just a few cattle that he milked by hand. He came in early in the morning from his whiskey still and milked his cows. He put the milk in cans and set them by the road. The milk truck would pick up the cans and leave empties. Uncle Dan also had a cream separator. It was a contraption with a hand crank and two spouts. As the crank was turned, cream ran out one spout and milk out the other. He set the cream container on the road with the other milk. After that chore was done, he ate, went to bed, and arose in the late afternoon for the afternoon milking. After dark, he went to his still to make whiskey and sometimes would be gone all night.

His still was on the bank of a spring-fed branch deep in the woods. Whiskey needed to be made near water, because the water was needed for the whiskey and to cool the steam lines from the boiler. He had several barrels filled with sour mash near the still which was fermenting to the proper age. I'm not sure of the details here, because I picked up this story from different ones who lived around there at the time. I do know the basics are a fact. After the mash had sat in the barrels for a certain number of days, it was poured into the still. The still had a pipe out the top, and as the brew boiled, the steam went out the pipe and coiled through the cool branch water then went back on the bank into jugs. He then had a clear mixture that was almost fifty percent alcohol called white lightning, hooch, stump hole, moonshine, and other names. They liked to call it anything except whiskey, because whiskey was illegal.

Uncle Dan would go up to the local store in the area to buy his sugar for the still. It took a lot of sugar. The store owner, who ran the store, knew what Uncle Dan was doing with the sugar, but it was never mentioned. The sugar would be ordered in one-hundred-pound sacks. One time, the sugar came in, and Uncle Dan didn't come that afternoon as usual to pick up his sugar. At closing time, the storekeeper drove up with Uncle Dan's sugar. Uncle Dan said, "Hiram, you didn't have to bring this down here. I would have come and picked it up."

Hiram said, "I figured you would have, but I didn't want the sheriff or some revenuer to come by and see all these large sacks of sugar sitting on my porch. They would have known what it was for, and I couldn't have come up with a lie they would have believed," he continued.

Uncle Dan started laughing, and the storekeeper told him that when he told him what day the sugar was coming, he had better be there to pick it up or he would have to order his sugar from someplace else. Uncle Dan didn't want to have to do that. The word might get out that he was making whiskey. He raised his own corn or bought it from other farmers under the pretense that it was feed for dairy cattle. Corn purchases were easily disguised, but the only legitimate reason anybody would want that much sugar would be to can foods. Even then, they would have to own a commercial cannery to need that much sugar all at once.

Even the delivery truck driver, who delivered the sugar, probably knew what was going on, but he never asked or even wanted to know who was using all that sugar. Everyone kept a tight lip concerning moon shining in those days. Their own family or friend might be making moonshine for all they knew, and besides that, if they didn't get their whiskey from moonshiners, they might not get whiskey at all. There were commercial establishments selling alcoholic beverages, but they were hard to find, and when found, they were expensive. Out in the country, it was cheaper and much easier to come by because of the stills.

Uncle Dan put food coloring in some of his whiskey to give it an amber color. He might have had other methods, but I don't remember him saying just how he did it, other than the food coloring. That gave the clear liquid an amber color, so it would look like store-bought whiskey. That was necessary if you were going to serve your friends. If it wasn't amber, they would know it was moonshine, and that was worse in some way. Even after Prohibition was repealed on December 5, 1933, people still bought moonshine, because it was cheaper and could be bought locally.

It wasn't easy to buy a jug of moonshine. If someone approached Uncle Dan to buy some moonshine, he would be almost outraged that they would even think he was involved in such a thing. He had a very few trusted people who sold his whiskey. One had to know one of those guys and buy a jug from him. That way, if they accidentally sold a jug to a spy or revenuer (Internal Revenue Service) and they were raided, a still would not be found. Stills were expensive, and the revenuers would bust up the still until it was completely destroyed. Revenuers were lawmen who worked for the federal government. Making whiskey carried a stiffer sentence than selling whiskey. People who were caught selling whiskey might get many days in the county jail, but distillers went to the Mississippi State Penitentiary at Parchman. Parchman was in the middle of the Mississippi Delta, where crops would grow in abundance. In the delta, large fields could be planted, several hundred acres in that flat delta land. Prisoners had to work for their living in the pen in those days. They raised cotton, corn, cattle, other crops, and all the food they needed. They made vehicle licenses plates, and the food wasn't anything special. Once a prisoner got out of there, he certainly didn't want to go back.

Uncle Dan had the milk cows for a front job, so he wouldn't be suspected of making whiskey. He had a brick pit behind his house with a disguised cover on it. That was where he hid his whiskey until it was sold. One day, the Jefferson County sheriff came by and parked out front. Besides the IRS, the sheriff himself could arrest moonshiners. The sheriff drove up, and Uncle Dan's wife had to get him out of bed telling him the sheriff wanted to see him. He said he almost ran out the back door but decided to go meet the sheriff head on. They were friends, because county elected officials needed to be nice, friendly local people to win an election. They spoke and sat on the front porch and did a certain amount of small talk for awhile. Uncle Dan said that was the longest time he had spent in his life. He was waiting for the sheriff to get to it. He finally just asked, "Bob, to what do I owe this pleasure?"

The sheriff said, "Come on with me. I want to go out here and look at your dairy cattle." They walked down the path toward the barn out of hearing of anyone in the house.

When they reached the point along the path to Uncle Dan's whiskey stash, the sheriff stopped. Uncle Dan was really nervous now. The stash was right there, and he thought the sheriff was going to raid it. He said, "Dan, you and I have known each other for a long time." He continued, "I know you are making whiskey, and I know where your still is located." Uncle Dan figured he must have known about the hiding place too for he had stopped right beside it. Uncle Dan said he almost hit the ground at that point; he just knew what was coming next. He had pictured himself picking cotton in Parchman and was wondering just how long he would have to be up there. The sheriff said, "I don't want to bust up your still, so you shut it down, bring it in, and store that thing in your barn or someplace around here."

Uncle Dan said, "I have a few barrels of mash aging. Would it be all right if I make that much more whiskey, but no more than that?" Uncle Dan couldn't believe what he was asking, especially what he was asking a lawman. Anyway, he had asked it and at the same time realized that in his nervousness, he had admitted to a major crime. He immediately thought the sheriff might be using him to get a confession. If he was, Uncle Dan had fallen headfirst into the trap.

Uncle Dan asked quickly, "If you think I'm making whiskey, why ain't you arresting me?"

The sheriff turned to Uncle Dan and said, "Dan, let me tell you something; you know this is an election year." Uncle Dan acknowledged that he knew that, and the sheriff continued, "If I bust up all you moonshiners, I'll lose this election for sure." When they reached the car, he told Uncle Dan as he crawled into his car, "You can make your mash that's on tap, but you had better get it done quick." As the sheriff poked his head out the car window peering upward from under the brim of his big straw hat, he said, "Don't make me have to come back, and this conversation never took place." He added, "You sure you understand me, Dan?"

Uncle Dan told the sheriff that he was shutting it down but might get started back after the election. The sheriff said, "Well, that's up to you, but you had better not get caught or you'll do some time in Parchman." After that, he drove on down the road, probably to the next shiner's house.

Uncle Dan finished turning his mash into whiskey, but he said it wasn't very good whiskey, because the mash was immature. He emptied the mash barrels and washed them in the creek and stored them along with the still in his barn. He never fired the still up again after that. He couldn't get over the scare he had from the visit with the sheriff. He had gotten off the hook once; he wasn't going to try a second time. Uncle Dan thought that nobody knew he was making whiskey, except his sellers, but he had been wrong. Even the sheriff knew he was making whiskey and furthermore knew where he was making it. Someone came along from Alabama and bought his still. How in the world did someone from another state know he even had a still? Uncle Dan was out of the business and would never make another drop.

The roads in the 20s weren't in real good shape for traveling. They had deep, washed-out places and other potholes in the road. Cars had to almost stop and ease across parts of the road. Another distant relative, Jake Brown (another assumed name) was working for a moonshiner. Jake didn't own the still; he just worked there. The revenuers raided the still, and Jake managed to escape by running through the woods. He reached the road and started walking down the road taking long, quick strides. Mr. Julius Shelton came by in his Model-T Ford and asked Jake if he wanted a ride. Jake said, "No, thank you, Mr. Jule, I'm in a hurry."

A man that my daddy had grown up with didn't like working for a living. He was a thief all his short life. There were general stores in towns near the cotton gin, or at least in the same town as the gin. People would bring their cotton to town to be ginned and would bring the money to the general stores to pay debts they had acquired over the year. They would also buy quite a few things that they had been doing without, waiting for the crops to be harvested and sold. The general stores all stayed open past nine or ten o'clock during that season. They had large safes to put the cash in for the night. Banks would be closed late at night when the general stores closed, and there were no night deposit boxes at the bank.

This guy, we'll call him Mike, would come around after midnight and rob those safes. He had been in Parchman more than once. One time up there, he managed to get a trusty job. A trusty is a prisoner who gets special treatment for good behavior. Mike was the chauffer for the warden. One day, he asked the warden for a leave, so he could come home and visit his family then come right back. The warden, of course, refused to give him that privilege, so Mike took matters into his own hands. Since he was chauffeuring for the warden, the guards at the gate let him drive through without getting clearance. They were just lax on the job that day, and Mike drove the warden's car all the way home from Parchman to his home in Jefferson County. He was smart enough to use the back roads, because he knew the major roads would be blocked with patrol cars. He might not get away with it today, but in those days, there weren't nearly as many policemen as today.

After he had spent a day or two at home, he just drove on back up to Parchman and tried to get in the gate, but the guards immediately arrested him and the judge gave him a little more time. Mike told the warden that he thought if he showed him that he would come on back, the warden might just give him special privileges. It didn't work; he had to serve out his time and was no longer a trusty.

My father hadn't seen his childhood friend, Mike, in quite awhile. Daddy was coming home from work in Natchez one afternoon and saw Mike standing on the street corner leaning against a power pole. Since Daddy hadn't seen him for a while, he stopped, walked up to Mike, and asked, "What's going on, Mike? I haven't seen you in a long time?"

Mike said, "Well, I've been in prison down in Angola, Louisiana. I just got out and caught the bus to Fayette. I'm trying to get a ride out to Mama's house." Their house was past our house, but Daddy told him he would take him home.

On the way, Daddy tried to chastise the boy a little bit. He said to him, "Mike, you know you ain't living right and you are not going to get away with stealing things that don't belong to you." He continued, "Now, I want you to give me your word that you are going straight, get you a job, and stop all that stealing."

Mike said, "Tom, I don't know if I can give you my word on that, but I can certainly promise you one thing for sure." He said, "I ain't gonna break the law in Louisiana anymore. I'm never going back to Angola. Those people down there are crazy." He told Daddy that when they marched them out to the fields, they didn't have them shackled like they did at Parchman. The prisoners were told to stay in line, and if they got out of line, they would be shot. He said that every once in a while, the guards would just shoot down beside the line to make their point.

Mike told about other bad things the Angola guards did to keep the prisoners in line. That makes me think if we had tougher prisons today, we might have less crime. Mike couldn't be rehabilitated, but he at least chose his prisons. If all the prisons were like Angola, that might have made a huge contribution to crime control.

One day, my brother J. P. and I stopped by to visit that family. Mike happened to be there, and one of his brothers that J. P. had grown up with was there too. I could see tires and different things through open doors to the bedrooms and other rooms in the house. It all looked new. They had crates of produce, like oranges, apples, bananas, and grapes. I was bold enough to ask for some grapes. J. P. scolded me for asking for anything, especially stolen goods. I didn't know they were stolen. Mike said, "Sure, boy, you can have some of these grapes and take you some of this." He got a grocery sack and filled it up with fruit. I was dumbfounded that he was giving me all that stuff. On the way home,

J. P. explained what was probably going on there. He told me the stuff was more than likely stolen. They had been generous with the fruit because he knew they couldn't eat all that before it ruined. I wanted to stop by there another day, but whomever I was riding with told me that we were staying away from that house. We might get swept up in an arrest or something. I guess they just picked up that produce on the way out of the store. It might have been a general store, since they had food and hardware. I never did know, but I felt kind of funny eating that stuff after I found out what it was. I managed to get it down, even though it wasn't proper to eat. It had to go somewhere, because it was going to ruin anyway. We couldn't return it; we didn't know where it had come from. If we had, I don't know how we could have explained how we came by it.

Not too many years later, Mike had joined a gang of outlaws in South Mississippi. He and two others hit a store up near the center of the state. The law was on to them and surrounded the building. When Mike and the two other outlaws ran out toward their car, lights came on and they were told to halt. The two other guys halted and were arrested peacefully. Mike ran around the store and toward the rear. There were cops around there too, yelling for him to stop; he was carrying a bag of money. He came to a high fence and tried to climb over. As he reached the top of the fence, he was shot several times. He fell lifeless on the other side of that fence, still gripping that bag of money.

My parents attended that funeral in Unity Baptist Church. Someone told Daddy that it looked like as many times as Mike had been arrested, he would have straightened out. Daddy told the gentleman that Mike wasn't going to straighten out and had told him as much one day on the way home from Fayette. They didn't open his casket at his funeral for obvious reasons.

27

The Beginning of my Education

In the fall of 1950, I arrived at United Vocational High School, Red Lick, Mississippi. At that time, Red Lick only had a post office, two stores, two churches, and the United Vocational High School. It was located about four miles east of Lorman on Highway 552. This town got its name from a salt lick used by deer and other animals. It was a red, sandy area that had boiled out of the ground for some reason. It was rich in salt. The animals would come there and lick the red sand, hence "Red Lick." So when the town was established, that was chosen for the name. Red Lick had been very well populated at one time. A railroad ran through there, and two large sawmills were built along beside the tracks. That brought in many jobs, and therefore many people. It was large enough for a large school. At the time of the school consolidation in Jefferson County, Red Lick was one of the three towns in the county that had a school. The post office, one store, and the school are no longer there. Mr. Henry Spencer owned one of the stores which has been closed for many years. The school closed in the spring of 1958. Although the school was called a high school, grades one through twelve were taught there.

The school was another consolidation move that had closed Blue Hill School and I don't know how many others. There were only three schools in Jefferson County at that time, Union Church, Fayette, and Red Lick. I think the new Red Lick School was built in 1936, but I'm not positive. There was an old building there before the consolidation.

The kids in our immediate neighborhood got to school on two buses until about 1956. One bus was Mr. Clint Shelton's pickup truck with a homemade body. The body was made of clap board siding with a door in the rear. To load, you stepped on the rear bumper, over the tailgate, and into the bus. The bus was six feet long with a padded bench on each side. There was an opening down both sides of the body just below the top about one foot high, and it ran the length of the body and was covered with one-half-inch mesh chicken wire. A canvas covered the top of the body and hung down both sides over the chicken wire openings and was tied there. In warmer spring and fall days, we would roll up the canvas and tie it above the chicken wire opening for ventilation. There was no heat or air conditioning in the body, but little children would ride in the cab with Mr. Clint on cold days. The cab was heated, but had no air conditioning. There was a little opening behind the pickup rear window so Mr. Clint could look back there and keep the peace.

This little bus did not run all the way to Red Lick. It would be called a commuter bus today. He picked up the kids on the spur roads off the main route. He ran from his house on Lucky Hollow Road to the Cooks', then to our driveway, then up Highway 552 to Uncle Jack's house on Blue Hill, then back down 552 to Mr. Jim Clanton's house stopping at the Shorts' driveway on the return trip back up 552. The bus's last stop was where Lucky Hollow Road intersects with 552. We would all wait there for Mrs. Jewel Tanksley's bus. Mr. Clint's bus was a contract bus, but Mrs. Tanksley drove a regular yellow county school bus. After many of the kids graduated and no more people were moving into our neck of the woods, the commuter bus was no longer needed. Mr. Clint got the job driving the county school bus and ran the whole route to Red Lick.

After Red Lick closed, he drove the route all the way to Fayette. At Fayette, there were two schools for white kids, Jefferson County Elementary for elementary and Jefferson County High for seventh through twelfth. I started in the ninth grade and graduated in 1962 from Jefferson County High School. These schools were the last of the consolidation of schools in Jefferson. Union Church School had consolidated with the Fayette school two years earlier. These two schools were the only white schools in the county. There were two separate schools for black kids also. The schools for the blacks were just as nice as ours. Liddell High School and Liddell Elementary were the only black schools in the county. Years later in 1960s, the schools were integrated, making our alma mater a junior high school with only seventh and eighth grades attending there. We never understood why the races were separated, because we all had about as many black friends as white ones. I know I did anyway.

Getting back to Red Lick, my first and second grade teacher was Miss Ella Brown, who must have been in her seventies and lived in Port Gibson. I was taught third and fourth by Mrs. Willie Sue Killingsworth from Red Lick. The fifth and sixth teacher was Mrs. Ella King from Fayette. Seventh and eighth were Mrs. Kling (English) from Red Lick, Mrs. Camille Brooks (science) from Lorman, and Mr. J. W. Herring (Mississippi history) who was also the school principal and basketball coach. Mrs. Bertie Mae Warren from Port Gibson taught math and other subjects.

Miss Brown drove a late 1940 model blue Chevrolet car. Port Gibson to Red Lick was a long commute for Miss Brown so she stayed in the school cafeteria building during the week and went home on the weekends. The cafeteria building had three sections. The right half was the cafeteria and kitchen, the back part of the left half was the science classroom, and the front part of the left half was the infirmary. It had a bedroom, bathroom, and a place for a small kitchenette. There was a refrigerator for storing medicine during vaccinations. Miss Brown used it for her food storage and a hotplate for a stove. I don't think Miss Brown ever married. She was truly an old maid school teacher. She was dearly loved by all the kids, especially the small ones.

The infirmary was necessary, because in those days, if a child got sick, there were very few parents who had a phone. If they had a phone, they probably didn't have an extra car to come to school and pick up their sick child. For the most part, the father worked and used the car, and there were very few two-car families in those days, at least in our part of the country. Some telephone numbers in towns were only two digits long. O. K. Cleaners in Port Gibson had telephone number 55 and Claiborne Hardware Co. telephone no. 43. Other businesses and homes also had numbers like that.

I used the infirmary on two occasions. One was when I cut a gash under my left eye at the school Easter egg hunt and picnic in 1953. The first through the sixth grades were having a field day in Mr. Anon and Mrs. Willie Sue Killingsworth's pasture behind Mr. Henry Spencer's store. Miss Willie Sue, as she was addressed, was the third and fourth-grade teacher at that time. We didn't have ice chests to keep the soft drinks cold, so we left them in the icebox in Mr. Spencer's store. After an egg hunt, it was time for the picnic lunch. The teachers told all the boys to go up to the store and bring back the soft drinks. We all started running, and I don't know why, except kids do run quite a lot.

There was a tenant house on Mr. Killingsworth's farm between the picnic area and the store. The resident in the house had a clothesline stretched from the front porch post to the top of a fence post. The clothesline was made of barbed wire. Barbed wire is normally used in fences to keep cattle from climbing through the fence. Most barbed wire is made of two strands of fourteen-gauge steel wire twisted together, and about every four inches, there are two short pieces of wire entwined perpendicularly through the twisted wire. These sharp, steel-wrapped wires are called barbs, hence the name barbed wire. It was on one of these barbs that I hung my left cheek about an inch below my left eye. I was running at top speed when the barb gouged into my face, and I fell to the ground on my back. My friend Charles Bryant saw me fall and stopped to see what was the matter. I jumped up and started to run again, because I didn't feel any pain. Charles grabbed me and said, "You have cut your face." He helped me back to the picnic area, and the first person we met was Mrs. Dorothy Mae Williams who was one of the parents helping the teachers with the outing.

Charles said, "Mrs. Williams, James has cut his face!"

I was holding my hand over the cut, and she said, "Let me see it." I moved my hand exposing the cut, and a handful of blood ran down my face. Poor Mrs. Williams' eyes rolled back in her head, and she started to fall backward. Luckily one of the other mothers or one of the teachers was close enough to catch her so she wouldn't hit the ground.

Two ladies who were helping with the outing, Mrs. Cain (my friend Woodrow Cain's mother) and Mrs. Bonds (another friend Clara Lea Bonds' mother) gave me a handkerchief and told me to hold it over the cut. They loaded me in their pickup truck, and we started to Fayette to the doctor's office. They asked me if I had any older brothers or sisters at school, and I told them my brother William was there. They went by the school and picked up William, and we all four went to Dr. Greene's office in Fayette.

He laid me on the table, sewed the cut with five stitches, and told me how lucky I was that I didn't lose an eye. Each stitch hurt and stung very much, but I never shed a tear. After all, I mean just think about it, those two ladies, the nurse, and my big brother were in there. There was no way I was going to let any of them see me cry. When we later told Mama how brave I had been, she wanted to whip me for all the times I had thrown a little fit over the least little bump or scratch on me that she had tried to doctor. I told her, "Well, that old Methylate in a cut hurts worse than a stitch." After sewing me up, Dr. Greene bandaged the wound from above my left eye to my chin. Then he gave me a shot and some pills and sent me back to school.

When we got back to the picnic area, all the kids were so nice to me. They had saved sandwiches, candy, a soft drink, and some other goodies and served me while telling me how sorry they all were that I had gotten hurt. When we all arrived back at the schoolhouse, the teacher told William to select one of his friends and take me down to the infirmary where I could lie down until school was out. After that, when it came time to get on the bus, Miss Willie Sue told William, "When ya'll get home, you run ahead of James and tell your mother that he is all right and that it is only a cut on his cheek, so she won't be so shocked when she sees the bandage."

William said, "Yes, ma'am," and so he did.

The school had an insurance company to write accident insurance for schoolchildren in those days. I doubt if very many families had insurance. I know we never had any health insurance. However, at school, one could buy an insurance policy that cost two dollars and the kid was covered for any accidental injury from the time they boarded the school bus in the morning until they got off in the afternoon. Mama always insured all three of us with that two-dollar policy, and she was glad she had done that. Dr. Greene had me coming back every Saturday for about four weeks. He was giving me a shot and pills to take each time. I do believe he was milking that insurance company out of every penny he could. Somebody had put that idea into my head, and I was going to tell him that, but Mama wouldn't let me. Dr. Greene was a good doctor, and I did admire him.

My next trip to the infirmary wasn't so dramatic. I had a bad skinned place on my right knee and kept knocking off the scab so it kept getting deeper. During first recess one morning, we kids had a softball game going in the graveled parking lot behind the school. I hit the ball and ran past first base. It was going to be a close call on second. I started to slide, and the first part of me to hit that gravel was my right knee. I tore my pants at the knee and tore that scab off again. It started to bleed really badly. Somebody ran and got Miss Willie Sue. She told me to go inside and sit down at a desk. It wasn't long before a crowd gathered around me. It didn't take much of an event to draw a crowd at school. I was hot from playing, and the crowd was competing for the available air to breathe. When that iodine hit my knee, my head went backward and the crowd became fuzzy. I said, "Miss Willie Sue, I can't see." She told the crowd to give me some room and had somebody fan my face.

When I finally came around, she sent for William and told him to pick one of his friends to go with him and take me to the infirmary. Since I was older now, I didn't need to stay in the infirmary very long, but William and his friend, Charles Ray Ross, wanted me to stay a while longer so they could skip class. If I remember correctly, we stayed in there until noon. Those were the only two times I ever did any time in the infirmary, and I can't remember any more accidents anymore serious than the cut cheek and skinned knee at school.

Mr. J. W. Herring was our principal, and he taught my Mississippi history class. He could draw a circle on the blackboard without using a compass. He used his shoulder for an axis and ran the chalk between his fingers. We would check it with the chalkboard compass, and it would be right on. He could also draw a straight line without using a straight edge. We would place the yardstick on it, and it would be perfect. Mr. Herring could multiply 3.5 by 398574362 in his head and write the answer across the board as fast as he could write. He could do other fractions like 2.5, 1.5, and I think 4.5. He would let any of us write the long nine-digit number on the board, and he would walk up there and in seconds write the answer. We knew it was some kind of trick, but he never told us how to do it.

When the school was built, it had outdoor toilets. My daddy was the plumbing contractor who added the restrooms inside the building sometime in the mid-forties, I think, after he came back from Tennessee. There was only one drinking fountain for the entire school, and it was located outside. The fountain was made of homemade concrete. It was about two feet tall and six feet long and had three water fountains sticking out the top with a hollowed-out place under them with a drain. It was not a watercooler. We drank it at ground temperature. By the time I started to school, only two of the faucets worked, and sometime after that, only one faucet worked. We hardly ever had to stand in line to get a drink except after recess when we would be thirsty from playing. Several people would be standing in line to get a drink, and the bell would ring, resulting in a scuffle to get a drink so we wouldn't be late for class. The water came from a well in the school yard. It was very rich in iron, tasted awful, and smelled to high heaven. The water was wet and delicious when you were all hot and tired from playing, though. I don't know if they had water filters in those days or if our school just didn't rate one. We never talked about what was in it, just how bad it was.

One year, I think it was 1956, we had a talent show in the gym. Elvis was just gaining popularity, and Dale Williams imitated him using a 45 RPM record player. That was very good, and I remember some of the girls could really sing and several did piano numbers. I was going to be in that talent show, but I couldn't find anybody to play my music. My song was "The Wayward Wind." I had heard that song on the television show *Wide Wide World* and thought it was very pretty. I remembered most of the words. During the talent show tryouts, I sang, "The Wayward Wind" in front of all my schoolmates, without music, over a microphone, and not one person told me they didn't like it. Red Lick people were like that; they had sympathy for stupid people. If I could have found somebody with the talent or guts to accompany me on a piano with "The Wayward Wind," we would have performed in the gym the night of that talent show, in front of all those parents. That could have been my big moment, you never know. The kids on Mr. Clint's school bus were not as sympathetic as the Red Lick crowd. When I would sing "The Wayward Wind," they would immediately tell me to shut up and tell me I couldn't sing. That was all right. I figured they just didn't recognize talent like the other Red Lick kids.

Red Lick had a lunchroom that sold lunch for fifteen cents. I could buy a one-month meal ticket for three dollars. Lunch included a half pint of milk; one could get an extra half pint for three cents. We had a choice between white and chocolate milk. I wasn't really crazy about the food at the Red Lick cafeteria so when I was older, in the seventh and eighth grades, and could handle money, I went to the store at lunchtime. I could buy a soda pop, bag of potato chips, and an apple for fifteen cents and use my extra nickel allowance for a candy bar.

One of my friends, Carl Sanders, had the job of taking out the garbage from the lunchroom after lunch was served. That job required two kids, because one couldn't carry a garbage can by himself. He would get the teacher's permission to borrow a kid to help him. We would bribe Carl to choose one of us, and he was very good about giving different ones a turn. He got free lunch for this job, and we never knew why they didn't give two kids free lunch since the job required two. We liked to help because the job was done after the lunch period, and this would allow us to miss class. The garbage was in two cans; one was the leftover food, and the other was the paper. Carl was only responsible for the paper; some farmer picked up the food scraps to feed hogs or hunting dogs. We had to carry the trash to the rear of the cafeteria and into the woods and burn it. We had to wait until the fire died down before we went back to school. It was a nice extra little recess, and we would do anything to miss school for a while.

The only sports at Red Lick were basketball and softball. I played basketball and enjoyed it very much. We had a lot of softball games and marble games at recess. Marbles were the main games for the boys from the first to the sixth grade. Some high school kids also liked to play marbles. We never had any marble games at Fayette, and we missed that very much. There was a Coca-Cola machine in the corridor on the high school side of the school, and the Cokes cost a nickel. Sometime around 1957, the price of Cokes went up to six cents. A small box was placed on the top of the front of the machine. One put a penny into the slot, then the nickel went into the usual slot. On the elementary side was a chest-type Pepsi-Cola soft-drink machine. I can recall four flavors of sodas in that machine: Pepsi, orange, grape, and Dr. Pepper.

I think there were a couple of other flavors in there also. If a student wanted a Coke, they had to go over to the Coke machine. If they wanted another flavor, then they came to the Pepsi machine. The entire school had access to both machines.

The Pepsi machine worked quite differently from the Coke machine. The cover lifted up on this machine similar to a chest-type freezer. There were horizontal bars across the box about an inch apart. The bottle necks slid in between these bars and hung there not quite touching the bottom of the box. To purchase a drink, one would slide the flavor down the bars to the end and down the space between the end of the bars and the wall of the box. There was a little door with a slot just wide enough for the bottle to sit in. Then a nickel was placed in the slot and the bottle could be pulled up and the door would release so the soda could be taken out. This box had a small box mounted on the left end to accept the money. When drinks went to six cents, the little money box was replaced with a box that had two slots, one for the nickel and one for the penny.

Some of us kids would go home with a friend to spend a night or weekend. I went home with my friend Ronald Phillips several times. On one weekend stay, his mother asked us to go into their pasture and check on the milk cow. The cow was due to have a calf, and Mrs. Phillips wanted to know how she was doing and if the calf had been born. We found the cow and could tell by looking at her the calf had been born. The problem was we didn't see the calf. Ronald said, "Let's look around and see if we can find the calf, and if we do, we'll drive the cow to the lot."

"We can make the cow find the calf," I told Ronald.

"Now, James, how are we gonna make a cow find a calf?" he asked very puzzled.

"You just watch this," I replied. Then I told him to come with me, and we would hide in the tall grass near where the cow was. Once we were hidden, I put my hand over my mouth and blatted, flapping my hand off and over my mouth making a sound like a calf in trouble. The cow immediately ran to where the calf was lying in the tall weeds. When she stopped, I told Ronald that was where the calf was. We went over there, and sure enough, there was the calf. We then drove the cow and calf to the lot and were very proud of ourselves for having not only found the cow, but found the calf and driven both to the lot. Ronald couldn't wait to tell his mother about how I had made the cow find the calf. Of course, his mother wasn't impressed for she had found calves that way many times and probably learned that technique from her elders. I had learned that from one of my parents.

Kite flying was a fun thing to do at school every March. Mr. Henry Spencer sold kites for a dime and string for a nickel. Some of us would go without sodas and chips for a week to save up for a kite and two balls of string. We would go out behind the school and fly our kites over the baseball field. Sometimes we would make our own kites with two cedar weed stalks and paper. A cedar weed is a tall weed with small limber limbs. The trunk is around a quarter-inch in diameter, and the weed will sometimes grow three or four feet long. We would find a weed from the previous year, so it would be dry and light. The weeds were tied together in a cross shape then a string was brought around the four ends of the sticks. This was then covered with the lightest paper we could find, usually newspapers which weren't very strong. Grocery bags made stronger kites, but the paper was heavier so the kite would fly very well, but not very high. After the paper was stretched over the sticks and string, it was folded around the string and glued. It was very exciting to see a kite that my friends and I had made actually fly. The tail of a kite is very important; it holds the kite in an upright position allowing the paper to ride the wind currents. While one held the string and slowly let it out, the kite would slowly climb to its highest possible altitude, which was a couple hundred feet.

As mentioned earlier, another game at Red Lick was marbles. Marble games were probably the most popular games among the boys on the grammar school side. The game was played by using a ball-shaped glass toy about a half inch in diameter. Marbles came in a bag of about ten for a nickel. The marbles had different colors embedded in the glass making them very pretty. There was a particular marble called a cat-eye. These marbles were clear glass with a splotch of color in the center shaped like the pupil of a cat's eye. The splotch was different in different marbles, and they were very popular. Some marbles were larger than others. I believe the largest I ever saw was about one inch in diameter. The most common one we used was the half-inch diameter marble.

One type of marble game was "ring" marbles. A ring about three feet in diameter was drawn in the dirt using a stick. A line was drawn across the center of the ring about eight inches long. Then the players, usually numbering from two to six kids, would decide how many marbles to put into the ring. Somebody would ask, "How many are we putting in?" Then somebody else would suggest a certain number, usually two or three marbles per player. Once the marbles were lined up in the center of the ring, it was time to lag to determine the order in which each player would shoot. A lag line was drawn a few feet away from the ring, and each player would throw his "toy" at the lag line. The "toy" was what we called the marble that the shooter would shoot with. The toy that landed closest to the lag line would get first shot at the marbles lined up in the ring. The toy lying the next closest distance to the lag line would be second and so on.

After the shooting order had been determined, the game would begin. The first player would kneel down with his toy in his shooting hand, resting the marble in the curve of the forefinger and thumb with his thumb toward the marbles located in the center of the ring. He must shoot hard enough that when or if his toy hit one of the marbles, it would knock it out of the ring. If this happened, the player not only got to keep the marble, he also got another shot. The second shot was not from the outside circle of the ring, but from where the toy had stopped.

This procedure of the toy stopping close to where it had hit the other marble in the ring was called "sticking." It was believed that if the marble would "stick," it would make a good toy. Many times, we would show off our toys, usually very pretty marbles. When you showed somebody your toy, he would automatically ask, "Will that baby stick?"

The response was always, "Shoot yeah, this baby will stick!"

The other party might want to negotiate a trade. If so, he might ask, "How much will you take for it?"

The reply might be, "You haven't got enough marbles to buy this toy."

The buyer would beg, "Aw, come on now. I'll give you, say, five or ten marbles for it."

The owner would reply, "Well, which is it, five or ten?"

"I don't know, just say eight maybe."

"No, you already said ten, but I might want fifteen marbles for this toy. I mean this baby will stick, now. I'm not kidding."

"Well, all right, ten marbles, it is, but I'm not going one marble higher."

The seller might then say, "Okay, you can have it," or he might say, "Come back and see me when you got twenty; that is, if I haven't already sold it." He might add that he had turned down an offer of ten already.

This would put pressure on the prospective buyer, and if the little lie worked, the buyer would say, "All right, I'll give you eighteen, but if this thing don't stick, I want my marbles back!"

The seller would say, "Aw, it's going to stick; that is, if you shoot it right," adding, "You just practice with it awhile, and you'll see, it's going to stick." I think the spin put on the marble when it left the shooter's fingers actually caused the marble to stop when it hit the other marble. I'm not sure what caused a marble to stick, but I do know some marbles were rounder and better balanced than other marbles. This made a good toy, because the marble would travel straight.

Getting back to the game—assuming the toy had stuck, the player would shoot from the spot in the ring where his toy had stopped. If he hit another marble and knocked it out, he would shoot from where his toy lay for the next shot. That was why sticking was important. If the player didn't knock the marble out of the ring, or if he missed, then he lost his turn and the second shooter would shoot. Marbles knocked near the ring but not outside would stay at that spot for the next shooter to shoot at. The game would continue until all the marbles had been knocked out of the ring and placed in the successful shooters' pockets.

The game "bananas" was played a little differently. A ring shaped like a banana about two feet long and one foot wide would be drawn on the ground. A determined number of marbles would be placed along a line drawn down the center of the banana. Aside from the banana, a lag line would be drawn. Each player would stand about ten feet from the line and toss their toys toward the lag line. The closest toy to the lag line would determine the first shooter, then the second, and so forth depending on the distance the toy had stopped from the line.

The shooter then would have to shoot from the lag line. This meant he very possibly wouldn't knock any marbles out of the banana from ten feet away, but he would carefully throw his toy so it would stop close to the lined marbles for his next turn. This action was called "laying up," which meant he had laid up his marble, so that on his next turn, he would have a close shot at the lined marbles. He kept all marbles he knocked out of the banana.

The second and third shooters' toys would be laid up to the lined marbles, and the first shooter would want to knock their toys away from the lined marbles. He would earn another shot if the toy he hit was knocked out of the banana, but he wasn't allowed to keep the toy. If the other toy was inside the banana, then it could not be targeted. Laying up would sometimes be allowed in ring marbles, and sometimes it wouldn't. If laying up was allowed, the shooter would announce, "I'm going to lay up." Then he would gently roll his toy as close to the lined marbles as possible, but he would lose his turn. Then on the next turn, he would have a close shot. That is if another player hadn't knocked his toy out of the ring.

Another game was "holes." In this game, about three holes were dug about ten feet apart in a row. The players lagged for their turn, and the game began. The first shooter would try to roll his toy into the first hole from the lag line. If he was successful, he then shot his marble at the second hole and then the third. The first person to roll his toy into all three holes was the winner. If a shooter didn't hit a hole, he would shoot his toy from where it lay on his next turn. No marbles were gambled in this game, so far as I know.

The fun of holes was you couldn't lose any marbles, and if the previous shooter had stopped outside the hole and if his toy was near where the present shooter's toy was, the present shooter could knock the other player's toy across the yard as far as he could. The present shooter would not get another shot for this, but he would be closer to the hole than his opponent and would have an edge on him. You only got one shot per turn unless you hit the hole; if so, you earned an extra shot. Depending on the players' desires, there were no limits on the number of holes.

Sometimes a game might not end until each player had hit all three holes, going and coming back to the lag line. This became difficult coming back, because the leading player's toy would be stopping near a toy of a player coming back. If this happened, the shooter could knock the leading player's marble across the yard and gain an advantage. It was a great advantage in the holes game to have a very large marble, even a steel ball if possible. This would make the marble roll more easily and farther, and small objects on the ground would not interfere with its roll as much. Besides that, another player could not knock the heavy marble very far away from the playing line.

My good friend Ronald was probably the best marble shot in the whole school. I went home with him several times to spend the night, and he had a large basket full of marbles. He must have had five dollars' worth of marbles, maybe more, in that basket. He didn't shoot his toy from the curve of his forefinger like most shooters, but the toy rested on the tip end of his curved-up forefinger and the end of his thumb. He placed downward pressure on the toy with his thumb. This method gave the marble more speed as well as a more accurate aim. Another good friend of mine Ray Brown could shoot a marble too. Ray, Ronald, and I, all three of us used the same method of holding our toy. Holding the toy on the end of the forefinger with the second knuckle of that finger on the ground caused the toy to travel downward when it hit the other marble. I believe this motion also helped the toy stick.

If a player could knock all the marbles out of the banana or the ring with one turn, he had "mopped up." Ronald, Ray, and I "mopped up" on many occasions. Sometimes other kids wouldn't play with us if we were all three in the same game. They also wanted first turn without a lag. It was hard to get a game started if one mopped up too often. We had to "hustle" them for a game by letting them win a game or two, and then we would win their marbles a few at a time. It was the only way to keep them playing. Sometimes this was called hustling. I'm sure that I never won as many marbles as Ray or Ronald, but I did all right.

"Chase" was another good marble game. There was a lag to determine who would get first shot. The one farthest away from the lag line was the loser, so he would drop a marble a certain predetermined distance from the lag line, and the winner would shoot at the dropped marble. If he hit it, he put it in his pocket and the loser would drop another marble to shoot at. If the shooter missed, the other player would shoot at the other shooter's marble, and the game would go on until the players were tired or one player had no more marbles to lose. There was no limit on where the game might travel. We just took turns shooting at each other's marbles no matter where they lay.

Ronald and I got into a game of marble chase one day that I will never forget. The weather was stormy that day, and the electric power to the school was off. Therefore, the class bells were not working. Since we were all inside because we couldn't play outside in the bad weather, Ronald and I decided to play a game of chase marbles. We started in the school corridor and chased up and down the corridor. At some point, one of us shot at the other's marble, and the marble was traveling toward the boys' restroom door. Somebody opened the door coming out of the restroom, and our marble went inside. Now, this was a disgusting situation, I know, but it was a marble game and marble games were taken very seriously. So, the game continued into the restroom. Since we were inside the restroom, we didn't hear the teachers telling everybody to go to class. We had forgotten that the bells were not ringing because of the power outage, and being deeply involved in this game, we were not aware of the time.

A teacher could hear us in there since the restroom and the classroom shared the same wall. They could hear our marbles bouncing around. The teacher immediately decided some students were playing hooky, so she went down to the principal's office and got Mr. Herring to go into the restroom and catch whoever it was. He stormed into the restroom, asking no questions as to why we were in there, promptly pulled off his belt, gave us both a few licks, and sent us to class. Boy, were we mad that nobody would listen to our story, much less believe it. Everybody thought it was very funny to be playing marbles in the restroom.

Since I had been punished unjustly, I decided to tell my father about it and maybe we could get that ole Mr. Herring fired. I'll never forget my father's reaction when I told him about the matter and that Mr. Herring had whipped me for no reason and I didn't deserve the whipping. Daddy replied, "Well, why don't you just chalk that one up for one of the ones you didn't get that you did deserve?" I now know parents were stronger concerning discipline back then. Parents let teachers correct their children when they thought they needed it.

Red Lick School closed in the spring of 1958, and that was the only year I hated to see school close. I missed that old school then, and I still miss it today. Those days were the happiest times of my childhood. Red Lick School has a reunion every year in the nearby town of Port Gibson, Mississippi, in Claiborne County.

In the fall of 1958, we went to the brand-new school in Fayette. Jefferson County High School was very well lit and the tile floors waxed and shining. It had new, shiny desks with no chewing gum stuck under them and no initials carved in the tops, and the chalkboards were all green. I had never seen that before, and I thought they were very neat and pretty. There was a cafeteria inside the building. There would be no more going outside and running down the sidewalk on rainy days to the lunchroom. This cafeteria being new, it had all new tables and four new chairs per table. There would be no more sitting in a dimly lit lunchroom on long picnic-type homemade tables. The food was superb at Jefferson High. We had two very good chefs. The meals were great, and we had very good desserts.

Consolidating with Fayette and Union Church schools was a little disturbing. We were concerned about going to school with strangers. The fact that we were from a little hick school like Red Lick might cause the Fayette kids to think we were a notch below their social level. At first, Ronald Phillips, Ray Brown, and I kind of stayed together; we had all known each other since first grade, and Ray and I before that. But it didn't take long to make new friends, and we fit in better than I had thought we would. Most of the Fayette School crowd were country folk just like us. They hailed from Church Hill, Rodney, Lorman, and little farm communities, just like we did. Everybody fit in, and we enjoyed our school days maybe even more than we had at Red Lick.

The science lab was very modern and well equipped. We had a very large, beautiful auditorium with a large stage. There was a brand-new gym out back with hardwood floors that shined like glass and nice comfortable bleachers. We had Ping-Pong tables and volleyball and badminton tables in there and showers in the locker rooms. Gas heaters hung from the ceilings in the gym and the locker rooms.

Out past the gym was a shop building for vocational technical training with all the latest and most modern saws, routers, planers, drill presses, welding machines, wood lathes, and other tools and a classroom as well. Out behind that was a baseball field, and down the hill in the flat was a football field with lots of bleachers. Yes, we thought we might just grow to like it there at Jefferson High. Maybe we shouldn't have been so disappointed about leaving Red Lick. Jefferson High was a very nice school with more conveniences, more comforts, and above all, better food.

I signed up for vocational technical training (shop), and I enjoyed every minute of it. Mr. Neal was our shop teacher, and he required every kid to have a project for building something. My project was a tool cabinet. I made a drawing of a tool cabinet. It was to be six feet tall with two doors in the top half, two pull-out drawers below the top doors, and two more doors that opened to the lower compartment. After my design was approved by Mr. Neal, he told me I would need help with a project that big. My friend Carl Sanders asked if he could share my project, and Mr. Neal told him it would count and Carl could still come up with a project of his own for next year.

Carl and I went to town and bought some two-by-fours, hinges, latches, and nails. We divided the two-by-fours into two parts lengthways on the table saw, making two-by-twos. Next, we nailed the two-by-two pieces together, making a frame. We went out behind the shop where some old scrape plywood was stacked. We pulled out a few pieces and sawed them into shapes for the sides, the rear, and the doors. After all that, we made two drawers then cut out the four doors and put on the hinges and latches, and our project was completed. This took most of the year working only one hour per day and not every day because we had class only on certain days. Carl and I were so proud; we had overcome all the flaws in the plan by ripping out, rebuilding, chiseling, dressing, hammering, and sawing. Finally, I carried the tool cabinet home and placed it in one corner of the crib. Daddy filled it with tools, and the cabinet is still sitting there today. I saw Carl about twenty years or so after we completed that project, and he asked, "Is that thing still together?"

I proudly told him, "You mean you have to ask? Of course, it's still as good as the day we drove in the last nail." And it is. I believe that cabinet is about forty-eight years old this year.

My next project was watering troughs for the cow lot. I found an old galvanized twenty-five gallon butane gas tank. I split it in half lengthways with the acetylene cutting torch. Then I cut some half-inch rebar rods and welded them on the bottom for legs on one trough. I cut some short pieces of angle iron and welded them across the other half piece of tank so it would sit on the ground. One half of the tank had legs so it stood up off the ground for the cows, and one half had no legs, so it lay on the ground for the chickens and hogs. I don't know what ever happened to my tall trough, but the one sitting on the ground was used for years. It was used to water chickens mostly since we had a pond in the little pasture that opened onto the lot for the cows. Finally, both troughs were gone; they probably rusted out over the years, but I enjoyed making those things because I enjoy building, and at that age, I hadn't yet built any really useful things.

The back porch screen door handle broke off at about that stage of my life, and with all my new self-confidence, I decided to make a replacement. Mama had wanted to pick up a new handle in town, but she couldn't remember to do that, so I just told her I would make one. I found an old piece of half-inch-diameter copper water pipe and sawed off about six or seven inches. I hammered the ends flat on the anvil and punched holes in each end for nails to pass through. Then I took two wooden spools that sewing thread came on and ran nails through the holes in the copper and through the spools and into the door. The spools served as standoffs, and the round copper pipe was the screen door handle. It was a very nice-looking piece of work, and I can remember Mama, Daddy, and maybe one other member of the family telling me what a great idea that was and adding it was a good job. I would tell anybody who was entering the door with me, "I made this door handle here."

Most of them replied, "Umm-huh." That was about all I remember anybody saying. I mean, they weren't really impressed. It was just a door handle, but I thought coming up with the idea and making it become a reality justified a little bragging.

We learned a little mechanic skill in the shop. When the fuel pump went out on Daddy's 1957 Pontiac, I thought, *Well, no use in taking it to Hiram Norton's garage down the road. I'll just change this pump myself.* After all, I was maybe fifteen, and I was taking shop at school. A kid was supposed to learn something, I reasoned with myself. Couldn't be much to it. There were only two bolts and two three-eighth-inch copper fuel lines on the simple little thing. Shoot, I could have that thing changed before we could get halfway to Hiram's and we would save that mechanic bill.

Hiram Norton was family. He was married to my father's first cousin Alice Rushing. His garage was located about four miles east of the Dennis Cross Roads on the north side of Highway 552 and about three or four miles from our farm. Hiram was a really nice person. I enjoyed hanging around his shop and watching him work. He had a sense of humor, and I liked to visit with him. I would ask him questions about mechanics since I was taking shop in school, and I learned a lot from Hiram. Things that I learned from Hiram have been valuable over the years, like how to time an engine and how to determine why an engine won't start. Hiram taught me to first determine if an engine is getting gas. Then determine if the spark plug is firing. If it's getting gas and the plug is firing, that puts fire and gas together and that will result in an explosion every time. That means the engine has to hit. It may not start, but the engine fails to crank because of one of those two problems most of the time.

I got the new fuel pump for our '57 Pontiac and found that it was simple to remove the old pump. Putting the new pump back on was more of a challenge. There was a lever on those old mechanical pumps that went through a hole and inside the engine. I couldn't see inside the hole because there was no way to get in the proper position to peer through the hole. The lever was hitting something, and the pump would not go in place, so the bolt holes were out of alignment. When I applied pressure, the bolt holes would line up, but I couldn't hold the pressure on with one hand and screw the bolt in with the other hand.

I tried tying wire to the pump, stretching it over the engine, and tying it off to hold the pump in place until I could get the bolts started. That didn't work, so I tried propping it up from the bottom with a piece of wood wedged between the pump and the ground. We could have gone to Hiram's and let him overhaul the engine and come back in less time than I spent getting that thing on there, but I finally got it on and it worked. It was a sweet sound hearing that engine run knowing the required fuel was being pumped by a fuel pump that I had installed. I felt pretty good about my mechanical abilities. I didn't know if I could do that, but I gave myself a chance and found out that I could mount a fuel pump on a GM car. The lesson learned is if you give yourself a chance, you might be surprised at what you can do.

One day, when I was hanging around Hiram's shop, I asked him, "Hiram, when you are replacing a fuel pump, how do you prop it up so the bolt holes will line up?"

He looked at me with a confused look on his face and asked, "What do you mean by 'prop it up'?"

Trying to sound kind of bold, like this was a conversation between one mechanic and another, I said, "Well, the other day, I was changing one out and I couldn't hold the tension while putting the bolts in."

I could tell by the look on Hiram's face that he couldn't quite grasp what in the world I was talking about. I had gotten his curiosity up to the point where he stopped what he was doing and started asking specific questions. I explained to him about my contraptions and told him about the frustrations I had experienced installing that pump. He kind of laughed saying, "I don't know how you ever got it on like that."

Then he explained, "There is a cam inside the engine that presses on that lever pushing it down with every turn of the engine causing it to pump fuel." He went on, "In your case, that cam had stopped just as it was coming in contact with the lever and that is what was holding it off." He added, "You could have bumped the starter to turn the engine and that would have moved the cam past the lever. After you got the cam out of the way, you wouldn't have had any trouble," so explained the professional leaving this young novice with a blank stare. All that time and aggravation could have been avoided by bumping the starter. Lesson learned: "Everything is simple, once we understand it."

Another time, one of the universal joints came out of the car. A u-joint is a coupling that attaches the driveshaft between the transmission and rear end. The rear axle is attached to springs to give the car a smoother ride. This up and down action has to be considered when applying power from the transmission to the rear wheels, hence a u-joint. Again, this appeared to be a simple mechanical procedure, and it was simple to remove the driveshaft and what was remaining of the u-joints. There are little caps on each end of a u-joint that are pressure fitted into the yoke of the driveshaft. I couldn't figure out how to remove those caps. I could hammer the joint through, but the "X" shape of the joint would catch on the hole before it pushed the cap all the way out of the yoke. I worked with it and beat it back and forth and tried every trick I could think of, but nothing worked. So, I drove down to Hiram's shop and asked him if he would show me how to remove a u-joint. He knocked the joint in one direction pushing the cap about a quarter of an inch out of the hole; then he placed the cap in his vice clamping it tightly and hit the yoke with his hammer and that was all there was to it.

I thanked him, and as I was walking out of his shop, I saw another person in his shop that day. I don't remember who it was, but Hiram said to him in a voice loud enough he was sure I would overhear, "That's called helping people beat you out of business."

I didn't say anything and just kept walking as though I hadn't heard, but the message was clear. Lesson learned, *'If you are going to do the job yourself and not let me have the business, don't come running to me when you get in over your head.'* In other words, it just wasn't fair to a businessman.

When Hiram first opened his shop, he was trying to get it equipped as cheaply as possible, so he didn't buy one of the new electric gasoline pumps to refuel vehicles. Somebody had recently replaced an old hand-operated pump with an electric, so they let Hiram have the hand-operated gasoline pump for his shop.

The gasoline pump was located between the road and the front entrance to Hiram's shop. When I was a small boy, I was fascinated with that old gas pump. The thing was a red pedestal about twelve feet tall, and it had a glass tank on top that held ten gallons of gas. There were metal tags with numbers from one to ten mounted in a vertical line down the glass tank, to measure gallons of gas in the glass tank. There was a steel lever mounted on the side of the pedestal that was about three feet long.

The lever moved back and forth to pump gas up into the glass tank on top of the pump. If the customer wanted five gallons of gas, Hiram would grab the lever, move it back and forth, and watch the amber-colored, leaded gasoline rise up into the glass tank until it reached the metal tag marked with the digit five; that would be five measured gallons. The pedestal had a gas hose attached to the bottom of the glass tank with a nozzle on the end, much like the ones today. Hiram would remove the nozzle from the cradle on the side of the pedestal, then insert the nozzle into the vehicle's gas tank, and drain the gas into the car. If the customer wanted more than ten gallons, Hiram would pump the glass tank full up to ten gallons. He would then drain that ten gallons into the car, pump the glass tank to the desired amount, and drain that into the car, adding up the quantity of gallons.

When I was a small boy, I would keep my eye on that pump watching for a customer to drive in. I would run out to the car and all exited ask, "How many gallons do you want?" The customer would tell me, and I would grab the lever and pump the amount into the glass tank. If you accidentally pumped more than the right amount, it wasn't a problem; you just opened the filler cap to the underground gas tank and drained the gas down out of the glass tank back into the underground holding tank. Sometimes, if no one came in while I was there, I would just pump the gas into the glass tank, then drain it back into the underground tank just for the fun of it.

Just east of Hiram's garage on Highway 552 was Nesler's store. He had an electric gasoline pump, but a hand-operated kerosene pump. The kerosene tank was a three-foot-square steel tank that stood about four feet tall. A pipe protruded about two feet out the top of the tank with a faucet on the end. To fill a kerosene container, you cranked the handle around and around until the desired amount ran into the container. The handle would only make a certain number of turns, and it would stop. This number of turns would pump one quart of kerosene. The handle had to be wound in the opposite direction until it stopped. It was then ready to pump another quart. That's how the kerosene was measured.

If the pump sat there very long without being used, the kerosene would drain back into the tank and would have to be pumped back up. The first pump round was turned until kerosene started coming out of the faucet. Then the handle was turned backward until it stopped. Then it would pump one quart on the next pumping.

On the front of Nesler's store was attached a device to patch tire tubes. The device was an L-shaped steel plate with the long part of the plate attached to the wall. There was a screw-operated press attached a few inches up the long part over the shorter part sticking straight out. To patch a tube, the area around the hole was scraped to rough up the rubber; then glue was applied on the rubber around the hole. After purchasing a "hot-patch," which was attached to a metal dish, from the store, one placed it over the hole. The patch and tube were clamped in the tube patching device, and the screw press was screwed down on the metal plate pressing the hot-patch tightly to the tube. The flammable substance was scratched a little and set on fire. The substance didn't flame, but it sizzled like a fireworks sparkler. This caused the plate to heat and melt the patch to the tube, bonding a very good seal.

One day, somebody was patching a tire, and the sparks from the hot-patch ignited the spilled kerosene on the outside of the kerosene tank. Since the fuel was spread over the tank, it made a very large flame. The tank was located just inches from the front door of the store and about two feet from the gasoline pump. Several people were inside the store when the kerosene ignited. The flames were blowing across the front doorway, and there was no back door.

The only way out was through a small high window on the side or a small low window on the front. Both windows were too small for Mr. Goza who was in the store at the time. He told me he embarrassed himself in his excitement by saying, "To heck with a place without a back door!!"

He said when they were talking about the incident later, Mr. Nesler told him, "Don't be embarrassed, Grover. I was thinking the same thing."

Somehow, they managed to extinguish the fire. I don't remember how, but the store had a back door before the end of the next day and the tire-patching device was moved well away from the gasoline fuel tanks.

I enjoyed my years at Jefferson High School, especially my senior year. Mr. Clint Shelton drove the school bus, and I was his substitute driver. He was a very cautious driver which meant he drove very slowly. The kids wanted to get home as soon as possible, and they all liked the days I drove, because I drove faster. I never drove dangerously, but I at least got up to fifty miles per hour on the highway and about forty in the flats on the gravel roads.

School bus drivers earned five dollars per day. The drivers had to furnish their own substitute. There was no set fee for a substitute, but it was customary to give the substitute three dollars. Anyway, that was the amount Mr. Clint would pay me. I told him that I would be happy to drive for nothing, because I had to ride anyway and I enjoyed driving. If nothing else, driving was less boring. He wouldn't have that. He said his conscience forced him to pay me at least three dollars per day. I was so excited about the money, I didn't argue with him about it. One month, he just wanted to take some time off and told me to keep the bus at my house. And so I did for twenty-three days. That was when I realized the amount of money could be significant. He gave me sixty-nine dollars for driving twenty-three days.

That bus was fun to drive, especially when it rained. Brady Road was about three miles long and not very well kept. There were strips along that road that didn't have a proper amount of gravel. It would be slippery, and that necessitated a lot of gear changing. This road ran from the old John Kling homesite to Red Lick, right through the woods. On some of the grades, I had to change gears twice. Even though the Chevrolet had a synchronized transmission which didn't require double clutching, you know, I just had to double clutch!

That bus had five speeds on the floor, and it would have been a shame not to clutch it, pull it into neutral, let out on the clutch, race the engine, clutch it again, and pull it into the next gear. That was fun, but the passengers didn't know I was living a childhood dream. In my mind, I was back in the ole hollow and six years old again. I would think about how wonderful it would be if we lost the muffler, so that baby could have sounded loud like those old Hood Lumber Company log trucks. The bus would pull off just fine from a stop so it only needed single low. Some kids' driveways connected to the road on uphill grades. Pulling off from a dead stop on a grade meant … you are right, double low! Double low, double clutch, single low, double clutch, second, double clutch, then high.

We had our twelfth-grade senior play at school. I tried out for the senior play and got beat by one of my classmates, John Noble. I never knew why Mrs. Nevels liked him better than she liked me, and I never asked. I just assumed that I couldn't act. I do know I was very nervous having to stand in front of all the kids who were trying out for the play. We had to read some lines from the script and try to do so without sounding like we were reading. The play was set in a hospital room with two beds. It came down to John and me for the orderly part. John won, and I thought that was that. But John played baseball. He was sitting on the bench one day, and a baseball hit him in the right jaw and broke the bone. They wired his mouth shut for six weeks, so he was out of the play. Since I had been in second place for the part, Mrs. Nevels came to me to play the orderly. I was all excited, but how would I get beyond my nervousness? I just don't know how I did get over it, but I was worried right up to opening night. Mrs. Nevels came backstage while the curtain was still closed, and she said, "I have peeped out there, and you all have a packed house." I didn't want to hear that, but I didn't say anything. Some of the seniors were talking about being nervous, and that somehow calmed me down a bit.

I wanted to be stronger than somebody. My part brought me on stage first; the curtain was opened with two kids on stage, one in each bed. I was to walk on as soon as the curtain was pulled with a vase of flowers and announce to one of the patients about the flowers and who had sent them. I was amazed at how calm I was. I was speaking loudly like I was supposed to do and thought, *There is nothing to this acting.*

I had to come on stage many times during the play. One of my parts involved coming on stage in a hurry to summon the doctor from the room. I yelled, "Dr. Jackson! Dr. Jackson, come quickly! Mr. Ogletree was eating his supper and got a chicken bone stuck in his throat!" That drew a big laugh, and I found myself actually enjoying acting.

Another time, I came on stage mopping the floor. One of the patients was a grouchy old man, and I had to ask him if he knew the difference between a sheep and a mule. He grouched out, "No, I don't know the difference between a sheep and a mule."

I then said, "Well, I would hate to have you for my butcher."

That line drew another big laugh from the audience, and I was feeling like maybe I should be an actor when I got out of school. I can't remember anymore lines, but I can remember giggles from the audience when I would walk onstage. They were expecting a funny line, and I was there to oblige. When the play was over, we went out in the hall, and I received many compliments on my part. At school the next week, many people told me they liked my performance. I had surprised myself as well.

I graduated high school in May 1962 with a C average in most of my studies, but I only passed English with a D and didn't do much better in science. I did much better in math, bookkeeping, and social studies. For some strange reason, I had mixed emotions about finishing school. I wouldn't see my friends very often and might never see some of them again. I would miss my teachers very much. Life goes on, and one has to face adulthood. It was time to accept more responsibilities and time to think about making my own way in the world. It was exciting in a way, but I did not look forward to it in other ways.

28

Serving My Country

One day during school, our eleventh-grade class had a meeting with a representative from the Port Gibson National Guard Unit. He gave us a pitch about fulfilling our military obligation. The draft was alive and well in those days, and if a young man didn't join a military service, he could be drafted into the army. Several of us boys became real interested in joining, but we were not supposed to join until we were finished with high school, the reason being, immediately after joining, we were supposed to go on a six-month tour of active duty.

My two older brothers and other people I knew had joined, so I was familiar with the Guard. Several of my friends at school were asking questions and considering joining. Finally, James, Ray, Dean, Terry, Carl, and I became very interested in the pay, which was about $40.00 or so every three months. The military draft was still in force in those days, and none of us wanted to serve our country for two or three years.

We still had this problem with staying in school and meeting our active-duty training at the same time. I talked to my brothers about it, and they advised me that we all should come over to the guard armory on Tuesday night, their drill night, and talk to First Sergeant Baker. He might be able to work something out. So, we all went over on Tuesday night and observed a drill. Sergeant Baker told us he could arrange the records to allow us to finish school before active duty, but since we were not yet eighteen years old, we would have to get our parents' signatures to join.

The guard was bending the rules a little, because the Mississippi National Guard was being built up at that time, and since there wasn't a war, very few people were concerned about the draft. Many people joined the guard to avoid the draft. This reasoning has been frowned upon, and national guardsmen have taken a lot of ribbing about being draft dodgers. In my mind, the national guard is a branch of the military and requires soldiers to man the effort. If a young man or woman decides to serve his or her country in the guard, they deserve the same respect as if they served in any other branch of the military. The draft only drafted people into the army and not other branches of the military. Once a person was drafted, they had a certain number of days to join any branch of the military of their own choosing. This fact would make any one serving in any branch of the military a draft dodger, except the ones who went into the army. Joining the national guard didn't guarantee no active duty. If the regular army had been called into a war, the national guard would have been activated and placed in regular army forts and trained for combat. Some guard units were later activated during the Vietnam crisis. So joining the guard didn't necessarily mean dodging the draft. It only meant staying at home while serving your country in the military.

The Port Gibson Armory was struggling to gain full strength which was about seventy or so soldiers, but I'm not sure of the exact number. They had started with about a dozen men, which made the two weeks of summer camp very tough. A guard unit has to perform training exercises, and it is tough with just a few men, especially if you are an engineering unit and you have to put steel bailey bridges together.

My friends and I all signed up before our senior year started, and when the time came to leave for active duty, Sergeant Baker called us into the office and said, "I have some papers for you men to sign."

We, of course, asked, "What kind of papers?"

He said, "This is the army, boys. You don't ask questions; you just follow orders. Now sign right here." He said all that in a joking way and then added, "Ya'll can read 'em if you want to."

Mine read something like I had fractured the tibia in my right leg during my childhood, and it was causing pain so I would need a few more months before I could report for active duty. I never asked, but I'm sure Johnny got that off my medical records I had filled out when I joined. The broken leg was accurate, but I hadn't had any problems. One person's read that he had planned to attend summer school, but his plans had fallen through, and he would have to attend regular school to finish his senior year.

I'm sure all the powers that be in the guard knew what was going on and Johnny was probably advised by some general to handle the matter that way. We never heard any more about it, and at 10:00 AM on June 16, 1962, one month after our high school graduation, we boarded a bus in Port Gibson and headed for Fort Jackson, South Carolina.

We rode all day and all night, and in the early afternoon of June 17, we rolled into Fort Jackson. With our gear in hand, we started down a sidewalk as directed and into a company area that included several buildings. Four were sixty-man barracks, and a soldier was standing outside one of the barracks. Seeing us new civilian-clothed young recruits coming down the sidewalk made him feel like having a little fun. He pointed at the front door of a barracks and said, "You guys go in that barracks!" He was wearing a uniform, so we had no reason to doubt his instructions, and we went in there.

Toward the rear of the barracks were a few soldiers cleaning the floors, and the one supervising was a big sergeant with many yellow stripes down both sleeves of his uniform. He yelled in a very loud bass voice, "Get the hell out of here, you idiots! Don't you have sense enough to pull your shoes off when you come in somebody's house?!!" We turned around and almost ran over each other getting back out the door.

Terry Goza was grinning as he looked back going out the door. That sergeant came out on the front stoop of the barracks yelling, "You behind there, the one grinning, you think it's funny? I'll have your silly self in here shining these floors, then we'll see if you think it's funny!"

That was our "Hello, so glad you came!!" welcome to the United States Army. The soldier who had told us to go in there was smiling widely, and I'm sure he was very proud of himself for being such a comic jester. Then he instructed us to line up in the street. We were then sorted out and assigned to a barracks. During the next ten days, they cut off all our hair, gave us several vaccinations, examined our teeth, gave us a complete physical and many tests, and issued us uniforms, packs, blankets, field mess gear, and whatever else a soldier might require.

Two hundred and forty of us were then loaded into the back of trucks and shuttled off to another company area. Hello, Company E, 18th Training Regiment, 5th Training Battalion. E-18-5, for short, would be home for the eight hot and grueling weeks to follow. All company areas were alike with seven buildings including company headquarters, a supply hall, a mess hall, and four barracks.

For some reason, they told us we were a couple of days early, and the company wasn't ready to receive us just yet. The CQ sergeant (charge of quarters) got on the phone and rounded up three or four sergeants who showed up in jeans, shorts, and T-shirts. They had been home relaxing and waiting for us, the next wave of recruits, to arrive in a couple more days. So they had run down there to help the CQ get us settled, at least for the night. They didn't look like soldiers, and at this point, we didn't know they were soldiers or what was going on. They were very nice as they lined us up on the paved road that ran between the barracks and divided us into groups of sixty, the number required for each barracks. We were then sent into our respective barracks. One gentleman in his late thirties wearing jeans and a T-shirt helped us line up and draw bed linens and hung around to be sure everybody had a bunk and knew how to make one up. He taught us how to put the sheets and the blankets on, etc.

The next morning about daybreak, the lights came on in the barracks, and a loud whistle, like a referee's whistle, shrilled out. It was this same gentlemen, only he wasn't wearing jeans and a T-shirt. He was all decked out in stiff, starched, and ironed fatigues (green uniform), with yellow stripes down both sleeves, spit-shined boots, shined brass belt buckle, and blocked fatigue cap and blowing that shiny brass whistle. After a few toots on that whistle, he had traveled to the rear of the barracks. He pulled the brass whistle that hung from his shirt pocket buttonhole on a shiny brass chain out of his mouth and started yelling, "Get up! Get out of those bunks and get your clothes on and be on the street in five minutes!"

As he passed by my bunk, I saw his name tag, "Mullins," and I thought, *Well, good morning to you too, Sergeant Mullins.* He walked in a long, foot-stomping stride back to the front door then swung around the stair banister and stepped up the stairs. We could hear him repeating the same instructions as the heels of his spit-shined boots thundered down the floor overhead.

When he came back down the stairs, everybody was pulling on clothes except two buddies from Georgia. One was on the top bunk and the other on the bottom. Sergeant Mullins bounded down the stairs and rounded the corner in our direction again. Seeing these two still in bed, he picked up the pace in their direction, yelling, "Get yore lazy butts out of that bed! You ain't home now, and this ain't yore mama!"

The man on the bottom started out the other side of the bunk, and Sergeant Mullins grabbed the mattress on the top and tossed the top man, mattress and all, on top of the other soldier. "Now, get your uniforms on and make up this bunk and get your sorry a** on that street or I'll have to get mean!!" the good sergeant shouted.

He definitely had our attention, and he wouldn't have to repeat that particular scene again for the rest of our tour of duty. We all lined up on the street and answered as our names were called out from a roster. The question was then asked, "Any sick calls?" Sergeant Mullins explained, "Sick call means is anybody sick?" He continued, "If you are sick, then step out and we will send you to the doctor."

I don't remember any sick calls that morning, and the Sergeant continued, "Well, if you ain't sick, let's get a little exercise. Pull off your fatigue jackets, fold them, and lay them on the street in front of you."

After that, he yelled, "Company, atteeention! Right face! Forward march! Left turn! March! Left turn! March! Hup yore left! Hup yore left! Hup yore left! Right! left!" We were marching in four ranks which means four lines with sixty men in each line. The left turn command meant the first four men turned ninety degrees left while we continued marching. The second left turn command turned the columns ninety degrees left again, and then we were headed in the opposite direction. One might ask, "Why not just make a left face and march off in the desired direction to begin with?" A company is made up of four platoons. Each platoon shares one barracks, and the platoons are lined up with the first platoon at the left end of the formation. A company always marches with the first platoon first then the second, third, and the fourth platoon last. To maintain this order, the company must always begin marching in the direction of the first platoon. If you want to go in the opposite direction, you must make two-left turn movements in order to keep the first platoon in the front of the column.

After we were straight, he yelled, "Double-time, march." This meant start jogging, and we jogged to the exercise field. There was a platform about eight feet high there, and the sergeant jumped up on it and yelled some orders to spread us out facing him. He then proceeded to lead us in different exercises. After about thirty minutes of that, he jumped down and got us back in formation, and we double-timed for about half a mile and back to the mess hall for breakfast. He lined us up outside the mess hall where there were a set of "monkey bars," a twelve-foot-long parallel ladder lying flat on four posts. He told us to hang on to the rungs and walk the thing. We were panting and struggling for breath by now, and very few could make the distance of twelve feet on the ladder.

He let us do the best we could, and then one by one, we filed into the mess hall for breakfast. After we finished breakfast, we filed back onto the street, put our shirts on again, and marched to different training sites each day to be taught hand-to-hand combat, map reading, small-weapons fire, machine-gun fire, and hand-grenade use; we learned how to crawl under barbed wire with machine guns firing overhead along with other combat skills. The exercise was tough at first, but I don't think it was as bad as it seemed. Most of us were kids just out of high school and pretty much in shape, especially the ones who had participated in sports. After a couple of weeks, we could already tell the difference in our physical abilities.

Each night after cleaning weapons and shining our boots and brass, we had a little time for ourselves. I wrote a letter home to Ruthie every night. I told her all about what we would be doing and how much I loved and missed her. At mail call every day, I got a letter from Ruthie. That went on for the entire time that I was in the army. We marched out to most of the training sights carrying an M-1 rifle which weighed nine pounds, a web belt, canteen, cup and cover, bayonet, an extra ammo clip, and a poncho raincoat. The M-1 was a 30.06 caliber semi-automatic rifle with a clip that held six bullets and one in the barrel for a total of seven shots. The web belt was a woven cloth belt about 2.5 inches wide with black eyelets spaced all the way around on top and bottom. The eyelets in this web belt were brass, the officers sanded off the black paint and shined these outlets for appearance. Each piece of gear had hooks spaced accordingly to fit into the eyelets of the belt so they could be attached. The poncho was folded and neatly rolled and placed around the rear of the belt. The canteen was metal and fit inside a metal cup that was mounted inside a canvas cover which hooked onto the belt. The bayonet had a blade about nine inches long; the handle was designed to fit on the muzzle end of the M-1. It came with a holster that hooked onto the web belt. That was where it was carried if not on the end of the weapon. The ammo clip, a spare for the M-1, hooked onto the web belt. We wore helmet liners most of the time that were fiberboard hard hats and were designed for a steel bulletproof helmet to fit on top. We never had to wear the steel helmets unless we were going to a firing range to fire the M-1 or on some other dangerous combat training mission.

Most of the training sites were on open ground. There was no shade, and after training a couple of hours, we would drink our canteens empty. They kept a lister bag hanging around there someplace. A lister bag is made of canvas and is shaped like a round drum with about six or eight spigots around the bottom. It has a canvas cover and ropes tied to the top so it can be hung. The older sergeants would say, "Don't drink too much of that water; it will put you out." We would look over toward that bag full of ice water, and that cold canvas bag would be sweating in the hot South Carolina heat. We would comment, "Go ahead, put me out; if a cool drink of that cold ice water is going to put me out, then out is where I want to be." Finally, they would let us go over and catch a drink in our canteen cups.

Our field first was Sergeant Mullins who had been taught how to take care of soldiers in the cold as well as the heat. He told us in the beginning, on our first day, as we stood in formation, "Now, men, it gets awfully hot this time of year on Fort Jackson. You will be marching and training and getting very hot. Some people," he continued, "get too hot and pass out. When you are out on these training sites, some of these old-timers are going to be telling you not to drink too much water!" He was shouting as he turned his head back and forth in front of the large formation of young soldiers. "Don't you listen to those old soldiers; they are from the old school," Sergeant Mullins insisted. "I have had courses in physical training, so I can take care of you. And I know what has been learned in recent physics." He continued, "You listen to me and take my advice and you will fare much better than if you listen to anyone else and that includes your own mother." He was jesting a little, and the troops chuckled. That was probably one of the reasons he loved his job. He then continued, "If your body is telling you it wants a drink of water and if you are not marching and if you are not in ranks, then pull your canteen out and take a drink." Ranks were formal lines of standing or marching order. He went on, "Your body is smarter than any of these old soldiers, so pay attention to your body and drink plenty of water so you won't dehydrate. Also remember to take plenty of those little salt tablets." After stressing his point, he yelled, "Company, attention! Right face! Forward march! Hup your left! Hup your left! Hup your left, right, left!"

We marched off toward some training site at sixty steps per minute, which is normal marching cadence. That was Sergeant First Class Mullins, a lean and mean machine, tough as whet leather and meaner than a striped snake, if you didn't do as he said. He was a soldier you could be proud of, and most every young man wanted to be just like Sergeant Mullins. He would say, "Troop, if you disobey my order, I will grab you by the nape of your neck and dart straight to hell with you!" And we just believed he might do just that.

I will never forget the fifty-caliber machine gun training site. A fifty-caliber shoots a bullet that is more than an inch long and about three-eighths of an inch in diameter. This gun will shoot so fast that it will melt the barrel. The machine gun is fired in five-burst rounds. That means pressing the trigger down for one second or so, then letting up, waiting for a second or so, and pressing the trigger again. This gives the barrel time to completely empty. If the trigger is held continuously, the gun will fire a string of bullets so fast that a steady stream of ignited gun powder will be in the barrel. This will melt the barrel. The barrel doesn't go limp, but it will bend enough that the bullets will travel in curves in the air and turn end over end. This, of course, can only be seen when firing tracer bullets. I observed this in national guard training at Camp Shelby, Mississippi, later in my military career.

At the fifty site one day, we were seated in the bleachers just like at the ball game, and about fifteen or twenty fifties were lined up out front. About two hundred yards in front of the guns were fifty-five-gallon drums filled with dirt which were used for targets. The range was flat from the gun out to the drums. The drums were lined up in front of a steep hill. The hill was the impact area for the fired bullets.

A fifty-caliber machine gun sits on a tripod, and this tripod has a bar across the back two legs. There is an adjustable rod between the rear of the gun and this cross rod. In the center of the rod, there is a wheel about two inches in diameter. Turning the wheel raises the rear of the gun up and down, and since the gun is center mounted on the tripod, this causes the barrel to rise up and down. This controls the elevation of the barrel, and the rod will slide left and right on the bar so the gun can be aimed from side to side. All this action together will allow the gun to be aimed. Since we had joined the national guard a year before our tour of active duty, I already knew how to operate the M-1 and the fifty-caliber machine gun. Some say a little knowledge can be dangerous, but I wanted to display how much I already knew about the fifty.

After sitting in the bleachers, we took turns firing the weapon. The training sergeant was instructing us on how to use the weapon, and he wanted us to learn one step at a time. The first step was simply to lie down at the rear of the gun and fire a few five-round bursts. He placed a man behind each weapon and yelled, "Commence firing!" We all started shooting, and my bullets were hitting below the barrel to my front. So I reached down and turned the wheel a few turns as I fired until I hit the barrel. I could see that no one else was hitting their targets, and this made me proud. This sergeant yelled, "Cease firing!" He then ran over to where I was and dropped one knee on the ground. He leaned his head over so his mouth was about six inches from my ear and yelled loud enough for the people in the top bleaches to hear, "What are you doing, troop?"

While I was trying to ask, "What do you mean?"

He yelled, "Get your dangerous, stupid self up off that ground and away from that weapon!"

I stood up facing downrange, and he yelled, "Ateeention, about face!" I turned around facing the stands and all the remaining troops (more than two hundred people). They were all smiling. They knew I was about to be chewed out, but neither I nor they knew why. The good sergeant in a very loud voice asked me, "What were you doing to that weapon besides firing it?"

I replied very shyly, "I was turning the elevation wheel, Sergeant."

"Who told you to turn a wheel?" Before I could answer, he asked, "Where are you from, troop?"

"Mississippi, Sergeant." With that, I noticed the troops in the stands were really grinning now, especially the New York and Chicago crowd.

I could tell this was what the sergeant lived for as he paced around me and kept yelling. To his credit, though, he had two hundred and fifty kids out there and fifteen or so very dangerous weapons. He was now making the point to the whole crowd that we should do only what we were told and we should unlearn anything we thought we knew. I was his example for the day. "Nobody told you to turn a wheel. You were told to fire the weapon!" he continued with the loud talking, "If I want you to do anything with that weapon, I will tell you what and when!" He had a two-foot pointer in his hand and swung the pointed end toward the stands and said, "Get back up there and sit down before you kill somebody!" I don't know if anybody else made another mistake that day, but I certainly didn't.

On the training site that taught us how to crawl under the wire obstacles toward the enemy, the machine guns fired tracer bullets that glowed in the dark. They could be seen as we crawled along under them. They were about ten feet high, but they looked a lot closer from under them on the ground. Of course, all these different types of training were not done in one day; this was over a period of eight weeks. After the exercise was repeated a few weeks, we could jog a couple miles and hang onto those monkey bars back and forth two or three times without breathing hard. Slim guys started putting on a little weight, and the heavy ones were losing weight. We were being whipped into shape and being served proper nutritious food. I can proudly say that I made very few serious mistakes while being trained to serve my country. I think this was due to the great pride I took in the training they offered. After the basic inception and basic training that took about ten weeks altogether, we were shipped home again.

We spent two weeks back home, and then we were off to Fort Leonard Wood, a base near Columbia, Missouri, for eight weeks of basic training in engineering. We boarded the train, the *City of New Orleans*, in Brookhaven. It was to take us to Columbia. For some reason, we missed our connection in Springfield, Missouri, and had to spend the night. The next morning, we caught a cab to the train station. The cab driver asked where we were going, and we told him Fort Leonard Wood. He said, "That's only ninety miles from here." Making us a deal, he continued, "I'll take you boys up there for five dollars each." There were five of us, and we all agreed to go with him. After going by his office to get an out-of-town permit, he took us by the train station and helped us get a refund on our tickets since the overnight stay was the train's fault. We arrived at the fort much quicker than the train and somewhat more comfortably.

Engineering training at Fort Leonard Wood consisted of building different types of bridges, tying ropes, and learning how to block rope lines with different pulleys. We also learned about land mines and explosives. This training was very interesting. We built a pontoon bridge across a small river and a bailey bridge. The bailey consists of steel transoms and steel girders. The whole thing goes together with pins; however, the parts are very heavy, so the work is strenuous. One amazing thing about it is that the bridge is constructed on the riverbank on top of rollers. As the bridge is constructed, it is rolled out over the river until it reaches the other bank. A soldier never gets wet building the bridge and doesn't have to cross the river before or during construction.

My Fort Leonard Wood outfit was D company, second battalion, and first training regiment, or D-2-1. Our first day there, they asked for volunteers for firemen to fire the coal-fired boilers for heat and coal-fired water heaters for hot water. I volunteered, and we went to school one day and learned how to do the job. We served in twelve-hour shifts. There were several men, so each person only served about four times during the eight weeks training.

We firemen would keep the fires going in the different barracks, the mess hall, supply building, headquarters building, about three buildings at battalion headquarters, and two or three buildings at the regimental headquarters. There was only one fireman per shift. There was a coal bin outside the door of each boiler room. A coal shovel was in each bin. To do the job, one would put a shovel of coal in each firebox. I believe there were two, maybe three, fireboxes per barracks and only one in each of the other buildings. We made the round every ninety minutes, and it took about twenty-five minutes to make a round. The coal had to be slung into the firebox and not piled up or the fire would smother. We had to pay close attention to the steam gauges so the boilers wouldn't overheat. If a boiler reached a certain temperature, we would open a relief valve to bleed off the pressure and only put in enough coal to keep the fire burning low until the next round.

They didn't accept everybody who volunteered for the job. They checked our records, and if they liked what they found, we went to school. We had to pass a test at the end of the day to qualify. The job was simple, but it had a considerable amount of responsibility as well. At firemen's school, they showed pictures of boilers that had blown up, and it sometimes took out walls and most of the time the ceiling of the boiler room. The ceiling of the boiler room was the floor of the second floor of the barracks where soldiers were sleeping. The platoon sergeant's room was over the boiler room, so only he and one more soldier slept there. Human life was at stake, and no boiler ever blew while I was there.

I was also selected to be a truck driver while at Fort Leonard Wood, and that was a fun thing to do. All the trucks were commercially built six-cylinder GMCs. They had four-speed transmissions, which were not synchronized, and that meant performing my favorite truck-driving skill, double-clutching. The truck could not be downshifted without double-clutching, and that was a trick when trying to get over hills. If the driver pulled it out of gear and didn't properly race the motor and clutch, it would not go back in gear and would start rolling backward; then brakes would have to be applied. The truck could then be pulled off from a standstill, but it was embarrassing for the driver to let the truck stall. Truck-driving school was only one day long. They taught us, then gave us a driving test, and if we passed the test, we got our licenses and were out of there. Double-clutching was learned from experience, and all that playing with the transmission during my school bus driving days paid off. There were very few of us who caught on easily, and the others got laughed at very much. I had an edge on most of the class because I had experience from hauling hay on Mr. Goza's truck, in addition to driving the school bus.

We did very little marching at Fort Leonard Wood. The training sites were separated by great distances because of the explosives and the need for river sites suitable for bridge building. For that reason, troops were trucked to the sites. Each truck hauled thirty men, so there were eight trucks in each convoy for each company. The sergeants rode on the passenger side of the cab. We would go to the motor pool, draw our truck, convoy back to the company area where we would load on the troops, then head to a training site.

After eight weeks on Fort Leonard Wood, I received orders to ship out to Fort Sheridan, Illinois, just south of Chicago. I stayed there only a few days. We national guard troops had only four weeks left on our six-month tour of duty, and there wasn't much left that we could learn in four weeks. We all were dispersed to different areas around the country for flunky details around Thanksgiving that year. I was shipped out to a post-engineering group in Milwaukee, Wisconsin. This was not actually a fort or training site. It was located within the city of Milwaukee. There were strategic missile ranges north of the city since that was the north border of the country.

This group of post engineers was commanded by a chief warrant officer. The rank of warrant officer is a promotion from a noncommissioned officer rank. Simply put, one must become an officer at a young age. If he doesn't choose to be an officer or can't make the grades to be an officer, he is promoted from private to corporal then to sergeant. There are six ranks of sergeant, and if at anytime he wants to become an officer, he must qualify for warrant officer. There are four ranks of warrant officer. All the warrant officers I have ever met in the army were gentle people and talked to a private soldier on a private's level. I believe this was due to the fact that the officer had come up through the lower ranks. In other words, he felt that he was one of us. A warrant officer is addressed as mister. All four ranks are misters.

Three troops that I knew, along with myself, were shipped to Milwaukee and ordered to report to Warrant Officer Smith. We four lined up in front of his desk, and he said, "Now just relax, gentlemen."

Gentlemen, I hadn't been called that since entering the army. Lighting a cigar, he continued, "You have been harassed enough during your first few months in the army." I remember this like it was yesterday, because

I was waiting for the other shoe to drop. He would start shouting any minute. I had witnessed that scene many times since my induction into the army. I didn't know at the time that officer wasn't going to order us around as the training sergeants had done.

He never raised his voice. He just got out of his chair, and as he walked around from behind his desk, he said, "You fellows only have a few more weeks, and I want you to enjoy the rest of your hitch." *Hitch* is army talk for tour of duty. He smiled as he asked, "Where are you boys from?"

I replied, "Mississippi, sir."

Willie Everett, my buddy from Laurel, Mississippi, said, "Me too, sir."

One guy was from Georgia, and I think the other one was from a state up north. After we told him where we were from, the officer directed his attention back toward the guy from Georgia, Everett, and me. He said, "I don't reckon you boys have ever been this far north, have you?"

We all smiled and said, "No, sir."

He said, "Well, this wintertime is going to take some getting used to." It was the end of November and extremely cold. The temperature was dropping below zero at night and only rising to twenty-something in the daytime. It turned out to be an unusually cold winter, even for that far north.

Mr. Smith told us we didn't have to be concerned about shining our boots or brass. He also said we didn't have to worry about being in uniform and that saluting wouldn't be necessary around there. He told us not to worry about starched clothes. He said, "Just wash, dry, and wear your clothes." There were washers and dryers on site.

After our little talk, he turned us over to one of his sergeants who showed us to our barracks. On the way, the sergeant told us where we were and gave us a little history about the place. The campus was actually an old military prison left over from WWII. Alcatraz prison in San Francisco Bay, California, was going to be closed in a couple of years. This prison in Milwaukee was being renovated to house some of those prisoners. Our barracks consisted of a small brick building that had been a guard's quarters when the prison was in operation. It was a well-built place and had no air leaks. There were steam radiators for heat. During cold, below-zero nights, we slept with just a sheet for bed covers. There were ten soldiers in our barracks, and all were privates, just running out the final days of our tours. We four were replacements for four that had been shipped home the week before. Every week, some would leave, and some more would come in as replacements.

The old prison kitchen wasn't open, so we dined about a mile down the road at a radar site. They had a small fancy mess hall. It had shiny tile floors and tablecloths. Each table seated four and had a little flower vase in the middle, just like in a restaurant. There was a milk machine and coffeepot in the dining area, and the rule was "all you care to drink." I wasn't too excited about the coffee, but I was ecstatic about the milk. We had not been allowed the privilege of enjoying all the milk we could drink since I left home. Being that I was a country boy, milk had been a mainstay all my life, and I had missed it very much. It was strange to us, dining with sergeants and officers in mixed seating all around in the same room. To these soldiers, running the radar site was just a job, sort of like civilian work.

There was a recreation room on the site, and we all watched television or played pool, Ping-Pong, or cards, and so on during off hours. Our jobs were helping the post engineers every day. *Post engineer* is the military name for civilian maintenance personnel governed under military command. There were several radar and missile sites within a short drive from the area, and we would haul asphalt and patch potholes in different roads on the sites. Sometimes, we installed culverts and things like that.

In front of the administration building was a very large lawn, maybe two acres in size, with large maple trees all around. I remember thinking how beautiful it was as we drove into it the first time. The leaves on the trees were showing an array of fall colors, and the many orange and brown leaves scattered over the lawn made a beautiful sight. Little did I know those leaves would have to be raked and hauled off, and it would be our job to take care of that task.

We all lined up, along with the post engineers, and moving our leaf rakes in unison, we raked the leaves in a neat wind row across the lawn. The wind was always blowing across Lake Michigan, bringing down maple leaves as we raked. We raked the leaves onto a tarp then loaded them onto a truck to be hauled off someplace and dumped. It took just about all day, and when we finished, the lawn was covered with just about as many leaves as when we started. After two or three days, we would rake and haul leaves again. We continued this until the maple limbs were bare.

All the steam radiators in the old prison had to be scraped and repainted with silver paint. There must have been several thousand window panes in that building and very many of those were cracked or broken out completely. One morning, I was assigned to an engineer and we went over to the supply building to check out a stack of windowpanes and cans of putty. He and I started at one window, and he said, "I'm going to finish knocking out these broken panes, and you start replacing them." As he reached into his toolbox for a hammer, he asked, "You ever replaced a windowpane before?"

I kind of cutely responded, "No, but I think I can learn pretty quick."

He must have been waiting for that. "Just look at one that's not broke and make yours look the same," he said smiling and looking at me kind of sideways.

Replacing windowpanes was very boring in the beginning, but then I remembered a lesson I had learned about life from my father. We get out of life what we put into it. Any chore can be fun and rewarding if you respect the task and put pride into your work. If you are a windowpane-replacer, then strive to be the very best windowpane-replacer there has ever been. Those are his words, except the windowpane part. With that in mind, I knew I had to fill the remaining days of my hitch doing something, so I decided replacing windowpanes wasn't a bad job. I was grateful to be away from the blowing wind and cold. I placed the pane in the steel frame, rolled the putty into long snakelike rolls and placed it around the pane. Then ever so skillfully, I smoothed the putty with my trusty putty knife. I went over and over the edges until each one looked exactly the same. The engineer told me at one point, "Smith, you should put your signature on those panes." We had a little chuckle, and I realized he didn't care how much time I wasted. He was working on a salary, and all he really had to do was keep the two of us busy until quitting time. That's the government way, the tax payers have plenty of money.

When I reported the next morning, this engineer told his boss,

"When you walk through the prison, you can spot every pane Smith installed."

The boss asked, "Is Smith doing sloppy work?"

"Why, no indeed," he said with a grin. "Smith makes an art out of replacing each pane."

They both laughed, and later that day, I was installing a pane when the boss slipped up behind me to watch. When I realized he was there, I turned and he just about flipped out laughing. "Smith, we want you to do a good job, but there is just going to be prisoners living here, not the Milwaukee socialites."

I said, "Oh, don't pay me any attention. I just don't have anything better to do."

After three days or so of changing windowpanes, we did something else for awhile. They were good about giving us different jobs and that kept us from getting too bored.

Finally, the day came for us to ship back to Fort Sheridan, so Everett and I were off. Our ride was in a pickup truck with a carrier. A carrier is a military term for someone who delivers things around to different offices. This carrier drove down to Fort Sheridan every day to deliver paperwork and small packages and returned with the same type of cargo. He was a staff sergeant, and it was his job to make the round-trip from Milwaukee to Fort Sheridan five days every week. It took him almost a full day to complete one round trip. He told us that he enjoyed it, but could transfer off the job anytime he wanted.

We processed out of Fort Sheridan on December 14, 1962. With our separation pay and discharge papers in our pockets, we caught a cab to the train station in downtown Chicago, Illinois. There, we boarded the mighty *City of New Orleans* passenger train and headed back to the warm Southland. As the train pulled out of the station, Everett and I sang a couple lines of "Dixie." Departing time was 7:30 AM, and I arrived in downtown Brookhaven, Mississippi, that night at 10:30 PM.

Everett had gotten off at the Jackson, Mississippi, station. We said our good-byes, and as the train pulled out, I waved to him through the window. He was a small man in stature, about five feet eight inches tall. We had met at Fort Jackson, South Carolina, in June of 1962 and became the best of friends. We had bid each other good-bye when we got off the bus in Jackson after our Fort Jackson days were over. When I got to Fort Leonard Wood, I was surprised to see Everett once again. We must have asked each other a dozen times, "Can you believe we are still serving together?" When we received our orders to ship out of Fort Leonard Wood, they were identical. We were both leaving for Fort Sheridan, Illinois. From there, we got identical orders again to go to Milwaukee, Wisconsin. It's amazing how that worked out.

Everett had joined the guard just out of high school and was serving his six months active duty the same as me. One Sunday in Milwaukee when it was snowing pretty heavily, we put on our swimming suits and sunglasses. We stood outside in our bare feet and had one of our buddies take our picture. I wish I still had that picture, but it got away from me somehow.

As the train pulled away from the Jackson, Mississippi, depot, I was looking out the window of the train car with my hand stretched out on the glass. Everett was standing there in his uniform with his luggage in one hand and waving his army cap high in the air over his head with the other hand. He waved the cap back and forth as he slowly disappeared from sight. That would be the last time I would ever see my dear friend, I thought. I tried looking him up in the Laurel, Mississippi, phone book a couple of different times when I would be in that area, but I never located him. Several years had passed, and my thoughts were that maybe he had moved from Laurel; none of the Everetts listed knew a Willie or Willis. Some would ask me to describe him, and I would say, "Oh, he is just a nice little guy who likes to laugh." One day in 2007, I was on the Internet and went to whitepages.com and found my dear friend's telephone number. I searched all the Everetts. I found one that was listed Tommy W. and decided to try that one. It was him; he had dropped the Willis and started going by Tommy. That had been the problem. We had a very long phone chat and swapped e-mail addresses. We sent each other pictures of ourselves, wives, children, and grandchildren. Of course, we couldn't believe forty-five years had passed. The days go by sort of slow, but the years, they fly by.

Once back at the Port Gibson Armory, we started learning important things—for instance, how to play poker without losing a card in the wind when riding in the back of an Army truck with the tarpaulin sides rolled up. It takes skill and requires attentiveness to do this. Place a folding card table in the center of the truck bed. Two players sit on the regular passenger benches on each side of the truck. One player sits on a metal folding chair riding backward, and the sixth player sits in a metal folding chair riding forwards. Each player keeps his money in his helmet liner while holding it between his legs. Each player holds his cards down with one hand while they are dealt. Try to have plenty of coins so the money won't blow around, and if you only have a bill, get it changed to coins. The bills will ride very well if they are kept below the laced headbands of the helmet liner.

Very few people believe that after many miles, over several years, we never lost a dollar bill or a card out the back of a truck. You see, as wind blows around a truck cab and into the back of a deuce-and-a-half (two-and-a-half-ton, ten-wheeled army truck), the wind turns downward toward the bed. The air then flows up and over the tailgate. If a card or paper bill blows off the card table, it will take a downward turn toward the bed before it blows up and out of the truck. The person sitting in the folding chair at the rear side of the table must turn quickly and dive on top of the card or bill.

Once per year in the springtime, a guardsman is required to qualify with a rifle and officers are required to qualify with their handguns. We would convoy to Camp Shelby, just south of Hattiesburg, Mississippi, or Camp McCain near Grenada, Mississippi. They had pull-up-type bull's-eye targets at, I think, two hundred yards. I always shot an M-1 rifle. When an M-1 is fired, it sounds very loud and kicks like a mule. It had open peep sights, and to hit a ten-inch-diameter bull's-eye at two hundred yards, it had to be held very steady.

An M-1 rifle is very accurate if the shooter holds it very tightly and squeezes the trigger very gently. The weapon has to fire unexpectedly, so the shooter doesn't flinch. If he flinches while pulling the trigger, he will pull the rifle off target. If it's done right, it will hit the bull's-eye seven out of seven shots. I shot that thing for eight years, plus all the shooting on active duty. I hit seven out of seven, more than once, but not often. The line judge had a telephone from the firing line to the target pits. On one occasion, I had hit five out of seven and six out of seven. When the line judge noticed how well I was shooting, he came down the line and lay down beside me. We were shooting from the prone (flat down on our stomach) position for that round of shooting.

He was a corporal, and I was a staff sergeant. He said, "Sergeant, I believe you could get seven out of seven today." He continued, "I'm going to make sure they are marking the target right and also find out exactly where you are hitting."

To further explain just what he was talking about, after a seven-round burst of shots, the pit man pulled the target down and pasted a patch over each bullet hole. He then raised the target back up and raised a round, white metal tag over the bull's-eye for each bullet hole in the bull's-eye. He then turned the tag over, and it was red on the other side. He marked the other places on the target where it was hit. If a person missed the target completely, a red flag was waved across the target for each bullet hole he didn't see out of seven possible holes.

When the tag comes up six times and he shows the shooter a red tag, the red might be just outside the bull's-eye. All shots might be just in one edge of the bull's-eye on the right, left, top, or bottom. If you know exactly where on the bull's-eye you hit, say a little low, you can aim just a fraction higher and get all seven shots in the bull's-eye. Windage matters also. If the wind is blowing left or right, the shooter has to move his sight against the wind, so the wind won't blow the bullet off target. That corporal wanted to know exactly where the bullet was hitting, so I could allow for windage. He yelled into the telephone, something like, "We want to pay close attention to number 37 …" (Or whatever the number of target I was shooting that day) "… let us know exactly where this sergeant is hitting. We think he can get seven out of seven today." Everybody wanted to see that done, because they all knew it was very rare to hold that rifle dead on for seven straight loud and kicking shots.

The pit answered, "Number 37 is all over the bull's-eye." That meant it wasn't the rifle off target, it was me. The extra attention built my morale, and I was having an exceptional day, so I held that weapon ever so easy.

I shot one time, and the corporal said, "Wait a minute, Sarge." He yelled into the phone, "Mark 37!"

The pit replied, "Thirty-seven's high and to the left," or something like that. I made the second shot, and they pulled and marked that shot. I had hit the bull, but I hadn't hit near the same spot, so I knew I wasn't holding the weapon steady. Somebody else needed to send a phone message, so while the corporal was busy doing that, I stood up and stretched.

After I lay back down, I said, "Corporal, tell 'em not to mark after each shot. I'm going to fire the last five."

He asked, "You sure?"

I said, "I'm all over the bull, so the rifle must be accurate."

He yelled into the phone, "Thirty-seven is going to shoot all five rounds. Don't mark until we tell you."

I shot the last five, and somehow, I just knew I had hit the bull's-eye with all five.

After the last shot, the corporal yelled into the phone, "Mark 37!" They pulled the target down, and the corporal asked me, "Do you have them?"

I said, "I have got 'em."

The target slowly rose back up, and they marked seven white tags. The corporal yelled at the tower behind the firing line where the big brass (officers) were, "Hey, Captain, take a look at 37!"

The captain yelled back, "Mark it!" The corporal yelled into the phone, "Mark 37 again. The big brass is looking!"

Again, the white marker came up seven times. The captain yelled, "Send that man up here. I want to shake his hand." After I was on the platform beside the captain, he yelled, "Give me your attention." After a few seconds, all heads were turned in his direction, and he continued, "I just want you all to see a man that can hit seven out of seven!"

I was proud of myself that day. It took things like that to keep the army interesting. I had seen it done quite a few times during my career and was very glad I was fortunate enough to do it before my time was up. I fired like that more than once, but never got that much attention again. All that depended on what officer was running the show. Sometimes they would give some kind of prize for a seven-out-of-seven shooter. Sometimes, they would pay no attention to it.

I served eight years for my country in the Mississippi National Guard and rose to the rank of staff sergeant. I enjoyed those years very much, and I have many good memories from those days. But as things usually have a tendency to do, the guard got boring, so after my eighth year, I made a decision not to sign up for another year. It wasn't an easy decision. I was up for a promotion to sergeant first class, and the guard wanted to keep us old heads in.

There had been an influx of soldiers into the guard, because of the draft for the Vietnam War. The guard had a lot of new troops, and they needed experienced sergeants to head up the training. I thought very seriously about staying in since my country needed me, but my company commander advised me to get out for a few months. He said I could come back any time I wanted. He thought I would feel better about serving after a leave of absence. However, I never did rejoin, but several people I know did get back in and served twenty years and some over thirty years.

29

Higher Education

Early 1963 was a time for me to turn another page of my life. I had graduated high school and completed my active duty in the national guard, a duty that had me feeling proud and patriotic, because I was serving my country.

Everything that I had done since my birth, in March of 1944, had brought me to this major fork in life. It was time to go to college or get a real job. My friend James Richardson and I decided to get a real job. We traveled from Natchez to Vicksburg and filled out applications in many businesses along Highway 61. Nobody wanted to hire us, and they all would say the same thing, "Why don't you boys go to college?"

We replied to this question more than once, "We are tired of school." We stopped short of the rest of our thoughts: We were tired of classes, tired of tests, and most of all, we were tired of not having any money.

James landed a job with Mississippi Plastics in Port Gibson, and I was hired by the Westinghouse Corporation in Vicksburg. My pay was one dollar and forty-nine and a half cents per hour. I never was able to figure out why one half of a cent less than one dollar and fifty cents per hour made a difference. I don't know, and I never did ask. I was so excited that I had a job. I rushed home to tell my folks and could hardly wait to report for work the following Monday.

When I walked into the plant's office, they first showed me how to punch my time card. Then they gave me directions to a doctor's office in Vicksburg, where I would have a physical examination. After returning about ten o'clock that morning, I was led out into the manufacturing area and introduced to my boss. My boss then led me over to a testing station and trained me to do a job. This training took less than three minutes, then my boss said, "If you have any problems, I'll be right over there," pointing to a desk where I had just met him.

This particular area of the plant manufactured fluorescent lighting ballasts. This ballast was an electric device about one by two by eight inches. It had about four wires hanging out each end. To the right of my test station was a wire basket on rollers, filled with these ballasts. The station was positioned about twenty feet from the end of the assembly line where the ballasts were manufactured. They were filling the baskets with the ballasts as they came off the line and rolling the baskets over to my test station. There were three lines and three test stations.

When my boss and I walked up to the test station, he mumbled something to the person running the station, probably assigning him another job. Anyway, the tester walked off, and my boss took over. My boss said, pointing to the basket, "These are ballasts. Pick one up, place it on this table, and place the green wire in the green hole and the red wire in the red hole, etc., until all the wires are in the holes." He was referring to a metal socket mounted on the front of the station. Continuing, he said, as he placed the wires in the perspective holes, "Now that all the wires are in the holes, it is time to test this ballast." Having said that, he reached over and flipped a light switch. The fluorescent light fixture in front of the station lit. He instructed further, "Since the light came on, this is a good ballast; place it in this basket," he said as he placed the ballast in the basket to his left. "If the light doesn't come on, place the defective ballast over here." He was pointing to a basket behind the station.

I started testing ballasts, and finally, I was down to about three or four ballasts left in the basket and without any instructions from me, a stranger rolled up another basket that was level full with ballasts. He scooped the remaining ballasts out of my basket and placed them on top of the newly arrived ballasts, and rolling the empty basket off, he said, "There is another one for you. How do you like this job?"

"Just fine." I lied. I stood there wondering, *Why can't we sit down?*

I could do this job while sitting on a stool? I was also thinking, *Do I want to do this job from any position, including lying down?*

Lunchtime came, and suddenly the plant got quieter as the motors running the assembly lines were turned off. The man running the test station on my right came over and said, "Let's get some lunch. My name is …" (whatever it was; it has been a long time). He said this as he reached out his hand for a shake.

"James Smith," I replied as I shook his hand.

"How long have you been at this?" I wanted to know.

"Just about three years," he said. While we were eating, I asked him if he had ever had any other jobs in the plant. "Yeah, but I like this one the best. It doesn't have any pressure, and it's easy," he answered.

No pressure and it's easy, I thought, neither of which interested me nearly as much as "interesting and challenging."

That afternoon, as I performed that think-less job, I had to make some serious decisions. Will this job or similar jobs be my life if I don't get an education or at least learn a skill? The answer in my mind was a resounding yes, of course. I had been told that more times than I could count. I remembered a few words of wisdom from my dad, "You only get out of life what you put into it." That analogy most definitely applied here. I didn't want to study, put up with having no money, take tests, and all the rest that is involved with college. By the same token, I hated this job more than all that. I had to put some effort into my life to learn how to do something or this and similar jobs were going to be my career.

I decided to give the job the rest of that year since the last semester of college had already started. I would save my money and enter Hinds Junior College in the fall (Hinds Community College now). Three thirty that afternoon finally came, and someone walked up beside me and asked, "You are new, aren't you?"

"Yes, just started today," I replied.

He said, "Well, I'm the next shift. I'll take over here, and I'll see you later." I lined up at the time clock, picked up my time card, punched out, and placed the card in the out slot. That would be the last time I would touch that card, although I hadn't planned that at the time. My plans changed as this new adventure played out. I thought I was coming back to work there until fall.

I got into my car and drove toward Vicksburg. Having a job meant driving back and forth every day while living at home or finding a place to live in Vicksburg. My friend, Pete Foster, lived in a boardinghouse, so I went by to visit him and asked for information on finding a place to live. Pete said, "There is a vacant room here for $15.00 per week."

I pulled out a pencil and found a piece of paper. I said, "Now let's see." I wrote down $1.495 per hour times forty that came to $59.80. "How much do you think they'll take out of my check for taxes, etc., Pete?" I asked.

"Oh, about $10.00 probably, unless you join the union down there; that'll be another dollar or two," he replied.

I continued figuring $59.00 less, say, $11.00. That was $48.00 less $15.00 room and board; that left $33.00. That totaled $132.00 per month leftover. Now I couldn't continue using my parents' car. I'd need say $50.00 per month for a car note; that left $82.00 per month leftover, thus far.

Pete was keeping up with my figures and my mumbling and added, "You need to figure gas for the car and oil changes."

"Yeah, let's see, another six bucks for that. I will have about $15.00 per week left."

He grinned as he said, "And now that you're workin', Ruthie is gonna expect more. Better just throw in the rest of that change to entertain her." Then he let out a big laugh.

I politely laughed along, but I was realizing that I was in for a very cramped lifestyle, so I didn't feel like laughing at all. I said, "I don't think I can get by on fifty bucks a week."

Pete always did like to kid around. He had noticed my seriousness and probably thought he could lighten me up a little. He said, "Well, James, if you don't think you can live on that, you should just ask your boss for a raise when you go in tomorrow." He laughed again, and I forced a smile to let him know I appreciated his humor. Fifteen dollars was worth much more of course then than now, but I had just begun to deduct. There were many more incidentals that I hadn't deducted yet. I knew there were many people living on that kind of money, some with families even, but I wasn't willing to settle for it.

I bid Pete farewell and drove on down to Harriston, Mississippi, to visit my friend James Richardson that evening. I told him about my job and that I wasn't pleased with my earnings. He said he had the same problem at the plastic plant, but he thought it would do until something better came along. I asked him why he thought something better would come along if we had only a high school education and no skills.

His mother said, "I have been trying to get you two to go to Hinds, and that's what ya'll ought to do."

I said, "Well, I have made my mind up, and I'm going this fall, if I can figure out how I will pay for it."

She said, "I checked into that before James graduated from school, and they told me you can start vocational school any Monday."

I said, "I'm going to talk to my parents and see if we can work something out."

James said, "I guess if you're gonna hit those books again, I will too."

That night, my parents said they would help all they could, if I would come home on weekends to help Daddy with the plumbing business. He would hold any work he needed help with for Saturday; of course, there would be no Sunday work. Then I had to work with him all summer long. I agreed. I wanted to be home on weekends to see Ruthie anyway, so this would work out great.

"What are you gonna study?" Daddy asked.

"I don't know, I never can decide," I responded.

The next morning, I called my boss at Westinghouse and quit. He asked, "What is the problem?"

I said, "I want to go to college and learn a skill."

He said, "Well, I'm proud for you my boy. I think that is the right thing to do, but understand, Westinghouse will probably never hire you again."

I told him, "I can appreciate their feelings, and for what it's worth, please tell the plant manager thanks for hiring me."

After a little more conversation about my check and other details, we hung up the phone. I actually needed that $11.96 real bad. I thought I might just carry the check up to Hinds, frame it, and hang it on my dorm room wall as a reminder of why I was there. I then called Mrs. Richardson and asked her about getting into Hinds. She told me that

James wanted to give Mississippi Plastics a two-week notice and we would go to Hinds after that.

The three of us arrived at the campus of Hinds Junior College in Raymond, Mississippi, around the first week of February 1963. We talked to the head of the vocational department, Mr. Phil Gibbs. He asked, "What do you boys want to study?"

James and I kind of glanced at each other and told the gentlemen we didn't know. He was leaning over toward us with his elbows on his desk and his two hands meshed together, smiling very politely. While pondering our answer, he didn't move, but his smile just faded. He responded, "You don't know?"

I said, "I just can't decide what to do with the rest of my life."

Mr. Gibbs sat back in his chair and started naming subjects. "We have mechanics, body and fender [car repair], business machine maintenance, air conditioning and refrigeration, machinist, electronics …"

"Electronics," I interrupted. "I think I would like Electronics."

James said, "That's gonna be pretty hard, Jim."

Mr. Gibbs said, "That's the most beautiful thing about vocational training: if you get tired or bogged down, you can change your major any Monday." He proudly smiled as he stated, "That also makes my job easier." He asked if we knew anything about electronics. I told him that I had looked inside a radio and even looked inside a television set as the repairman worked on it. He smiled and stated, "Well, at least you know what you are getting into; that's something." He continued, "All that stuff will be simple once you learn it." I had heard that before, but it was a lot to learn.

We walked outside. James was worried about learning electronics and how much studying it was going to require. I said, "James, just keep thinking about that dollar and something per hour we'll have to settle for if we don't learn it."

He agreed with an, "Oh, well, we'll give a try for the first week, I guess."

Mr. Gibbs got us a dorm room then introduced us to Mr. Hershal M. Cook, our electronics professor. Later on during our first day in class, Mr. Cook introduced us two new students to the rest of his class and gave us the most important advice that he could ever give. "Boys, in this class, you have to pay attention. Electronics is like building a house: you drive nails into one board at a time." We later understood that you must first understand the atom before you can understand the electron or the proton. You must understand the ohm (that is a unit of resistance), before you can understand resistors. If you don't understand the magnetic field caused by alternating current, you will not understand the workings and reactions of a transformer. Capacitors charge and discharge rapidly, and that must be understood before you can grasp the electronic filtering effect that capacitors have in an electronic circuit. I studied ahead in the campus library, so when Mr. Cook went over the material the following day, I would have my questions prepared. The library was quiet and away from all the distractions around the dormitory.

College was fun. We were all grown up and could do anything without our parents' permission. One of the things we did was shoot pool in Jackson. The pool room was Tall Man Pool. The room must have been named after the owner, because he was tall. I don't remember his height; it was not quite seven feet, but almost. I had a couple of friends with cars. We picked up Coke bottles alongside the highway and turned them in for two and three cents each. Soft drinks came in glass bottles; the bottles could be returned for a two-cent deposit. That later became three cents per bottle. That kept us in gas money and pool money. Gas cost thirty-two cents or thirty-four cents per gallon. It only took eleven or twelve bottles to buy a gallon of gas. I got to be a rather good snooker player and was also good at nine ball. We never bet any money, but I think I might have been good enough to win a little.

There was a nice lake at Hinds College. We would go out there to suntan and ride in boats, if we could find somebody who would let us ride with them. We were at the lake one day and a car salesman was out there with the college president. He was trying to sell the president a car that was also a boat. It was a convertible the size of a Volkswagen. It had two propellers on the rear and was steered by turning the front wheels. The front wheels acted as rudders. It didn't go very fast on the water, but it was okay for fishing. The idea was to load your fishing gear, and when you got to the water's edge, you didn't have to launch a boat or move the gear from the car to the boat. You didn't even need a boat in the first place. The fisherman just drove out in the water and went fishing, then drove out and went on home. He gave us all a ride. If we had had the money, we would have definitely bought one. That would have been fun, riding around in a car, then going fishing in the same car. Those cars aren't around anymore; they just didn't catch on, I guess.

One of my dear friends at Hinds was a boy from Macon, Mississippi, named John Tennet. He had a white 1957 Oldsmobile. I didn't have a car my first year at Hinds, and I rode around with John and a couple more buddies. John would take us all to Jackson for a meal, movie, pool, or whatever, and we didn't have to chip in for gasoline. The only thing was John liked to keep that white Olds looking good all the time. He had gas money, but he made us wash and wax his Olds as a payback for the trips to Jackson. The campus body and fender school building had a place, hoses and all, for washing cars. Usually three or four of us guys could do a pretty good job in a short time, washing and waxing John's Olds. We were proud of the job we could do on the white sidewall tires and shining the chrome. We did a good job cleaning the inside as well.

There was a drive-in restaurant in Jackson back then, like Sonic now. They served fried dill pickles. We would bring our own beer, because it was cheaper in the C-stores. We would stand around outside our cars eating fried dill pickles and drinking beer. That was the very first time I had ever heard of fried dill pickles. They battered each slice of dill pickle and deep fried it, like French fries. I don't know if they were very good or if it was just something new. I haven't noticed them in years, but it was worth a trip to Jackson in those days.

James left Hinds after one semester and landed a very good-paying and interesting job with Michael Baker Corporation that summer and didn't come back to Hinds. I came back that fall and stayed the full year.

I finally got the privilege of using a car at college, quite by accident. I had been hitchhiking a ride home on Friday evenings and came back to school with friends who went to school there. I didn't catch a ride home with them, because they could not leave until late in the evening after school. I got out at two o'clock on Fridays and was anxious to get home to Ruthie. That occurred every weekend. I caught some interesting rides. Two black ladies picked me up one day, and I thought that was strange considering the race relations in the 1960s. They told me that if one of their sons was hitchhiking, they would like for someone to give him a ride. I laughed and told them I certainly would, if I knew he was their son; they thought that was amusing. Then they told me the real reason for picking me up. They weren't sure they could change a flat tire. They had prayed that they wouldn't have a flat, and since they were going all the way to Fayette, they wanted to have somebody with them to change a tire. They thought I was the answer to their prayers. I hoped I wasn't, because I could do without changing a tire. We made it without a flat tire and had some real good conversations.

One Friday evening, I was picked up by a convoy from McCullough Tool Company. They tested oil wells for oil companies. They had two large trucks and a pickup following them. The pickup stopped and picked me up. They were going to Natchez and had to go through Fayette. I always hitched to Fayette and caught a ride from there to the house. The convoy stopped at a beer joint along Highway 18, and I sat at the bar but didn't order anything. The guy in the pickup asked me if I wanted a beer. While riding in his pickup, I had told him all about me going to college and that my weekly budget was bare. He said, "Aw, man, I'll buy you a beer." We sat there and drank two or three. They were all going home for the weekend, and he had picked me up, so he would have some company for the ride. They moved only about fifty miles per hour on that two-lane road.

One Friday afternoon, November 22, 1963, I was squatting beside Highway 18 just south of Raymond, Mississippi, and the Utica High School principal picked me up. He was listening to the news on his radio. He told me the special news on the radio was telling us that President John Kennedy had been shot in Dallas, Texas. I'll always remember where I was and what I was doing that day. I got out in Utica and wished I had turned down that ride. If I was stranded in Raymond, I could walk back to school. I had turned down rides before, because I didn't want to be stranded on the highway. For some reason, I hadn't been thinking clearly and had accepted a ride to Utica. At least I had been dropped off outside a truck stop. Maybe I could flag a ride with a trucker. There was bound to be one going to Fayette.

No sooner than I was out of the car, I saw the mail truck coming. I had heard people talk about riding to places on mail trucks. I didn't expect him to stop, but it didn't take much effort for me to stick my thumb up. I did, and he stopped. That was one of the worst rides I ever flagged. He was going to Fayette all right, but he had to stop at all the little post offices along the way. There were post offices in Carlisle, Carpenter, Hermanville, Port Gibson, Pattison, Lorman, and then Fayette. We had to drive seven miles out to Pattison and back to Highway 61. Fortunately, he didn't tarry long at each stop. He had to open the back of the truck, get a bag of mail, enter the post office through the back door, set the bag of mail down, and pick up the outgoing mailbag. That only took a few minutes. That old guy carried on good conversations. He had been in the war in Korea and told me all about that. I say he was an old guy; he must have been in his early thirties. He was old to this teenager. He told me about all the auto accidents he had experienced along his route. He traveled from Jackson to Natchez and back six days each week. He delivered newspapers along the way. He had quite a few newspapers in the cab and replenished them from the back when he stopped at post offices.

One weekend, there was a movie that some friends wanted to go see, and they asked me to go along. I decided I could hitchhike home Saturday morning and never gave a thought to calling home and telling my parents. About eleven o'clock that night, I thought about calling home. My parents were sick with worry. They just knew I had been harmed out on that highway hitchhiking. They never liked the idea in the first place, but somehow allowed it. I know Mama thought the Lord would take care of me, but she had decided the Lord might have let her down. They had stayed by the phone at home while my brothers went out looking for me. We didn't have a phone in the dorm room, and not many people were around to answer the pay phone outside on Friday night. It had to be answered by someone on that end of the dorm. They were the only ones who could hear it ring. Evidently, no one was there on that end. Mama had rung it several times without an answer.

J. P. and William had driven to Port Gibson to the police station. The police radioed the highway patrol, and they radioed a car near the campus. That patrolman came to the dorm and knocked on doors until he got someone to tell him where my room was. He came to my room telling me that my family was worried and out looking for me. I apologized and told him I had forgotten to call home, but I had already called awhile ago. He radioed the news to the Port Gibson Police Station that I had never left the campus. I went on to bed, and later in the night, my brothers came knocking on my door. They had called Mama, and she told them to come up there and bring me home. She didn't want me hitchhiking anymore. Being Mama, she thought the Lord was giving her a message or something. The old Plymouth was gone; it was not safe enough to drive that lonely highway all the way to Hinds anyway. They had Daddy's pick-up to ride around in, and I could use the family car to go to school. That all had worked out real well for me; however, I wasn't proud of myself for the reasons it had worked out. I got over my ill feelings for putting my family through all that misery. I had my own car now and could go and come as I pleased. The only thing lacking was money for gas. I had a real tight budget for that. That ole '57 Pontiac barely got fifteen miles per gallon even when I drove it easily.

Sometime around February or March 1964, Mr. Cook had a talk with me. He said, "James, you have applied yourself and you have learned electronics well." He continued, "There is a lot of field to cover, but you will do well from here on out; everything from here on will be familiar to you, so it will be easier to understand what you are trying to learn. Therefore, learning and understanding will be easier," he continued.

I was thinking, *Hurry up and get to it, Mr. Cook. You have my attention.*

He said, "Western Electric has us teachers searching for students with the potential they desire to hire and train to install and service their telephone gear." Mr. Cook continued to explain, "Now, Western will only hire people with a first-class communications license. The Federal Communications Commission will only license people in a certain order; that is, you have to get a third-class license, then a second-class, and finally a first-class license."

I asked the obvious question, "How long does it take to acquire all these licenses?"

He said, "Well, now, that is mostly up to you, I mean, how much you study for the test and all. They give the tests four times each year, but there is a waiting period between second and first-class licenses," he explained.

"I don't want to stay in school that long, Mr. Cook," I responded.

"You don't have to stay in school; you can study on your own for the test. They don't ask any questions that aren't in your electronics book," he said.

After our little talk, I thought about it for a while and felt it was time to be moving on. I asked Mr. Cook if he would put a word in and help me land a job. He advised that Mr. Gibbs got telephone calls all the time for students who were educated in electronics and other fields, so I should just tell him to send me on interviews. I told Mr. Gibbs to add my name to his list, and one day, he sent for me. "I got you a job interview here, boy," he stated as he held out a piece of paper in my direction. "Call this number and they will set up a time for you to come in. If they hire you, please give me a call so I will know," he continued advising.

The name of the company was Jackson Patrol Service. It had been formed by a former Hinds County patrolman named Robert Thomas. Mr. Thomas's brother was a Hinds County deputy sheriff who later became Hinds county sheriff. Their other brother, Maxwell, was the warden at the Hinds County Penal Farm in Raymond. Mr. Thomas, whom we all called Bob, had expanded his patrol service (sometimes called "Rent-a-Cop") business into the electronic security business. Bob needed another electronic technician, so he had called Hinds Junior College. The interview went rather well, and he hired me on the spot. The pay was $75.00 per week to start with a promised $10.00 per week raise as soon as I proved myself.

I went back to Hinds and bid good-bye to all my friends then cleaned all my things out of my dorm room and moved in with my brother J. P. and his wife, Frances, in Pearl, Mississippi. I paid them fifteen dollars per week for board and started paying my parents for the 1963 Chevrolet car I was driving. The rest of my life had begun, and I was off on a new adventure.

This decision would turn out to be the best decision I ever made. After a while, the electronics industry no longer required licenses except for the communications part of the industry. We could all install and service electronics if we had the capability. It was very interesting work, and I didn't realize it at the time, but it would be just exactly what I would want to do for the rest of my life.

30

My Career

The very first real job I had was working for Jackson Patrol Service on Terry Road in Jackson, Mississippi. The company moved to Gallatin Street in 1965. We installed and serviced security systems, both residential and commercial.

We were moving our monitoring gear from the old Jackson Police Department to the new communications office north of town. I was working in the old Police Office helping switch the monitoring gear. One day, an alarm went off that I wasn't switching, and I told the police dispatcher that I hadn't caused that alarm. The dispatcher told me that it was a holdup alarm at the Poindexter branch of the First National Bank. He announced on his radio for any unit close to the bank to respond to a holdup alarm. He got a reply from an officer who was talking on his handheld radio. The officer was working traffic and said he would just walk over there. The dispatcher told him he would send backup, and so he did.

The radio became quiet for a few minutes, and I went back to work. All of a sudden, policemen started screaming into their radios with code numbers. I asked one of the dispatchers what was going on, and he told me they were shooting at each other out there. The highway patrol and the sheriff's department radios were monitored at this police station. They both started dispatching cars. Different cars were being directed to set up roadblocks. Descriptions of the bandits, the clothes they were wearing, and the getaway car were announced.

An ambulance was dispatched, and I heard that a policeman was down and one suspect was dead. I heard one suspect was on foot, running with a bag in one hand and a gun in the other. Being a young country boy and having grown up in a quaint atmosphere, I just about had a heart attack with all that sudden news. It wasn't anything I hadn't seen in the movies and on television, but this became suddenly real and I, in some way, was part of it. I had just announced that alarm to the police dispatcher.

There were two dispatchers there. One looked in my direction, smiled, and told me to take it easy. I asked him what he meant by taking it easy; he said I looked a little faint. One dispatcher told the other to find out who the policeman was that was down and his condition. Then there was some code jargon on the radio, and the phone rang. A cop was phoning in a response to the radio dispatcher's request for information, because they didn't want that information over the radio.

He advised the policeman's name and said he had been shot in the arm as the bandit was running out of the bank. Before he could say "halt," there was gunfire, and the policeman had killed one bandit and wounded another with a shot that had paralyzed him. The third robber ran with the money. The policeman recognized a bystander. He gave the individual his gun and radio and told him to not get too close, but to keep an eye on the robber and help the police keep up with his whereabouts.

The robber ran through a playground where children were playing and in between houses. The man chasing him kept the police units informed of the robber's locations, and they surrounded the place. Finally, the robber ran out on the sidewalk and started running down the street. The police ordered him to stop, and he didn't, so the police shot and killed him as he ran.

The policeman fully recovered, but I never heard about the wounded robber. The driver of the getaway car changed cars a few blocks away and escaped through the roadblocks. He was captured a few days later and identified by the policeman, who had been wounded. After all that, I had to shut down our operation. I was so weak you could have knocked me out with a wet noodle. I got my boss on the phone, and he told me to just go home and come back the next day. This event happened in 1964 or 1965, I'm not real sure.

My friend James Richardson got tired of his job and started looking for something else. I got him on at Jackson Patrol Service early in 1966. After James had worked there a few months, he told me about his uncles who worked for the Ethyl Corporation in Baton Rouge, Louisiana. They told him he could get a job there making more money than he was making at the time. He offered to get me on down there. I decided that the money I was making at the time, one hundred and twenty-five dollars per week, was satisfactory, but I could use a change. I was getting a little bored with all the traveling and thought I would like to stay in one place all day. I asked James to check with his uncles to see if they could find an opening for me and if so, I would go along with him. James arranged a meeting on Lake Bruin, Louisiana, at his one of uncle's lake house. We went over one Sunday afternoon, and I met his uncle. We filled out some Ethyl paperwork, and we were both hired a little later. I gave Jackson Patrol Service a two-week notice, and Ruthie and I loaded everything we owned into a U-Haul truck and moved to Baton Rouge, Louisiana, in October of 1967.

We lived down there seven months, and the instrument department job came up four times. I never reached the testing stage. One night, the phone rang, and it was Johnny Burwald from Jackson Patrol. He had been their salesman, and he and I got along real well. He wanted to know what I was doing and how I was. I asked him how he found my number, just out of curiosity, and he told me he had called all the James Smith's in the Baton Rouge phone book. That was funny, and I asked him if he had been searching on the phone since October when I left Jackson Patrol. We were jesting about the name James Smith, knowing there were many anywhere you went. He went on to explain that he had started his own business, and I jokingly asked what that could possibly have to do with me. He wanted me to install his electronics in hospitals and nursing homes.

Ruthie and I went to Jackson to visit with him and his company owners. I was hired, and we moved back to Jackson in April 1968. Ruthie was excited about the news. She liked Jackson much more than Baton Rouge. She didn't like shift work, because she didn't like being home alone in a strange large city.

I enjoyed working with Burwald at Signal Systems. He had served in the Marine Corps in WWII in the Pacific Theater of Operations.

His outfit had surrendered to the Japanese Army and was in the Bataan Death March in May of 1942. Some 60,000 American prisoners were forced to march seventy miles to prison camps, and about 10,000 died along the way. At Signal Systems, I still had the same compassion for Burwald that I had had at Jackson Patrol Service. I wanted to help him all I could for the company's sake and for him as a person, because he was responsible for keeping my country free. I knew he was a good individual and a good salesman. He just needed help with his paperwork.

To make photo copies we went down the street to a printing shop and used their copier for ten cents per copy. Only printing shops and very large companies had copiers. There were no fax machines, there was a teletype machine. You typed a message in the teletype machine and pressed the telex phone number where the message was to be sent. When a telex was received the typewriter on the machine typed out the message. The paper was on a roll and it just rolled through as the machine typed. Phone calls were expensive. There was a minimum charge, then a certain amount per minute.

Ruthie and I started our own business, Electronic Controls, Inc., in April 1976, website: electroniccontrols.biz. We started out in our dining room and moved to a two-room office on Terry Road in Jackson, Mississippi, then to a three-room office at the same address. Jimmy Carter had been elected President and he and the Democrats was letting the economy drop into the dirt. Business was bad and we were looking at bankruptcy. We then decided to move to the country and to some scaled back living. We kept our house and rented it to tenants. We bought a mobile home and put it on eight acres of land near Ruthie's parents' house that they donated to their Ruthie.

After moving our business to the country, Ruthie and I trimmed our overhead to the bone. We moved to Route 2, Box 52A, Pattison, Mississippi. Ruthie's parents gave us eight acres of land on a beautiful rocky hill area. I built a small building beside a mobile home we had bought and parked there. As mentioned, we rented our house in Jackson to tenants. Ronald Reagan was sworn in that same year. He had come along just in the nick of time and cut payroll taxes, giving people more money to spend. That created jobs and brought interest rates down so the economy started moving again. He increased spending in the defense budget, and people started back to work as the economy surged forward.

A colonel in the Mississippi Army National Guard contacted me one day and asked me to come see him. He was the commanding officer in charge of the national guard armories in Mississippi. All armories had weapons rooms and vaults that had security systems. One of his responsibilities was installing and maintaining security systems in the arms vaults and supply rooms. He told me he was dissatisfied with the company he had been using and gave me the service contracts on every armory from just north of Highway 82 south to the coast. This contract continued for many years to come. That helped our business tremendously.

We were holding on, but we needed something with real money in it. An electrical engineer I had known for quite sometime asked me to help him design a fire-alarm system for the Ellisville State School campus in Ellisville, Mississippi. This institution also took care of patients with mental disabilities and poor aged people. It had been established before Medicaid and Medicare. It was a government facility. They wanted to install fire alarms in every building on campus and tie each one to the guardhouse, which was continually manned. I helped get it designed, and it came out for bid. There was a problem; my business wasn't strong enough for a bid bond, let alone a performance bond. A bid bond is bonding your bid amount for five percent. If you are awarded the contract and do not accept it, your bid bond will pay five percent of whatever your bid was to the owner. A business has to be well established to find a bonding company that will handle it. A performance bond is a bit more difficult. That bond guarantees, in this case, Ellisville State School, that if we do not finish the job, the bonding company will pay another contractor to complete the job at no additional cost to the school.

In order to acquire these bonds, a company has to have a pretty good track record, as well as pretty good assets. I had neither, just yet. I had assets and a track record, but not enough for a job that size. The contract would run over a hundred thousand dollars, and I had done nothing near that at the time. So, I would have to find an electrical contractor to bid the job, and I would be his subcontractor. I went to the school and told them what was going on and asked who they liked in the area. They referred me to a contractor named Valentine in Soso, Mississippi, just down the road a piece. He was a nice ole country boy like me. We got along like old friends, but he told me that in those tough times, bonds were hard to come by. He went through the Mississippi Small Business Bureau. They did just what their name implied; they helped small businesses, for one thing, acquire bid and performance bonds.

Valentine and I scouted the campus with the plans and specifications and put a price together. He was a little reluctant at first, but when I explained that I had helped the engineer design the job, he felt comfortable about us getting it right. Finally, the bid time came. Bids were to be turned in at 2:00 PM on that bid day and not a second later or the bid wouldn't be opened. That is normal for government bid work. Most private jobs are that way also, but not always.

Mr. Valentine and I were on the phone the whole morning of the bid date. I was in my office, and he was in his. We were checking and rechecking our numbers to be sure we had it all covered, including as much profit as possible while remaining the low bidder. I was calling the factory that manufactured the fire alarm system and begging for cost reductions. I would talk to them about how times were tough all over and I would have stiff competition. They would trim a little off the cost here and there and come up with a cheaper pull station, horn, smoke detector, or some device to get the price down. We were splitting hairs, but dragging cost out of the job almost pennies at a time. Finally, it came time to hand over the bid envelope to the school, and whatever was to be, would be.

I was working in the office in Pattison, and Valentine was on the phone inside the bid room at the school. It would be about forty-five minutes from the time we decided the final amount around one thirty or so until I received the call from him stating whether we had gotten it or we were high. Minutes crawled by like hours. I needed that job and real bad. Finally, the phone rang; it was Mr. Valentine saying we had gotten it! I asked why it took so long to open the bids. He told me that about five minutes after two o'clock, a bidder had walked in, stating that he had had a flat tire on the way to the bid opening and that was why he was late. They felt sorry for him and offered their condolences, but his bid could not be opened. He asked if he could open it anyway under protest. They had to let him do just that, but they knew the only way they could accept it was by throwing the bids out, advertising for new bids, and establishing a new bid date, and that would take three weeks by law. They had the contractor they wanted, and they liked us, because we had helped design the systems and the job was within the amount that had been budgeted for the project. The man opened his contract, and he was lower than we were. We had gotten that job because of a flat tire. It would cost them money to rebid the job. Besides that, they needed to get started.

Before this time, Ellisville State School had a fire, and that was the reason for installing fire alarms. They had a nursing home that was made of concrete blocks with glazed tile on the walls and a concrete ceiling. I had been inside that building and would have thought it was impossible to burn it down. It didn't burn down, but a lot of smoke was created inside the building. It was a dormitory with two wings and a central administration area. There was a small room in the center of the building where the laundry was folded and sorted. Then the laundry was taken to the wings and distributed. Laundry was done in a separate building on campus and trucked to the dorms. The laundry truck came in and dumped the laundry on a table in the center of the room just like they had done for years. The laundry wouldn't be attended to until the next morning. The laundry was hot, right out of the dryer. As it lay on the table in a pile, it ignited by spontaneous combustion.

The fire was contained in that one room. The campus fire department was on the scene in minutes with a five-hundred-gallon tank. That tank was emptied, and another tank was brought to the scene and emptied but that fire was still smoldering. Most of the clothing was made from cotton, and cotton is very hard to extinguish in a pile. There was a lot of smoke; one wing was closed by smoke barrier doors. The rescuers used air tanks and masks for breathing while they evacuated the patients. Some patients could walk out; some could be taken out in a wheelchair, but some had to be taken out on stretchers. Once they were out of the building, there was a delay in getting the patients placed in a safe place, where they could sit down or lie down to allow the wheelchairs and stretchers to return for other patients. I think about six or seven lives were lost in that one wing.

The other wing had no smoke inside. The smoke was hovering in

---

the middle of the administration area, but not drifting into that one wing. The nurse in that wing closed her smoke doors and turned on the lights. Since there were no doors or windows open in that wing, there was no draft to pull the smoke inside the wing. When the first wing was evacuated, the rescuers came over to the second wing to evacuate the patients. When they opened the fire exit door at the end of the wing, it created a draft to suck the smoke into that wing. One of the smoke barrier doors that the nurse had been very thoughtful to close had a broken latch, and the drafting force pulled the door open and allowed the smoke into the wing. This powerful draft was caused by the heat from the fire pressurizing the air inside the administration area. Opening the fire exit at the end of the wing released the pressure and allowed the smoke to travel into the wing. The nurse had only switched on the emergency lights. She never knew which lights the two switches on the wall controlled. One switch turned on the emergency lights, and the other switch turned on the domestic lights. She had switched on the emergency lights. When the room was lighted, she didn't think about switching on more lights. The emergency power wires were in a conduit that ran over the top of the room that was on fire. The heat from the fire heated the metal conduit and melted the wires. They shorted out and tripped the circuit breaker for the emergency lights. The rooms in that wing went totally dark and were filled with smoke. The rescuers' air tanks were empty, because they had been exhausted in the first wing.

Rescuers were holding their breaths and trying to evacuate people as best they could. Their eyes were burning from the smoke, since they weren't wearing the air masks. Several more people lost their lives in that wing. If I remember right, there were fourteen deaths caused by that fire. Ellisville School put a tape around that building and invited the public to come in and see just how disastrous a fire can be. They had employees directing tours to explain to hospital and nursing home administration people how simple things can mean life or death when a large building is on fire. I took the tour, and it was just mind-boggling how many little things one can misunderstand about fire safety. The nurse had a copy of the document that she had filled out to get maintenance to repair the broken smoke door latch, so the maintenance department was blamed. The engineer who had specified the wrong wire for the emergency circuit was blamed. With the news in all the papers, the state was trying to find a scapegoat. I don't remember just how many were fired, but there was enough blame to go around.

The silver lining in that cloud was that many lives have been saved, because a lot of fire alarms were installed and safety issues addressed because of that fire. Precautions were taken in facilities all over the United States. Fire inspectors with the State Bureau of Buildings and Grounds, fire marshals from different states from all over the nation, and anyone else who wanted to come see the mistakes came to tour the building. This was usually done by the NFPA (National Fire Protection Association), so new fire codes could be written and techniques for fire safety could be learned. After this, the school was installing fire alarms and fire safety equipment in all their buildings. We completed the contract in record time. We received praise from the electrical engineer over the project and from the state and the school.

Mr. Valentine asked me to help him with another job in Mendenhall. They were adding a floor on one of the buildings of the Boswell Rehabilitation Center. The building had a certain brand of system, and the fire alarm on the additional floor had to have the same fire brand. He had installed the conduit and installed the wires in the pipe. He thought they were supposed to install the equipment. He said he called them to come install the equipment and said, "They sent a man down here with a necktie on." I thought that was funny. Anyway, we went over and installed the equipment for him.

With the money from the Ellisville contract, plus the service work, the installations on the armories, and rental income from the Jackson house, Ruthie and I had a comfortable living again, and it felt good. We had been building our country home out of our pocket, and our pockets were getting bare, we had not made a lot of progress. We now had funds to finish the house, and we finished it in 1984. We had started that house in 1978 while still living in Jackson. We were coming down and working mostly on weekends. We ended up having to borrow twenty thousand dollars to complete the house. We borrowed the money on a five-year note and paid it off by 1989.

We had fun building that house; we had help from friends, in-laws, and our children. In making the move to McBride, I had some serious considerations about the business. We kept the office in Jackson open, but only had a salesman handling the office. All our customers in Jackson would have to phone us, long distance. Most businesses want local service. Being out in the country, I wasn't sure how the customers would accept it. They all said they didn't care where I was; they only needed a phone number. Customers who had to call long distance to Jackson wouldn't mind the difference anyway. My business would have a rural route for an address. I surveyed several of our customers to find out if all this would matter; it didn't matter. I was reminded that people do business with people they like when possible.

The Delta Regional Medical Center in Greenville was doing some renovations, and the contractors had fallen out over the fire alarm. They called me in to help. We had a sit-down meeting, and I told them we would visit each device in the facility and activate it, in other words blow smoke into smoke detectors and pull manual fire alarm pull stations. We would keep a log of what worked or did not work properly. Each device would have a number. Then we would meet again and determine who was responsible for which numbers. Then I would repair the devices and invoice the contractor, hospital, or architect for the service depending on who was responsible for the problem. There was a lot of grumbling about my plan.

Someone asked, "Do you have any idea how many fire alarm devices are in this hospital?" I told them it might be a few hundred. They complained about the time it would take. The administrator was the highest-ranking gentleman in the room. He told them that he had asked me to help them solve the problem, and I had come up with an excellent idea. He went on to tell them that if anyone had a better idea to let him hear it. The room fell silent. After a few seconds with no suggestions, he said, "Let's get to it."

We started around nine thirty that morning, checking every device in that four-story building. It took until around midnight to finish, but they all stayed with me until we were done. I later put two employees on the problems and got the system back in order. The system was inspected by the Mississippi Department of Health for Licensure and Certification. The system passed the inspection, and everybody was happy.

King's Daughters Hospital in Greenville had problems with their nurses call system and inquired at Delta Regional about who did their nurse call and fire alarm. They recommended us, and we got a lot of business from that hospital and still do to this day. King's Daughters added a five-million-dollar addition, and we did all the electronics in that addition. Then we got a contract to change out all the nurses call and fire alarms in the old part of the facility. Corrigan's distributor in Jackson was having problems with too many customers. So, Corrigan turned all of his lines over to me, and I was the only distributor for Corrigan in Mississippi.

The business was doing quite well. It had been growing and improving for 27 years, so in October 2003, Ruthie and I decided to move to Olive Branch, Mississippi, so we would be near our children and grandchildren. Once we had grandchildren, we understood why they call them grand. We asked our employees if they could run the business without us being there. They jokingly said they could do a much better job if they could get us out of there. I told them if they wanted to keep their jobs, they would have to see that the company kept going. They have all done a great job. They stay in touch with us by facsimile, computers, e-mail, snail mail, cell phones, and landline phones. We visit only a few times each year and less than we had thought we would need to.

I've had a wonderful career, because I enjoy what I do. There is no other job I know of that I would rather do than work in electronics and own an electronic business that operates with very little help from us.

Genealogy of James Edward Smith Senior

Daddy's paternal ancestors:

Wilford Smith, b. 1794 (Florida), d. 1894, m. Nina or Nona Martinez, b. ?, d. ?

James Monroe Smith, b. March 1845, d. 1920, m. Nancy Courtney Sermon Blunt, b. Feb. 1840, d. 1919

John Hiram Smith, b. April 1, 1875, d. Nov. 20, 1956, m. Annie Elizabeth Trevillion, b. Feb. 11, 1883, d. Sept. 1, 1962

Thomas James Smith, b. Dec. 16, 1905, d. Nov. 15, 1979, m Annie Mae Beesley, b. Feb. 7, 1917, d. Feb. 9, 2002

James Edward Smith Sr., b. March 18, 1944, m. Ruthie Jewell Goza, b. April 24, 1947

Children of James Monroe and Nancy Courtney:

Alice, b. 1879; Herbert, b. 1872; Willis, b. 1874; Otis, b. Oct. 1876; John Hiram, b. 1875; Ida A., b. 1864; Aubrey, b. ?; Carrie, b. 1869 (1870 and 1880 Census Records).

Daddy's maternal ancestors:

The name Trevillion has nine different spellings that I know of, Travillion, Travillian, Trevilion, Trevilian, Trevilion, Trevillian, Trevillion, Trevillyan, and Trovillion. The first Trevillion (our family spelling) came from Cornwall, England (*The Silver Horse*, by Ray A. Trovillion).

The earliest ancestor known to me is Richard Trevillion. He was born in 1748 in Hanover County, Virginia, and died in 1800 in the Mississippi Territory, now called Pattison, Mississippi. Richard served in the Revolutionary War. He was in the battle of King's Mountain, South Carolina (Pension Records in the North Carolina Library, Raleigh, NC).

Richard and his wife, Patsy Stots (French, pronounced "states" in English), migrated from North Carolina to Rodney, Mississippi, in 1788 (Mrs. McBee's Natchez Records, Vol. 11, page 219). Richard and Patty bought land in Mississippi, on August 6, 1783 (Natchez, MS, Court Records 1767–1805, Vol. 11, page 20; Book A, page 143). Temple States Trevillion (b. April 15, 1771, d. 1845) served in the Battle of New Orleans in 1814, under Andrew Jackson, as a surgeon's mate. Temple married Nelly Nevels on November 23, 1807, and his second wife, Eleanor, on April 26, 1818, and his third wife, Martha A. Herlong, December 17, 1833.

Son of Temple States:

Phillip Barnes Trevillion, b. Dec. 27, 1819, d. 1862, m. Matildia Valines Rogillio, b. Nov. 11, 1857, d. Feb. 6, 1910.

Phillip Barnes Trevillion started the Trevillion Cemetery in the Blue Hill community sometime around 1860 when he buried his twenty-one-year-old daughter on a ridge to the rear of his home. Trevillion Cemetery now has an association and meets on the first Saturday of May at 11:00 AM. There are about one hundred graves in the cemetery.

Children of Phillip Barnes and Matildia Valines Trevillion:

Alice, John Thomas, Temple States, Hiram Henderson. Guardianship for these children was given to Uriah S. Humphreys after his marriage to Matildia Valines Trevillion in approximately 1865 (Jefferson County Chancery Clerk's Office, Fayette, Mississippi).

John Thomas Trevillion, b. April 13, 1858, d. Dec. 28, 1935, m. Fransonia Abigail Humphrey, b. Nov. 11, 1857, d. June 7, 1936

Children of John Thomas and Fransonia Abigail:

Annie Elizabeth Trevillion, b. Feb 11, 1883, d. Sept. 1, 1962

Children of James Monroe and Nancy Smith:

Ida, b. 1865; Alice, b. 1869; Herbert, b. 1872; Willis, b. 1874; Otis, b. October 1877; John Hiram, b. July 1878; Walter, b. Dec. 1882; Aubrey, b. July 1884

Children of John Hiram and Annie Elizabeth Smith married January 7, 1903:

George William, b. Jan. 23, 1904, d. Feb. 5, 1969

Thomas James, b. Dec. 16, 1905, d. Nov. 15, 1979

John Benton, b. Aug. 20, 1907, d. April 8, 1962

Jessie Harold, b. July 31, 1909, d. Approx. 1970

Authur Barnes, b. April 18, 1911, d. May 3, 1931

Whitaker Woodrow, b. May 21, 1913, d. April 26, 1931

Lillie Inez, b. July 24, 1920, d. Feb. 9, 2001

Bessie Elizabeth, b. Sept. 21, 1930, d. May 30, 1933

Thomas James Smith married Annie Mae Beesley Dec. 26, 1934

From this union were born:

John Pearl, b. Sept. 30, 1936

William Arthur, b. Aug. 29, 1939

James Edward, b. March 18, 1944

Son: (No name) stillborn, b. Aug. 18, 1947, on a Wednesday, the same day of week as J. P., on the same day of the month as James, in the same month as William.

Bessie Mae, b. May 23, 1952

Paternal lineage of Annie Mae Beesley Smith:

The first (?) Beesley came from Wales; his wife was a Vardeman and came from Ireland.

Jimmy Beesley, b. 1800 GA, m. Annie born in France

George Washington Beesley, b. Jan. 9, 1833, MS, d. March 15, 1909, MS, m. Ophelia Jane Butler, b. 1851, GA, d. Aug. 25, 1903, MS

Pearl Beesley, b. Jan. 18, 1881, MS, d. Oct. 4, 1969, MS, m. Ada Love Klar, b. July 12, 1888, d. Feb. 13, 1976, MS

Annie Mae Beesley, b. Feb. 7, 1917, MS, d. Feb. 9, 2001, MS

James E. Smith, b. March 18, 1944

Children of George and Ophelia Beesley:

Child stillborn b. 1867; Willie, b. 1869; Mary Annie, b. 1872, d. 1936; James (Jim) b. 1874; Henry, b. 1876, d. 1956; Pearl, b. 1881, d. 1969

Lewis McQuere, b. 1883, d. 1954; Wiley, b. 1886, d. 1941; Nannie Mae, b. 1890, d. 1963; Walter b. 1893

Maternal ancestors of Annie Mae Beesley Smith:

Jacob Klar Sr. came from Germany.

Jacob Klar Jr., b. 1854, d. 1904, m. Mary Victoria Singletery, b. 1867, d. 1935. He lived in Rodney, Mississippi, and was in the casket business.

Ada Love Klar, b. July 12, 1888, d. February 13, 1976, m. Pearl Beesley, b. January 18, 1881, d. October 4, 1969.

Annie Mae, b. Feb. 2, 1917, d. Feb. 9, 2001 m. Thomas James Smith, b. Dec. 16, 1905, d. Nov. 15, 1979

Children of Pearl and Ada Love Beesley:

Pearlie Victoria, b. Aug. 11, 1907; Ruth, b. Nov. 26, 1908; Paul, b. March 9, 1911; Lewis, b. June 18, 1913; Annie Mae, b. Feb. 07, 1917; Walter, b. Oct. 06, 1922; Walter's twin stillborn, Oct. 06, 1922; John Henry, b. April 18, 1924; James Wiley, b. 1926, d. 1926; stillborn boy, b. Nov. 25, 1928; Bennie V., b. March 3, 1930

Children of Annie Mae Beesley and Thomas J. Smith:

John Pearl, b. Sept. 30, 1936; William Arthur, b. August 29, 1939; James Edward, b. March 18, 1944; child stillborn Aug. 18, 1947; Bessie Mae, b. May 23, 1952

Children of Ruthie and James E. Smith:

James Edward Jr., b. Feb. 22, 1970; Kimberly Lea, b. Dec. 31, 1974

Children of James Jr. and Ashley Harwell Smith:

Jackson Parker, b. May 3, 2002; Samuel Thomas, b. Dec. 13, 2004; James Benjamin, b. March 13, 2007

Children of Kimberley Lea and Seth McCaskill:

Shane Allan, b. May 13, 2008

Random family information, I'm not sure who these Trevillions are:

Albert Trevillion, Grandma Smith's uncle (great-uncle, I think), b. July 22, 1825, d. ?

Mildred Trevillion, b. August 6, 1917 (I don't know who she was.)

***

The information listed above was found in the old song book and on some pictures my cousins Georgia (Reynolds) Owens and Blanche (Reynolds) McGillis gave me. These were Aunt Ressa's daughters who lived in Memphis, Tennessee, at the time, which was around 1984.

Great-Grandpa James Monroe Smith mustered into the Confederate Army in Company E, 7th Mississippi Infantry in Franklin County. That unit was later organized into the 7th Infantry Regiment at Corinth, Mississippi, in April 1861 with men from Marion, Amite, Pike, Franklin, Lawrence, Yalobusha, Holmes, and Covington counties.

> He served on the Mississippi coast, saw action in Kentucky, then was assigned to Generals J. P. Anderson's, Tucker's, and Sharp's Brigade, Army of Tennessee. The 7th participated in many conflicts of the army from Murfreesboro to Atlanta, marched with Hood to Tennessee, and fought in North Carolina. It was mustered into Confederate service with 911 officers and men, and sustained 20 casualties at Munfordville, 113 at Murfreesboro, and 75 at Chickamauga. The unit was briefly consolidated with the 9th Mississippi Regiment in December 1863 and totaled 468 men and 252 arms. On April 26, 1865, it surrendered with 74 men. The field officers were Colonels William H. Bishop, E. J. Goode, Hamilton Mayson, and A. G. Mills; Lieutenant Colonels R. S. Carter and Benjamin F. Johns; and Major Henry Pope. (Copied from some Civil War records that I found on line)

Grandpa James M. Smith mustered in as a private and came out a sergeant. He was paid $168.00 for his service from May through

October 31, 1861. He received his pay on December 15th, 1863. He survived the war. He then entered the cotton gin business in that portion of Pike County that is now Lincoln County. He later got out of the cotton gin business and relocated to Franklin County were he met and married Nancy Courtney Sermon Blunt. This marriage occurred by the time of the 1870 Franklin County Census (1870 Census of Franklin County, MS).

Great-Great-Grandpa Phillip Barnes Trevillion was mustered into the Confederate Army—I'm not sure where—and died of pneumonia, either in the Confederacy or at home.

Great-Grandpa James Monroe Smith was born in Alabama. His father, Wilford Smith, came from Florida. They moved from Alabama to Pascagoula, Mississippi, then to Pike County, Mississippi. Grandpa James was married sometime before 1870, because he and Grandma Nancy are listed on the 1870 census as living in Lincoln County.

Pike County, Amite, Jefferson, and Copiah Counties had to give space for Lincoln County. Lincoln County wasn't established until after the Civil War, so Grandpa could have been living in the same spot, but his county was different. The 1880 Census still has him living in Lincoln County. The 1900 Census has him and Grandma Nancy living in Jefferson County. According to family rumor, they lived in Franklin County at one time.

LaVergne, TN USA
08 November 2010
204026LV00004B/12/P

BIOGRAPHY & AUTOBIOGRAPHY / PERSONAL MEMOIRS

James E. Smith grew up, beginning in the 1940's in Jefferson County, Mississippi. He spent his early years listening attentively to stories from his parents and grandparents. Everyone can learn from the simple life he and his relatives once lived.

While the author mainly wrote this book to preserve his family history for his grandchildren and other family members, it also is meant to inform lovers of history and those seeking to learn lessons from the past. Learn about:

- What life was like growing up on a farm;
- Eating traditions;
- How people dressed in the 1950's;
- Social gatherings of the past;
- Life on the home front during World War II;
- And much more!

Step back in time to a different era, and along the way, discover the beauty of life the way it used to be and what it meant to grow up on a farm. Find ways to achieve happiness every single day with *A Grandfather's Gift*.

James E. Smith grew up in south Mississippi. In writing this book, he mentions several things that really matter in life. He is semiretired, and he owns his own business in Brookhaven, Mississippi. He likes to tell true stories.

US $20.95

ISBN 978-1-4401-4144-7

www.iuniverse.com